BY THE SKIN OF MY TEETH

JOHN SHAILER

FOREWORD

Photographs and documents are integrated into the Page Number sequence and are listed in Appendix C.

An Appendix is included, which provides armament data of all warships served in by the author, and was obtained from Jane's Fighting Ships, 1943-4 and 1944-5.

A bibliography is included of books from which the author obtained factual data concerning Arctic Convoys, Fleet Air Arm sorties, the Reptiles of Ceylon (Sri Lanka), the Falkland Islands and the Falkland Islands Dependencies.

True identities are not always applied to everyone named in the text. This is done, although not invariably, to save them and maybe the author from any possible embarrassment.

Published by ULITHI WORLD
Copyright 2008 John Shailer
ISBN 978-0-9559465-0-9

DEDICATION

In memory of my late beloved wife, Glad, for giving me so much, for taking so little and for her love, loyalty and support, especially during my long absences.

*   *   *   *   *

THANKS

To my dear daughters, Janet and Gillian and their families, for their unfailing support.
To my dear sister, Pat, for her diligent proof reading and memory jogging.
To my brother-in-law, author Dennis Conroy, for his encouragement and helpful advice.
To my son-in-law, Paul Whitehurst, for his computer advice and the setting up of equipment.
To Rhianna, for her advice on word processing.
To Stephanie and James, my helpful neighbours.
To Carolyn Tanfield for her professional proof reading and advice.
To Lydia for putting up with the whims of an old man in designing the cover.
Finally, to my three grown-up grandchildren Jamie, Stacey and Damian for their cheek !

*   *   *   *   *

THE AUTHOR AS A YOUNG MAN

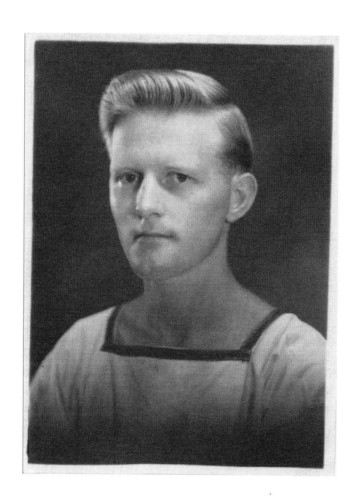

TABLE of CONTENTS

continued ....

TABLE of CONTENTS (continued)

continued.........................

TABLE OF CONTENTS (continued)

continued........................

TABLE OF CONTENTS (continued)

continued..........................

TIME is NOW but with a DIFFERENCE.

J . S . Shailer,
(2007)

CHAPTER ONE

A NEW KID ON THE PATCH

I was born in Narrogin, Western Australia, on the 5th February 1925, of English parents. Needless to say, it was not an event that caught the attention of the world. They had left England the previous year as participants in a government scheme which encouraged people to emigrate to the colonies, particularly Australia. The scheme offered free passage, together with a small cash incentive. No doubt it was the government's intention to alleviate the growing unemployment situation in Britain. Both parents soon found work ; Mother in a local department store in Narrogin and Father with a local dentist-farmer, Mr Campbell-Miller. Father was already a skilled dental mechanic and a proficient extractor of teeth. There was insufficient dental work in the area to keep my father fully employed. He managed to find additional work with Mr Campbell-Miller on his wheat farm, humping sacks and tending the horses. Life must have been hard for my parents at that time. My father was already a skilled horseman, having frequently ridden on his parent's farm, back in England. He often rode bareback. In World War I, at the age of fifteen and a half, he volunteered to join up and because of his equestrian skills became an instructor in the 2nd Cavalry Division of the 2nd Signal Squadron, the Royal Engineers. He soon found himself in the trenches in France as a sapper.

In later years, my parents told me of one or two `incidents` in Australia, in which I was directly involved, but of which I was far too young at the time to remember. Apparently, the kindly wife of my father's employer asked to see the new baby. I was placed in the pram, a wicker affair with large wheels. Mother set off for the farm. After proudly showing me off, and chatting about things women chat about over a `cuppa`, Mother headed for home. En route, she had to push the pram across a large field. With about fifty yards to go to reach the gate, she suddenly became aware of a large bull charging across the field. She ran for the gate, desperately pushing the pram, and just managed to get through the gap in time. Thankfully, I was completely unaware of this incident, which was just as well, otherwise I might have presented her with an extremely dirty nappy !

One summer afternoon, Mother spread a blanket on the ground and we both sat . By this time I had reached the crawling stage. Mother dozed off for a short while. When she awoke, I was nowhere to be seen. Houses in that part of the world were usually constructed of timber and if built on rising ground were built on stilts, to compensate for the slope. Our house had two stilt supports at the back. This gave a considerable space underneath, which encouraged the free circulation of air and only partially helped to deny access to the sometimes large `creepy crawlies`. For example, very large spiders. Yes, you have guessed. I had managed to crawl under the house. No amount of coaxing would persuade me to come out. In a panic, Mother ran into an adjacent field to fetch my father, who luckily was working nearby. He came running and getting down on his hands and knees, peered under the house. He could see me in the gloom, but could not reach me and failed to persuade me to come out. By this time I had reached that part of the slope where it meets the base of the house.

In Australia there is a spider the Aussies call a `Red back`, the bite of which is potentially fatal. It seemed I was going out of my way to meet one. Desperately my parents continued to try and coax me out, but I was not having any and just sat there demonstrating my freedom. It was probably hunger that finally got the better of me in the end and eventually I crawled out into their waiting arms.

*   *   *   *   *

A HORTICULTURAL EXPERIENCE

In 1927, each household placed an order on the local dairy farm for their daily delivery of milk. A billycan was strategically placed beside the road outside each property. A cart would appear, bearing a large milk churn. The milk was ladled into the billycan. On this particular day Mother went to collect the billycan and found it to be almost empty. She took the can inside. Then, realising that the house was quiet, went to look for her toddler son. She discovered me with a tin in my hand which bore traces of milk. She knew I could not possibly have drunk that amount of milk. She took a good look round. It did not take her long to discover that her plants had been given a treat. Whether they eventually produced blooms of magnificent proportions and fragrance I very much doubt. After all, have you ever smelt the aftermath of spilling a bottle of milk in your car? On second thoughts however, fertilisers of one sort or another stink to high heaven, so perhaps I am wrong.

I am unaware of any other babyhood `incidents' on my part, but I do have an old studio photograph of a blond, blue-eyed baby boy in a loincloth, sitting on a large Glaxo tin. This was not the way I was normally seen, either by my parents nor by our neighbours. Rather I imagine, they saw me as always delving into things that were not my concern, frequently getting dirty and constantly being cleaned up afterwards.

*   *   *   *   *

CHAPTER TWO

CHILDHOOD DAYS

In 1928 we left Australia as a family on the P and O liner Ormonde. I was then three and a half years old. My grandmother was fretting for her son and had written several times asking my father to return to England. She had not yet seen her grandson . I have no recollection of my life in Australia as a baby. So far, I have related matters as told to me by my parents. I can vaguely remember, however, two things about the journey to England. I mentioned these to my parents in later childhood. They seemed quite amazed that a child of so few years could have any recollection of such details of the journey. I recalled seeing several dark-skinned men manhandling large wooden boxes onto the deck from the top of the ship's gangway. Mother assumed these to be the large tea chests being taken on board at Colombo, Ceylon (now Sri Lanka).

My further memory of the journey was of a train steaming past tall palm trees. At that age of course I would not know what I was seeing. Mother assumed this was in Egypt, as we slowly progressed north through the Suez Canal. The palm trees would have been observed from the port side of the ship.

It was to be some sixteen years later before I would again set foot in Australia, but not via the Suez. This time it would be via the Panama Canal, as a sailor of His Majesty's Royal Navy.

On our arrival in England, the intention was to stay initially with my great grandfather, at Sipson, near West Drayton, until my parents were able to set up their own home. It was not long before we were living in a rented house in North Ealing, on the western outskirts of London. My father soon obtained employment as a qualified dental mechanic with a dentist in Chiswick. His wage for this highly skilled work was two pounds per week.

Eventually, the time arrived for me to attend my first school. That first day turned out to be horrendously tragic and clearly left a scar on my mind with the horror of it. My mother went to work in the mornings, to help make ends meet. This necessitated her making arrangements with an older boy, John, who attended the local senior school, to take me to school on my first day. A young mother who lived further down the street got to hear of this arrangement. She asked John if her son, who was also starting school that day, could accompany us. He agreed.

When the time came, we two small boys said our tearful goodbyes and clutching the older boy's hand, set off down the road .The new brown leather satchels strapped to our backs swung erratically from side to side, causing our new pencil boxes to rattle. We approached a T-junction where our road converged with a steep hill. As we were turning right at the corner to descend the hill, the other small boy was attracted by something and ran out into the road. He was instantly run over by a laundry van. Even now, after seventy five years, I can still see the scene vividly, as though it was yesterday, of a wheel going over his neck and fluid spurting out of his ear. This terrible accident occurred outside the house of a priest. I remember this man rushing from his house, picking the boy up and carrying him in his arms into the house. He found the boy to be dead. The older boy and I stood on the pavement in a state of shock.

My mother, who was preparing for work, hearing the commotion coming from the end of the road, ran to the scene. She must have been in a terrible state of apprehension, which soon turned to tears when she learned the truth. She took me home, washed my tearful face and taking me by the hand, took me to school. On reaching the school she told the teacher what had happened .

Nowadays we scarcely raise our eyebrows when we hear of a road accident, except when it is on our own doorstep. Understandably, I do get angry when I see very young children playing in the street without supervision. What are the parents thinking of ? After all, it only takes an instant for a short life to be tragically snuffed out before it has hardly begun and our lives to be shattered by the shock and pain of our loss.

In 1930, shortly after I commenced my schooling, my parents decided to move a few streets away to another street in Ealing - Fowler's Walk. We moved into a two-bedroom semi`. Now perhaps is an opportune moment to mention that during my formative years we moved house no less than seven times. This did my education no good whatsoever. In fact, upon reflection, there are a number of events which interfered with my learning, although I hasten to add I do not give these as an excuse for my academic shortcomings. I propound the contributing events thus ; the frequent moves from one dwelling to another ; the outbreak of World War II and my evacuation to the country ; the break up of my parents` marriage and my subsequent return to London at the height of the Blitz. To cap it all, from the age of seven I was badly afflicted with severe bouts of seasonal hay fever.

We soon settled into our new home in Ealing. I was delighted to discover an open field behind the houses opposite. On the very first occasion in my life to be allowed out on my own, I made for the field. The first thing to catch my eye was a magnificent tree. It fascinated me with its swaying branches and rustling leaves. This was to be my first experience of tree climbing. I vaguely remember standing up on the first branch with my arms tightly clasping the trunk.

As soon as I returned from school the next day, I had my tea (bread and jam or dripping in those days) which I ate as rapidly as I could and asked to leave the table.
"Can I go to the field Mum?".
"Yes John" she said , "but be back before dark." I slid down from my chair, raced out of the house and crossed the road into the field. The tree appeared larger than the day before. I started to climb. I had reached a third branch when suddenly I experienced vertigo and wanted to come down, but was afraid to move. Some considerable time elapsed, when to my relief I heard my mother calling me. I shouted back and she soon appeared beneath the tree. She peered up anxiously, looking for me.
"What are you doing up there? Come down now," she coaxed. Her voice gave me confidence and I slowly descended to the ground. In later years Mother told me, with a chuckle in her voice that my reply to her anxious call was, "I am a cuckoo". I always smile about this now.

On another occasion that year, my mother was about to take me with her to do some shopping.
"I must get some eggs from Lyons" she said. With surprise in my voice I exclaimed, " I did not know that lions laid eggs, Mum !" Such is the innocence of a child.

Further along Fowler's Walk lived two small sisters. Their surname was Parrot but I cannot remember their first names. We soon made friends and used to set off on `expeditions` On a particular day in the summer the `Trio` walked onto a triangular plot of waste ground, set between two rows of semis`. One of my playmates bent down and picked up an oval piece of dried dog excrement. She sniffed at it and

4

pinched her nose

"This egg has gone off " she complained and threw the offensive piece of waste into the long grass at the side of the track.

We progressed along the path. I discovered a hole in a small soil bank, where I had seen a wasp enter. I poked my stick into the hole, not realising the danger. Immediately angry wasps streamed out. I put my foot over the hole to prevent their escape, but of course did not succeed. Firstly, because my foot was too small and secondly, I had not thought about the returning wasps. To add to my difficulties, I was only wearing short trousers. I was badly stung, mostly on the legs. I ran home screaming and was still being stung occasionally on the way. The two small girls followed me. Luckily, neither came to any harm. Amazingly, I suffered no permanent after effects from so many stings.

To the far side of the field where my favourite tree stood was a large house standing in its own grounds. The `Trio` often went over to the house, to peer into the gloom of the shrubbery. In May we saw the glory of the rhododendrons in full bloom. From the opposite end of the field, the house presented a somewhat forbidding appearance and the cold iron railings that followed the perimeter of the grounds did nothing to soften the view. One day, we were playing in the field when one girl spotted something white in the direction of the house. It appeared to be moving .

"Look at that !"she exclaimed, pointing anxiously.

"It's a ghost !" her sister said, fearfully. It certainly came across to me as a human shape, clothed in white. I began to feel uneasy. We discussed excitedly what we could see and what we should do. Although I was frightened by now, I probably did not want the girls to realise this and so, with a display of bravado, I said,

"Let us get closer and see". We timidly advanced towards the white shape. As we approached, it moved. We stopped dead. After some hesitation we advanced again. Finally, when we were some two hundred feet from the railings, I suddenly realised what it was.

"It's a newspaper !" I shouted, very relieved. The partially separated pages had been lifted by a breeze and ensnared on the railings. Our reaction was to throw back our heads with relieved laughter.

Whilst still living in Fowler's Walk, I attended a Sunday school at a Methodist chapel in Pitshanger Lane, North Ealing, London. We had been rehearsing for a Christmas concert. It was the organisers` intention that I should learn and recite a poem. The day of the concert duly arrived. All seemed to be progressing well and after much singing it came to my turn. I was hustled on stage to recite my poem. I struggled through it and received some polite applause. Enjoying the attention, I remained on stage. The organisers did not realise I knew several other poems by heart, but they soon found out. I launched into another recitation. Frantic coaxing from the wings to come off fell on deaf ears. It was when I was nearly through my second rendition that the curtain was hastily dragged across the stage, cutting me off from my audience and abruptly ending my first attempt at stardom.

As I have already mentioned, every summer from 1932 I suffered from hay fever, in June and July. In my case, the pollen from a particular grass was the cause. I have read somewhere that hay fever, eczema and asthma are all related. Some people assume hay fever involves persistent bouts of sneezing accompanied by a running nose. Yes, these are the two main symptoms but there can be others. Sufferers experience various symptoms at different levels of intensity. To summarise these; the nose runs virtually continuously causing the lining of the nasal tract to become inflamed. The eyes stream and the tear ducts itch intolerably, causing the lids to become red, sore and swollen. Severe nose bleeds can occur, as a result of violent sneezing. There are sometimes asthmatic breathing symptoms. The glare of the sun tends to make matters worse, so the wearing of sun glasses is definitely beneficial. Depression and irritability may result, which can badly affect school studies. It certainly caused a loss of concentration on my part.

Luckily in my case, we lived next door to a nurse. This lady was a heroine of World War I, having been decorated with the RRC [Royal Red Cross] for tending the wounded under fire in the trenches. It was not uncommon for me to lose a jam jar of blood from my nose in one evening. If my mother was unable to stem the bleeding she would call for help from our kindly neighbour. The nurse would come round and plug my nose with considerable wads of cotton wool.

It was not until I reached late middle-age that I was to be freed of this accursed allergy. An exception was during my seagoing time in the Royal Navy. Then I was well away from the source of my distress - the pollen.

*   *   *   *   *

THE GAMES WE PLAYED

In the 1930s most families were poor and children of that time often devised their own amusements. A favourite pastime of mine was to assemble a simple toy parachute. Firstly, Father had to be persuaded to part with one of his magnificent, large, white cotton handkerchiefs. This he did with alacrity, knowing by his generosity he would engross his son for hours in harmless play. It would also, of course, keep me from getting under his feet.

To assemble the parachute was simply a matter of neatly tying a suitable length of string to each corner of the handkerchief. The four loose ends were then tied to a weight. A metal washer or steel nut was ideal. Finally, the handkerchief was folded, corner to corner and a small hole was cut in the centre. On completion, there was an impatient rush out into the street.

The completed toy was screwed up in the palm of the hand and thrown hopefully aloft, the higher the better. If it behaved according to plan, it would catch the air, billow out and float gracefully to the ground. More effort seemed to be exerted with every throw. Other children in the street and at school took up this pastime. Soon there were numerous squares of white cotton floating in haphazard descent. I remember one boy with a bent for engineering. He devised a gadget to fire the parachute higher than anyone else. He showed ingenuity in overcoming the problem of the cotton material billowing out prematurely, before the parachute had reached its zenith. To the envy of us all, his toy reached spectacular heights. He refused to divulge the workings of his invention, despite our pleas.

Another popular game of the time was `Cigarette Cards`. Picture card sets, each card on a common theme, were given away with packets of cigarettes, one card to each packet. They were colourful and educational and were avidly collected, especially by children. Most sets were made up of fifty cards. Much swapping went on to help complete a set. Many people smoked in those days, especially the men, so there was no shortage of cards.

The game could be played by several children, but was normally played by two. One child stood a row of their own cards up against a wall. The playmate, using their own cards, flicked them one at a time at their opponent's cards, to try and knock them down. Often, they soon won back a card they had previously lost. There was much excited shouting and it was not unusual for a dispute to occur. These usually ended amicably, but one child might head for home with a heavy heart, having lost their most treasured cards.

Marbles was a popular game at that time too. The cheaper ones were made of baked clay and had a glazed surface. They tended to break up. Glass marbles were more popular. They were more resilient, colourful and cheap. A particularly attractive coloured marble was highly prized. Should the proud owner of such a marble lose it to their opponent, they would naturally do their utmost to win it back .

*   *   *   *   *

CHARIOTS

One day in 1933 I was taking my usual walk to the local shops. It was a fine day. Suddenly I saw trundling down the road a quarter-scale version of an Austin Ruby car. It was correct in every detail, except pedal-power had taken the place of the internal combustion engine. This superb toy must have been expensive. Peering inside I asked the driver, a small boy, if I could have a go. He declined. Disappointed, I turned around and made for home. Excitedly, I told Mother what I had seen. "We cannot afford to buy you expensive toys," she said. "You must make your own fun." Reflecting on her words later in life I realised my parents, by their attitude, did me a great favour. They taught me, if you want the material things of this world they have to be earned by hard work, and then they are appreciated. I resolved to build my own transport.

Prams were in common use in those days and at the end of a useful life were cast onto the local rubbish heaps as scrap. I set about scouring the local patches of waste ground for prams and for any other discarded useful scrap. Eventually, I found what I was searching for - a pram with sound wheels. The body was damaged but that did not matter. It was only the wheels and axles that were needed. Other parts were begged from my suffering father.

Having got everything together, I now set about laying out all the parts on the back yard in some semblance of order. A stout board for the main suspension, a wooden box for the body, two wooden axle-supports for front and back, the front and back wheels and axles of course, some stout cord, a sturdy nut, bolt and washer and finally plenty of nails. When the cart was assembled, there was just one more part to fit, a stout flat piece of wood secured with a large pivotal bolt to the side of the body. This acted as a brake lever. It was to be used frantically and frequently on many occasions but proved to be totally inefficient.

Eventually the crude contraption was wheeled out onto the pavement. My small sister Pat, was placed in the box. Grabbing the steering cord and with me also pushing from behind we set off on our first precarious journey, which started on the flat but soon became a downhill run. There was much shouting, squealing and relieved laughter, as we negotiated each hazard at speed. From the moment we reached the start of the downhill gradient I jumped up onto the tailboard and hung on tightly to the cord. I applied the brake as we neared the bottom of the hill, where there was a T-junction. We nearly ended up in someone's front garden on the other side of the bottom road. The cart proved to be great fun downhill but was hard work for me to pull back uphill whilst my sister, who was letting out constant squeals of delight I might add was still ensconced in the box. I soon found out from other children that a few drops of oil in the right place made all the difference to the cart's performance.

Most boys of that time built similar such contraptions. Some added some quite sophisticated refinements, such as a steering column. The main snag with a steering wheel was that it could present a serious hazard if there was a collision. I preferred to steer with the cord and my feet. Other indulgences were a brake applied to both wheels and a longer tailboard. Also the seat was usually padded (splinters in the bum can be painful !). Here was a toy contraption that cost virtually nothing yet gave many hours of harmless play to so many children of the time. Surprisingly children sustained very few cuts and bruises from this strenuous activity.

*   *   *   *   *

A WIRELESS BROADCAST

By this time in 1933, we had moved yet again. We were now living in Ashburton Road, South Ruislip, Middlesex. My parents decided I should join the choir at Ruislip church. It is a Norman church. I remember across the road there was a manor house, complete with moat. I had been endowed with a reasonably good boy-soprano voice. Well, my parents thought so and so did the choirmaster. That was a mistake.

I attended a music class at school. I took a dislike to the new music teacher and often deliberately sang out of key, just to annoy him. I can visualise him even now, with pale face, dark hair and a Hitler-like moustache. He wore wire-rimmed spectacles. He was quite a humourless man and was unpopular with the other children as well. Eventually he decided enough was enough and called me out in front of the class.
"Hold out your hand," he said. I obliged, holding my hand out, palm upwards. "No," he said, "Turn your hand up the other way." This I did, turning the back of my hand upwards. Exerting some considerable force he brought the edge of a wooden ruler down onto my fingers, just behind the nails. The pain was excruciating and took some time to diminish. I really loathed that teacher from then on, but I hasten to add, I no longer sang out of tune.

The class choir eventually achieved an acceptable singing standard . From then on we constantly practised a set programme. This culminated in a school charabanc trip to the Alexandra Palace, which in those days had become a BBC studio. There was a mass rendition of the programme we had been practising, by four thousand young voices. The broadcast must have been heard by many a proud parent.

*   *   *   *   *

POCKET MONEY AND THINGS

The highlight of the week took place on Saturday, when I received my pocket-money. I would then head eagerly for the local sweetshop and cast an observant eye over all the tall glass sweet jars, which stood in a long row on a shelf behind the counter. I would often chose a sherbet dab or a liquorice stick. Sometimes, there were liquorice whorls, with a gaily coloured round sweet in the centre. Often, I bought a gobstopper or a bag of aniseed balls. Also on offer were ; liquorice allsorts, lollipops, chewing gum, jelly babies, thin chocolate bars in a wrapper, toffee apples and acid drops. Others that come to mind are coconut-ice and carob seed pods, the latter being chewed until all taste had gone. They were then discarded. Many of these sweets can still be bought today, although I suspect many of the old colouring dyes used in those days have been superseded by safer ones.

Many of the sights and sounds of my childhood have been overtaken by so-called `progress` but in my opinion, not always for the better. I can see in my mind's eye, a silver sixpence in the Christmas pudding, or the wish-bone from a chicken or Christmas turkey, being pulled with great determination with one finger . If you won it you were allowed to make a wish. Furniture glue boiling in a pot. Feather-filled pillows and eiderdowns. Paraffin lamps and wax candles. Boxes of matches. Small bundles of firewood and buckets of coal. Wind-up gramophones and the essential gramophone needle, which frequently needed replacing. Woollen blankets and flannel sheets. Telegram boys, sit -up-and-beg bicycles, trolley-buses and trams. Steam trains and steam rollers. The shoemaker's last. Gaslight with its glowing mantle, which often had to be changed. Dolly-tubs and the old brick copper. The scrubbing board and those large hand-operated mangles with wooden rollers for wringing out the clothes. Large bars of soap and hot water bottles (no detergents or electric blankets then).

Plastics were yet to come, except for bakelite, which tended to be brittle. As a consequence, many electrical items soon became unsafe, not only because of the fracturing of the bakelite but also because electric cables were rubber insulated and this soon perished.

As I have mentioned previously, people in the main were poor. This does not mean we did not enjoy ourselves as children. Family poverty led to hardship, neighbourliness, resourcefulness, tolerance and compassion. It made people tough and resolute, which stood us in good stead during World War II. Used as hoops, discarded bicycle wheels and loose tyres gave hours of fun. A cheap common toy often seen in the street was the wooden whipping top. Hand-made catapults were usually in vogue with the boys. Nowadays, they would not be tolerated.

To a child, November the 5th, Guy Fawkes Day, is one of the highlights of the year and so it was then. In October 1933, I was returning home from an errand in North Ealing. Approaching St Barnabas Church, I spotted two boys playing with fireworks in the adjacent field. As I walked past, they placed a penny rocket in a bottle and lit the blue touch-paper. I paused to watch, expecting to see it heading skywards. It didn't ! Instead it travelled horizontally and headed straight for me. It landed on my shoulder, still violently ejecting fire and smoke, where it stayed. In a panic, I swung my right arm across my chest to knock it off. It burnt the end of my thumb and dropped to the ground. The pain was intense. I ran home. My mother showed concern for me but also found the rocket had burnt a hole in my shirt. She was not pleased, which was understandable. To replace a child's shirt meant taking quite a slice out of the meagre family weekly income.

*　*　*　*　*

AWAY FROM HOME

It was still 1933. At that time my parents were having serious difficulties with their marriage. The fault lay mainly on my father's side. He socialised with the wrong crowd and became involved with other women. One day, my mother answered the telephone. A women at the other end of the line, in a hysterical state, said that if she could not have my Dad she would shoot herself. Personally, if I had known about this, I would have been pleased to give her the gun ! I knew nothing of this until Mother told me about it when I was fourteen. She also told me that when I was eight my father went to hit her, when there was a row going on and that I ran into the room and stood between them. Apparently, I said,
"Don't you hit my Mum,"
and my father backed off. What could I as an eight year old have done, if Father had attacked her ? I don't remember this incident myself. Possibly because I was probably in a state of shock, my childhood having been happy until then. Even so, I loved both my parents and later in life, because my father had served in the trenches in WWI from the age of fifteen, I tended to make allowances for his behaviour. I firmly believe that all those men who returned to `Blighty` from the fighting were not the same mentally as when they first went out to France. And so it is today, whatever war they happen to have been involved in. It doesn't excuse my father's behaviour.

To help to make ends meet, my mother got an evening job as an usherette at the Duke of York theatre in London. Strangely, only women with auburn hair were considered for employment there.

My parents decided they needed some space to air their thoughts, to try and save their marriage. Father decided therefore to board out Pat and myself . My sister and I ended up in a boarding house for children in Southampton, run by a strict, tall, middle-aged woman. She prepared our meals and provided a bed, a bath and a toilet. All the boarded children attended a local school. Unfortunately the lady was a dog fanatic and owned over a dozen Pekingese lap-dogs. These were led out into the garden and did there what they naturally had to do. Not a single square yard of the garden was suitable for a child to play on. We children really looked forward to going to school to get away from the place.

The landlady had a peculiar attitude towards children concerning the functioning of their bowels. Woe betide any unfortunate child that suffered from constipation! They would be made to stay on the toilet for an indefinite period, even if it meant being late for school. I gained the impression that her attitude to us was the same as her attitude to her Pekingese. In fact, it was a wonder that constipated children were not told to squat in the garden.

This unhappy state of affairs came to a head when Mother visited us. She realised at once that all was not well. Having listened to our complaints she asked to inspect the garden. Seeing what an unhygienic state it was in, and to our great relief I might add, she immediately decided to take Pat and me back to London.

*   *   *   *   *

CHAPTER THREE

THE ELUSIVE FISH

In 1934 my parents moved to my grand parents` house in Hill Rise, Greenford, Middlesex . My first day at Greenford School went smoothly until the time came to go home. I had initially approached the day with butterflies in my stomach but I need not have worried, as the school was fine. Everyone was helpful, or so I thought.

When setting off for home, I was joined by an older boy.
"If you go along that path," he said pointing, "you will come to a small bridge over a stream." "There are some fish in it." I readily followed him along the path eager to see the fish. We came to the bridge and stood looking down into the water. "Can you see the fish?" he asked. I stared hard but although the water was clear I could see nothing. "I can't see anything, " I said.
"We will climb down to the bank You will see them from there," he said. We walked off the bridge and descended the bank to the waters edge.
"There they are," he said, pointing.
"Where? I still can't see them."
"Over there," he shouted, in an exasperated tone. I leaned out further, peering. Suddenly he shouted "You will see them better if you are in the water," and gave me an almighty shove. I fell into the stream, face down. The water was freezing cold. I stood up in the shallow stream, gasping and spluttering. He was already running off, across the bridge, letting out hoots of laughter.

I walked home cold, wet and miserable. I was concerned about my clothes and my leather satchel. I did not tell my mother about my attacker but merely explained I had slipped into a stream. Going to school the next day, naturally I was on the look out for that boy. It turned out he was sick, away from school with a heavy cold. As far as I was concerned that was judgement on him. I learned from other children, he was the school bully. Several children had cause to complain about his actions. We put our heads together and decided when he returned we would gang up on him. We agreed, if he should pick on any one of us we would converge on him but not speak to him. In other words, `send him to Coventry`. It worked ! We didn't have any more trouble from him. In fact, if I recollect correctly, he turned into quite a reasonable lad. I did not receive an apology from him, but then I was not expecting one. I had been tricked, good and proper.

*   *   *   *   *

THE CABBAGE PATCH

Walking home from Greenford School one day I passed a mulberry hedge in a small front garden. I noticed the hedge was smothered with hairy caterpillars. I ran home to fetch a jar. Returning to the hedge, I plucked as many of the insects as I could and popped them into the jar, together with some mulberry leaves. With some feeling of satisfaction, I ran home and placed the jar in the kitchen window. For some time I was engrossed in watching the caterpillars munching the leaves at an incredible rate. This surprised me. I decided to fetch more leaves. I got back to the kitchen as my grandmother entered. She soon spotted the insects and in a voice of shocked horror, sternly told me to take them outside. I didn't want to see the creatures die, so I took them down the garden and released them on Grandfather's cabbage patch. Mistakenly I thought they would happily live on brassica. Luckily for Grandad and me (especially me) they preferred mulberry leaves, their staple diet. When Grandad found out what I had done he was very cross and from then on made frequent inspections of his cabbages but found no damage. He eventually calmed down, when he realised his precious vegetables would come to no harm.

*　　*　　*　　*　　*

GRACIE

My grandmother was a staid, kindly, stern but humourless lady. I put the latter down to her deafness. On this particular Sunday, the table was being set for dinner. The wireless was on. Gracie Fields was singing. At the end of her song Gracie made a quip which had everyone laughing, including me. I did not understand her joke but laughed with the rest, as children tend to do. Poor Nanna however, had not heard the end of the joke and so missed the point.
"What did she say ?" she asked, turning to me. "Soppy sod !" I shouted because that is what I thought I had heard. My grandmother was outraged and I was sent to my room. Worst of all, I had to forgo my Sunday dinner.

Not far from Granddad's house was a racecourse. Trotting races were held there. To me the course was like a magnet. I could not resist paying it frequent visits. I would climb on top of the perimeter fence and watch the horses exercising. Especially enjoyable was the sight of a horse-drawn sulky, with the horses flashing hooves and flying mane. The whole action seemed to be so rhythmically smooth.

On a summer's day I walked over to the racecourse as usual, but was shocked to find there were no horses to be seen. I walked back home, dragging my feet all the way with disappointment. A few months later I became aware of the sound of revving engines coming from the racecourse. I made a dash for the course and climbed up onto the fence. Wonder of wonders ! Brightly coloured racing cars were gathered in front of the grandstand and were soon hurtling round the track. Clouds of dust arose and hung in the air. There were a few more meetings that year. The following year, much to my disappointment, the racing cars failed to materialise. After that the track fell into disuse and soon became overgrown with weeds. Eventually it made way for a housing estate.

On my visits to the racecourse, it was necessary for me to pass a particular house. Somehow, my grandfather had become acquainted with the occupant, an artist. He turned out to be a follower of Sir Oswald Mosley, the hated leader of the British Fascists : the `Blackshirts`. The artist often made journeys up to London to attend political meetings and rallies of that organisation. On each occasion he wore a black shirt. When I passed his house one day I noticed his curtains had not been drawn. I told Grandad and he went round to the house. He discovered that the Blackshirt was in a sorry state. His face had been slashed with a razor and he had been beaten up. He wasn't seen about much after that and soon left the district.

*　　*　　*　　*　　*

TOFFEES UNDER CANVAS

In that same year, 1934, my parents decided I should join the Boy Scouts. As I was only nine years old, I was obliged to join the Wolf Cubs. It was during the summer holiday the troop set off for a camping week at Beaulieu in Hampshire. This was an enjoyable event and one that is fondly remembered. When we arrived at our destination there were the usual comings and goings associated with such a function. Our first task was to set up camp. This involved marching to a field, locating a suitable water source, erecting our tents and lastly, setting up a latrine. The days that followed comprised a well tried programme of demonstrations, followed by practical applications by the boys. How to build a shelter. How to light a fire, using gathered dry sticks. The preparation of meals and how to cook the food on the open fire. The tying and use of various knots. We were often taken for long treks through field and woodland. On each of these walks the Cub master would insist on whistling or worse still, singing such tunes as *Colonel Bogey* and *Oh Jemima.* We were encouraged to join in, although I must say, not all the boys were filled with the same enthusiasm.

The day before we were due to return home, we went on our last trek. We eventually came to a small village. The local shop sold just about everything. Thankfully, that included sweets. Luckily, I still had some money left over from the money my mother had given me for the camp. I decided to buy her a large tin of Mackintosh toffees. I happily carried the tin back to camp. Early the next day we were all busily involved in packing our belongings and taking down the tents. Soon a charabanc arrived and we all clambered aboard for the station .

The journey home entailed a train to London, followed by a short trip on the Northern Line to join up with the Piccadilly Line and thence travelling west to South Ruislip, where my grandfather, a widower, now lived. The tin of toffees was too large to pack. For most of the journey I sat clutching the tin on my lap. During the first leg of the journey I succumbed to temptation. Opening the lid, I stuffed a toffee into my mouth and discreetly put several in my pocket and then quietly closed the lid. After having sucked my way through the `spoils`, we reached London. We soon alighted and were herded together by the Cub master, who checked to see that none of us was missing. Then we headed along the platform towards the barrier. It was when I had passed the ticket collector that disaster struck. As I was stepping onto a large escalator, the tin of sweets slipped from my grasp. As it bounced and clattered down the moving staircase people looked back over their shoulder to see what the racket was. Then the lid flew off and all the toffees spilled out. My heart sank. "Mum will not get any toffees now," I thought, but I was wrong.

When I finally reached the foot of the escalator there was a battered tin and a bent lid, which had probably been stepped on. Thankfully however, most of the toffees were still intact. They were bobbing up and down, at the point where the moving staircase disappears into the floor. Jumping off, I put my pack and small case down and turned to face the oncoming rush of human traffic. Hastily grabbing the battered tin I managed to retrieve the bent lid and the shunting toffees. Much of the remainder of my journey was taken up with trying to fit the lid back on the tin. Eventually, by diligent straightening with fingers and thumb, I more or less succeeded.

Finally I reached home, tired but happy. My mother was so pleased to see me. When I presented her with the toffees, tears came to her eyes. I owned up to the fact that I had helped myself to a few. She made no comment but just smiled knowingly. However, she was not very impressed with the poor state of the tin, and said so. We both laughed when I explained the reason for the dents.

* * * * *

A ROYAL CONNECTION

In 1935 when I was ten, my father took me to Windsor to see a great aunt, whom I had not previously met. She ran a small tearoom, which was situated at the bottom of the hill that runs down from Windsor Castle. As I recall, it stood opposite the King George the Fifth monument and was part of a very old building - probably listed. It should still be there, unless the developers have had their way. At the rear of the main tearoom were a couple of stone steps, leading up to a dark floor area. Stacked in the far corner was a large heap of coal. Not what one would nowadays consider to be a suitable vista for customers.

My father and his aunt sat in the tearoom in front of a blazing fire and conversed for some time. Eventually auntie said she would have to fetch some more coal. Father ordered me to help her, much to my relief as I was becoming bored. I was handed the empty coal-scuttle and ascended the steps with auntie following me. After I had filled the scuttle my father carried it down to the fireplace. While he was doing this, Auntie pointed to a bricked up doorway in a brick wall at the side of the dim room. "That is where a tunnel leads down from the castle. It was intended as an escape route but the authorities had it bricked up," she said. I thrilled at this, imagining figures of importance way back in history making good their escape from the castle. It could have been an escape tunnel, but on the other hand it might have been a sally-port.

Further to the right of the bricked-up doorway was a rectangular opening in the wall at about shoulder-height. It held several iron bars. By jumping up I could just make out a dark room beyond the bars. It was too dark to pick out any detail. "They used to keep lepers in there and pass food to them through this opening," Auntie said. Whether that was true I cannot say, but the bars had been put there for a purpose. Also when I think about it, there must have been an access to that room, possibly leading in from the side of the tunnel via the bricked up doorway. I have often wondered whether it is still there.

* * * * *

THE NOXIOUS MIXTURE

It was at this time in my life that I learnt how to make up an explosive. It would be unwise of me to disclose the chemical ingredients I used in the mixture, or to specify the precise proportions required of each constituent. It is sufficient for me to state that I had involved myself in a very dangerous practice, although, I did not appreciate the danger at the time. My father was oblivious to my warlike activities and I was careful not to play around with the chemicals when he was not at work.

As soon as I was paid my pocket money I would rush down to the shops at South Ruislip and call in at the chemists. There I would buy the necessary ingredients. These came in separate paper bags. The chemist never thought to question why I was buying these chemicals, even though I paid him a weekly call. It was important not to mix the different powders before reaching home. Such an unstable mix, if shaken, could well explode.

Arriving home, I would tip all the powders into one jam jar. Then I had one of two options. I could either ignite the mix, when it would burn fiercely with a magnesium-like white-heat intensity, at the same time giving off clouds of poisonous, brown smoke. Or alternatively, I could take a small quantity of the mix and place it in a heap on the concrete back-garden path. I would then strike it with a hammer to cause a deafening report. Needless to say, I usually went for the second option, it being the more exciting and less wasteful. When I could afford it, the neighbourhood must have been like World War I, or so I imagined. No wonder my father often seemed to be mislaying his hammer.

Eventually Father observed several white patches on the path. He asked me what they were. My warlike activities soon came to light. From then on, much to my chagrin, I was forbidden to buy any more such chemicals. Thinking back now, I find it quite strange that my mother made no attempt to curtail my warlike exploits. She often said that `boys will be boys`, which was her way of making allowances for me I suppose.

$$* \quad * \quad * \quad * \quad *$$

GANG WARFARE

Our `gang` tended to make for the local shops, by South Ruislip Station. Some time during the summer of 1935, I shut the gate behind me at my home in Ashburton Road and ran towards the shops to join the `gang`. Those shops were like a magnet to us children. Much of our time was spent pressing our noses to the cold glass shop windows, gazing at things we would have liked but could not afford. After a period of shop gazing we would decide to go and watch the trains. We ran underneath the railway bridge to a convenient field on the other side of the track. By climbing onto the perimeter fence, we had a good vantage point. The field was often used as a dumping ground for a variety of scrap. All sorts of discarded metal objects, bits and pieces, old prams as well as cardboard boxes etc,.

We had only been in the field for a short while, when our enjoyment was interrupted by another group of children. They were of similar age to ourselves but were an ill-bred lot. They started to hurl insults at us and lob the odd stone in our direction. We were not going to stand for that. I took it upon myself to act as spokesman and suggested to them that we have a proper battle, from entrenched positions. They agreed to this. The two groups separated and started to lay their hands on various items of scrap. Our group managed to find an old corrugated iron sheet . This was set up as a protective screen for the four of us. It had one drawback however. To see the `enemy` we had to either look over the top or around the ends. We scouted around for some missiles - mostly stones. These were set up in small piles behind us. While these preparations were being made, there was much shouting and dire threats hurled between opposing camps.

Battle commenced. Most of the incoming missiles bounced off our `fort` with a loud clatter, and fell harmlessly to the ground. We experienced a feeling of satisfaction that the iron sheet gave such good protection. It was rather like being in a thunder storm. If you heard the thunder you knew the lightning had already passed. Although we were well protected, to take effective aim we had to show ourselves. The protection afforded to our opponents was just a couple of large cardboard boxes.

It was during the battle that I peered over the top, just as a piece of brick was lobbed towards us. It hit me hard on the forehead, just above the hair line. There was blood everywhere. The sight of the blood running down my face frightened our opponents and they ran off. I was quite proud of the blood and deliberately smeared some more over my shirt. My companions looked concerned. I decided to make for home. My sister Pat greeted me at the front door.

"Mum, Mum, John's bleeding," she hollered. My mother rushed out of the kitchen and after getting over the initial shock, she expressed her concern and became quite cross about my shirt. I still have a slight scar on my forehead. Whenever I touch it or notice it in the mirror, I fondly recall my childhood `battle`.

*   *   *   *   *

A FRUSTRATED INFATUATION

At this time, I was attending a mixed elementary school at South Ruislip. Many childish infatuations blossomed there between the boys and girls. It was common practice during lessons to furtively pass notes to one another across the classroom. I recall an attractive, dark-haired girl in my class called Barbara Swain. She sat quite near me and I used to scribble notes to her. Unbeknown to me, so did one or two other lads as well. On one occasion I scribbled her an innocent note to tell her that I would meet her on a small common that was conveniently on my route home. Secrecy was essential, as I wished to avoid the taunts of the other lads. Barbara nodded back to me when she had read the note. I took this to be confirmation that she would be there.

When I reached the common on my way home, I was shocked and disappointed to find she had another lad in tow. My reaction was immediate, unfortunate and cowardly. I angrily slapped her face. It was at that precise moment my father started across the footpath on his way home from work. He had witnessed the incident. "John, I have told you never to hit girls," he barked angrily. "Go home now and I will deal with you later." I set off for home with a heavy heart, knowing that I was for it, whilst my father stayed behind to apologise for my cowardly action.

When my father arrived home he gave me a spanking and sent me up to my room. As I reached the landing, he shouted after me, as an afterthought, "You can write me one hundred lines -`*I must not hit girls*`". I much preferred the spanking to the lines. The discipline certainly worked, because from that day onwards I never again struck a member of the opposite sex.

*   *   *   *   *

THE BIG DRAG

As children, we lived at a time when two thirds of the population smoked. None of the `gang` had done so. One day the children decided to walk along an alleyway at the back of the shops in South Ruislip. It was now 1936 and I was eleven years old. When we came to the back of a newsagents and tobacconist we noticed a heap of rubbish in the yard. We spotted amongst it a number of packets of Wild Woodbine cigarettes - a very popular brand in those days and fondly tagged `Willy Woodbines`. They were packed five to a pack, in a green paper sleeve.

The cigarettes we saw were spoiled stock, which had become either too old, too dry or too damp. Whatever the reason, to us it was like finding gold. We ran off with a packet each and made for `our` field. We all sat on the ground behind some bushes. `Bigs`, the fattest member of the group, produced a box of matches from his grubby jacket. We lit up. There was much laughter, coughing and of course, smoke. We attempted to smoke all five of our cigarettes but it wasn't long before we started to turn several shades of pale. One lad said he felt giddy and soon started to throw up. None of us felt very good, so we chucked the rest of the fags into the bushes and set off for home. "Never again" we said, expressing our disappointment at this silly, overrated adult pastime. I didn't tell my parents what I had been up to.

Unfortunately in my late teens I did become a smoker, so that was one childhood experience I failed to learn from.

*　　*　　*　　*　　*

CHAPTER FOUR

A CHRISTMAS HICCUP

No doubt I was a nervous child when it came to officialdom, pomp or ceremony. It was with some trepidation therefore that I responded to the choirmaster of Ruislip Church choir, when he asked me to sing solo at a BBC Christmas service. The service was to be broadcast live from the church and BBC musicians were to take part. I was to sing the part of the Page in the carol `Good King Wenceslas`. A professional baritone would be singing the part of the King. For the life of me, I cannot remember his name. In fact I don't think I was told it. During several practice sessions the baritone's part was taken by the choirmaster. It was only at the live broadcast that the baritone was to perform.

I had little sleep on the night before the broadcast. Next day I set off early for the church, full of apprehension and experiencing a very dry throat. So dry in fact, that I doubted whether I would be able to sing a single note. My proud parents came with me. Then came the moment I was dreading. We entered the church. Already, there was a large congregation. Mother and Father were ushered to a front pew, while I headed for the vestry. Several of the choristers had already arrived and were busily changing. I donned my cassock and surplice. We were forbidden to speak. The only noise to be heard was from the gathering congregation and from the BBC. engineers making final adjustments to their equipment. Presently we heard several musicians tuning their instruments.

The vicar led us out into the aisle and the choir filed into the stalls. The vicar stood by the pulpit and the choirmaster mounted a rostrum. The church was packed. A hush fell over the congregation. My gaze was drawn towards the musicians and to the BBC. equipment. Oh for calm nerves ! Just then the choirmaster tapped the rostrum to gain our attention, the vicar announced the first carol and the service had begun. This allowed me to exercise my tonsils and after a shaky start, my voice seemed to gain strength. We sang several carols, during which the celebrated baritone joined in. He had a fine, powerful voice and gained my immediate respect . The choirmaster half gyrated on the rostrum, waving his arms about like some flightless bird. It was very apparent the effort he was making in keeping the choir and the congregation singing as one. It was a joyous sound. Soon it was my turn to sing with the baritone. Then my legs turned to jelly and my throat dried up again. After a shaky start my voice cleared and soon, I swear `Good King Wenceslas` was never rendered better by anyone. That is until we came to the second verse: `Hither page , and stand by me`, the baritones part, but I continued to sing. The choirmaster nearly had an apoplectic fit on the spot. Seeing him glowering at me, I immediately realised my mistake and stifled my voice. I must say the professional singer carried on as though nothing untoward had happened. He had such a strong voice that I doubt if my mistake had been noticed by the congregation, as it was only for a brief moment. After the service no one made any comment other than the choirmaster. He was none too pleased. When I told them what I had done, my parents were very sympathetic and said how much they had enjoyed the service.

*   *   *   *   *

LITTLE ANGELS

During choir practice the choirboys were like `little angels`. It was only when we came out of church afterwards, that we often got up to mischief. Our favourite prank was to tie a black thread to a front door-knocker, pulling the thread gently through the hedge and then also tying it to the door of an adjacent house. Then, as a group of three or four young boys, we would crouch on the pavement behind the hedge. The thread was then tugged. We waited to see what effect this had on the occupants. We found it difficult to control our mirth, so as not to make any noise and prevent discovery. The unfortunate occupants reacted in various ways. Some would open their door, look around and shut it again. Others would both open their doors at the same time. We often heard shouted, "Those bloody children !"and the door being slammed. On one occasion when we tried the same prank, the front door opened and a large Alsatian appeared on the doorstep. We scattered in all directions in considerable panic.

*   *   *   *   *

SKATES AND THE AXE MAN

Whilst still living in Ashburton Road, South Ruislip, my parents bought me a pair of roller skates as a birthday present. It was not long before I became quite adept in their use. So much so, that I used them regularly to travel to school and back. Thankfully pavements then were reasonably level. Otherwise the journey of some mile and a half would have been fraught with danger. The skates clattered rhythmically as I progressed down the street, from one paving to another. Being quite noisy the skates gave warning to pedestrians of my approach. The type of skates I was using had metal wheels mounted on ball-bearings and so were quite fast. They did however have one main drawback in that the metal wheel rims soon wore down and had to be frequently replaced. Replacement was simple, as long as one carried a spare wheel and a special spanner. I also tended to carry a can of 3-in-1 oil in my pocket. This lent itself to smooth running or should I say, smooth skating.

A few doors away lived an elderly couple, Mr and Mrs Cooksley. They had recently moved from Marlow. Both were in their eighties. I did not know them then but happily recall how we became friends. I was skating back from school and came down our street doing a good turn of speed. Suddenly a man whom I had never seen before, ran out of his front garden straight in front of me, waving an axe! To say that he scared the living daylights out of me would be an understatement. I swerved into the road, nearly losing my balance. It was Mr Cooksley. He laughed jovially and lowered the axe to his side.

"Sorry I frightened you ," he said. This was his way of introducing himself. Certainly eccentric, but amusing, when once I had got over the shock. "I am Mr Cooksley," he announced, beaming.

"I'm John," I said, gazing up at him respectfully. His tanned face was weather-beaten and lined but he exuded cheerfulness.

"Would you like to meet Mrs Cooksley?" he asked me proudly. I removed my skates and followed him up the short path leading to the house. We entered a small kitchen and from there I was shown into the drawing-room. Seated in a rocking-chair sat his wife, a silver-haired, jovial, portly lady with a radiant smile and rosy cheeks. Her hair was done up in a bun. We had a short chat and then, by way of dismissing me, she said "It has been nice talking to you John. You must come and see me again." I left the house thinking what nice people they were.

After that I often called on them on my way home from school. I learned from Mr Cooksley he had been a sailor for many years, serving on board the old sailing ships. He told me many tales of his seafaring days. I listened very attentively. Something he related to me has always remained firmly fixed in my mind. Apparently when he was a young cadet on a sail-training ship, the cadets had to line up on deck for a daily cleanliness inspection. They were expected to be spotlessly clean. He explained that if any cadet had the slightest suggestion of dirt under their fingernails they were dragged off by two brawny seamen and scrubbed down with sand. Harsh treatment indeed ! It goes without saying that I had a great respect for the old mariner and his kindly wife.

Sadly whilst we were still living in Ashburton Road, Mrs Cooksley died and her old sailor husband followed her a few days later, probably from a broken heart. When returning from school I always glanced at their house when passing. They were sadly missed.

* * * * *

DENTURES FOR THE FAMOUS

As a dental mechanic (nowadays called a dental technician) my father rented a dingy cellar below the pavements of Chiswick High Street, West London. He used this as his workshop. He was not his own boss however, but was employed by a dentist. This man had on his books several famous names as customers, people from the stage and film world. On Saturday mornings my father used to take me with him to his workshop. We would enter a short passage between two shops. On one side was a door leading to the cellar. Father would produce an impressive bunch of keys and unlock the door. We would descend a flight of very narrow wooden stairs, ending up in a cold, dim room. The only natural light glimmered above from a thick glass pavement grid. There were no windows. I used to sit on an old wooden stool and gaze up at the pavement, fascinated by the moving dark shadows of the pedestrians in the street, as their feet clattered over the glass.

When Father switched on the light - a single shadeless bulb - an interesting array of equipment was revealed. On the floor stood a vulcaniser. This had a similar function to a pressure-cooker but the pressures reached were much higher. It was fitted with a brass pressure gauge and when under pressure, it hissed ominously. Releasing the pressure valve caused great clouds of steam to pervade the whole room. Condensation started to glisten on the walls . My father would then undo some clamps and after raising the heavy lid of the vessel would remove a set of false teeth. These had previously been teeth set in moulded rubber platelets but the vulcanising process had hardened the rubber.

This new set of teeth was now ready for grinding and polishing. A grinding and polishing machine was permanently mounted on the workbench. After some skilful grinding, my father would change over to the polishing stage. This was a particularly messy process. A plate of false teeth would be held against a high-speed, rotating cloth wheel. The wheel had to be continually fed with a water-grit slurry, which was given to flying everywhere, on the ceiling, on father and on myself, as an onlooker.

A shelf at the rear of the workbench held many sets of teeth. To me they all appeared to be grinning. Plaster casts, short lengths of wire and pink wax were also on the shelf. The wax gave off a pleasant smell when melted. My father aggravated these awful working conditions by smoking heavily. Sometimes he worked with gold, although I never found out where he kept the precious stuff. His wage, as I have said before, was about two pounds per week, which, considering the skills required in producing a decent set of teeth, was a poor wage. I know my father made teeth for some of the celebrities of the time, including several film-stars. Amongst these were Jessie Matthews and Robertson Hare. It was probably through his work that he came to play cricket with film-stars C.Aubrey-Smith (The Four Feathers) and Nigel Bruce (Dr.Watson). I always remember my father describing an incident concerning Nigel Bruce. Bruce was apparently in the trenches in WW1. He was always up to some mad caper. On one occasion he suddenly stood up in his trench and cocked a snook at the Germans, who promptly shot him ! He survived this but was invalided back to Blighty. And so it did him some sort of good, but I can think of better ways to get sent home !

*   *   *   *   *

NATURAL PHENOMENA AND ATMOSPHERIC POLLUTION

Two spectacular natural phenomena occurred, whilst I was living in Ashburton Road. I think the first happened at night, in 1936. There was a wonderful display of the aurora borealis. This phenomenon (The Northern Lights), usually seen at more northerly latitudes, is rarely observed as far south as London. What was so unusual, too, was the colour - a pinkish mauve, presumably due to the heavily polluted atmosphere that frequently hung over the capital and the surrounding area.

The second phenomenon (can`t be sure if it occurred in the same year) took place in the back garden. My father had constructed a rustic trellis and set it behind the lawn. It was an oppressive day which culminated in a severe thunderstorm. During thunderstorms I would stand by the window, waiting to see the next flash of lightning. On this occasion I was gazing out of the kitchen window when I became aware of a strange, faint blue, luminous glow on the trellis. It soon became brighter. I called my parents. We stood and watched, fascinated by this ghostly-blue light, which eventually outlined the entire trellis. We were to learn later that we had seen an electrical display - St. Elmo`s Fire ! I was to witness such a display again, ten years later in the Pacific, when the entire mast and rigging of my Royal Navy destroyer was similarly outlined with this weird glow.

Mention was made earlier of the polluted atmosphere of London. I well remember experiencing those awful fogs of the thirties (now called smog). The fog was unbelievably dense. So dense in fact, that if you stood beneath a street lamp and peered upwards, all you could make out was a faint orange glow. People out and about would be constantly apologising as they bumped into others walking in the opposite direction. I do recall reading a newspaper item at the time which referred to an incident that took place in a London `pea souper`. It involved a large house which had a long, semi-circular drive with two roadside entrances. A bus driver mistakenly drove his double-decker bus up the drive. To make matters worse, several cars behind followed him. This shows how bad those fogs were. The situation at the house must have been chaotic. God knows what the occupants of the house thought if they were in residence! If they were not at home perhaps they could not reach home because of the fog. Or perhaps they were on that bus !

21

BEYOND THE WOODS

You could say I was a budding naturalist. I used to go for long treks in Ruislip Woods. At the time my interest was directed more towards the fauna than the flora. Insects in particular fascinated me. Sometimes I walked many miles. I can remember one trek when I walked to Rickmansworth and back - some seventeen miles. During my woodland treks I would often encounter the perimeter fence of Hillingdon Hospital ; at that time a tuberculosis hospital. If I remember correctly it was called Mount Vernon Hospital. Mostly however I usually made for Ruislip Reservoir, which was on the far side of the wood. This stretch of water had much to offer both in scenery and for water sports. There was a very good lido near the approach road.

One day as I advanced through the wood towards the reservoir, I heard the murmur of many voices and the roar of engines from across the water. I hastened my steps. As I emerged from the trees I saw a hydroplane race in progress. To a young boy the sight and sound of those noisy, bouncing, streamlined craft, skimming over the water at great speed was very exciting. I was thrilled. I had never seen such craft before and enjoyed seeing their spray being flung out in all directions. What crazy angles they achieved as they rounded the marker-buoys.

A famous road-racing driver of the time Captain George Eyston was competing in one of the races. Suddenly his craft was flung into the air and capsized, settling on the water completely upside-down. It was with great relief the spectators heard over the public address system that he was unharmed. Information was also imparted that his craft would not sink because the hull was packed with some 15,000 ping-pong balls. I could not get home fast enough to tell my parents what I had witnessed.

*   *   *   *   *

A HORSE AND CAR

It was on a Sunday in the late winter of 1937, that my father decided to take us for a spin in the car, a Riley Nine. The car had a rounded, shiny radiator cowl, which I used to take great pride in polishing. If you put your face close to the radiator your reflected features appeared to be comically distorted, similar to the effect of a fairground mirror. We set off on our journey and eventually found ourselves in Brighton. On the return journey when we were about one-and-a-half miles from home, the engine started to cough and we came to a jerky stop. The car had run out of petrol. Father decided as it was getting late and we were not far from home, to leave the car at the roadside for the night. In those days it was fairly safe to leave your car anywhere, without risk of it being stolen or vandalised.

Next morning Father obtained a can of petrol and we set off for the car. After filling the tank he tried to start it, using a starting-handle to crank the engine. The car refused to start, probably because the engine was cold. While my father was engaged in this exertion, he suddenly noticed a large pool of oil on the ground, immediately beneath the engine. He crawled underneath the car and discovered the cylinder block had cracked. This must have been caused by the very low temperature during the previous night. The water in the engine water-jacket had frozen, bursting the block. Antifreeze had not been heard of then.

There was nothing for it but to abandon the car and walk home again. As we reached home we saw a coal cart. A huge cart-horse stood patiently between the shafts, while its master unloaded the heavy sacks of coal. Father told the coalman about the sorry state of the car. He offered to pay him if he would unhitch the horse and tow the car back home. A deal was struck and much to my delight, I was given a ride on the back of this huge animal. When we reached the car, the coalman attached a rope to the front of the Riley. I was lifted down from the horse and climbed into the car. Father took the wheel, whilst the horse was led by the bridle. The car started to move. This magnificent animal towed our car all the way back to the house. It performed seemingly effortlessly, including negotiating a long, gradual rise approaching the house .

The horse was put back between the shafts and the coalman was rewarded. Our lives returned to normal. It was a wonderful feat and good thinking on my father's part When I consider this event, I suppose to the horse it was really no different from pulling a loaded coal-cart, except there were certainly fewer stops and starts.

*   *   *   *   *

ELASTIC-POWERED FLIGHT

One of my childhood hobbies was the construction of model aeroplanes. The fuselage and wings were made of balsa-wood sections, each strut being cut out from a pre-printed balsa-wood sheet. Working to a detailed plan I glued the fuselage framework together. The fuselage was then covered with a tissue-paper skin. This was treated with `dope`, a sweet-smelling varnish, which always reminded me of pear drops. Varnishing the paper skin toughened it, making the assemblage more rigid.

When a new model was completely assembled I could not get out of the house quickly enough to give it its maiden flight. Propulsion was achieved by a wound, elastic-powered propeller. The usual method of winding the elastic was to rotate the propeller with the index finger. This method had one or two drawbacks. Firstly it was extremely slow. Secondly, if the finger missed a rotation during winding, the propeller would reverse at high speed, giving one some painful knocks on the finger. Often the skin was broken and there was certainly some bruising. Worse still, winding had to be started again, from scratch.

The culmination of all my efforts was of course the first flight. Each model seemed to have little quirks of its own, but once I had sorted out the teething troubles, they usually flew with some grace, if not duration. Most models were launched with a controlled throw into the wind. The elastic unwound completely in a few seconds, whereas the rewinding took a minute or two.

The fact that my grandfather's house in Victoria Road, South Ruislip, was very near to RAF Northolt probably prompted me to take up this hobby. Little did we realise that the clouds of war were fast approaching. Northolt Aerodrome would become the home of No. 111 Squadron, a famous Battle-of-Britain squadron, defending London during WW11.

*   *   *   *   *

MY FIRST FUNERAL

At the age of nine I was taken by my parents to West Drayton to attend a funeral. It was the first funeral of my life. My great grandfather, Grandad Squire, was lying in his coffin in the drawing room. Two great aunts, both dressed in black, went into the room to say their farewells. I was not allowed to enter.

"He looks beautiful," said one of the aunts as she came out of the room. This was my first realisation that life is not eternal and we are all accountable and so I was quiet with my own thoughts for most of the funeral.

The hearse was horse-drawn and immaculate. Two black horses had large black plumes attached to the head gear. The pallbearers walked along each side of the hearse, with the family including myself following on behind.

Funeral services seem to me like a bad dream, a trance-like ceremony in which, however good the preacher, all the mourners are glad to converge on the exit to get some air. When we leave the church, it is as though a weight is lifted from us, unless we are closest to the deceased. Then of course time has to be our best friend and our greatest healer.

*   *   *   *   *

WILLIAM BROWN STORIES

Apart from reading comics, boys magazines and the like, I particularly enjoyed two publications : Arthur Mee`s -`Children`s Newspaper` and Richmal Crompton`s - `William` books. `Just William` was my favourite title and at times I imagined myself as William in several of the situations I found myself in. The William Brown character was a popular icon for most boys of the 1930s, of my age.

*   *   *   *   *

THE CRYSTAL SET

Living so near to Northolt Aerodrome it was inevitable that the family would attend the annual air display. Planes, such as the Gloucester Gladiator, the Avro Tutor, the Whitley Bomber and the Hawker Hart, were often in the display. So too was the Avro Anson. There was always a static display within one or two open hangars. I was overawed by everything, especially the sheer size of the huge hangar doors.

At home I made a wireless crystal set and used to don a pair of bakelite headphones. I spent hours fiddling with the cat`s whisker, hoping to pick up a signal from the airwaves. I was quite successful, although it took a lot of patience. On one occasion I was really thrilled when I picked up a transmission from the airfield.

*   *   *   *   *

24

THE BIRDMAN

In 1937 I was still living in Victoria Road, South Ruislip. I can remember a brave American whose name if I recall it correctly was Clem Sohn. He hit the headlines in Britain when he started to leap from aeroplanes. He had special wings made which were fitted to his wrists and ankles. He also carried a parachute strapped to his back. When he jumped from a Farnham plane at 10,000 feet he would free fall until he was at a height of about 4,000 feet. He would then open his arms and legs. This allowed him to glide about for no more than a minute, because his arms would soon tire from the terrific strain exerted upon them. Even so his was a thrilling and spectacular display. When the minute was up, he would bring his arms to the side of his body and close his legs. As he plummeted to earth he would open his parachute, gliding gracefully to the ground in the normal way.

Clem Sohn became an idol of every schoolboy in Britain. I well remember the Daily Express newspaper selling a cardboard model of this hero. It cost one shilling and sixpence and was launched with a catapult. When fired, the wings would open and it would glide effectively for a short distance, before crashing into the ground.

Sadly Clem came to a similar sticky end. On 3rd May 1937 he was taking part in an air circus at Vincennes in France, in front of 100,000 spectators, when his parachute became entangled with his wings and he plunged to earth. I was told he broke practically every bone in his body with the force of the impact.

*   *   *   *   *

LETTING OFF STEAM

My present for Christmas 1937 was a small, working model steam engine. My father showed me how to operate it. The engine required a small amount of water for the boiler. A small can, filled with methylated spirit and housing a wick, was pushed under the boiler. The wick was then lit. When the water eventually boiled it produced a steam pressure sufficient to move the piston up the cylinder. The energy thus produced was transferred to a large wheel, by means of a piston connecting rod, causing the wheel to rotate. I used this power to operate various mechanical toy models constructed from meccano metal strip.

There is a problem with using methylated spirit as the fuel for the boiler. It burns with an almost invisible blue flame. I say this because a few days after I had been given the engine, Grandfather happened to look out of his kitchen window and saw his shed was on fire ! With bucket and basin to the fore, the family ran out into the garden and doused the flames. Not too much harm was done as the fire had been spotted early. Needless to say I was not allowed to fire up the steam engine in the shed any more. From my point of view this was a pity as I could only play with the engine in the garden. And so I needed fine days and certainly not windy ones, otherwise it would have proved almost impossible to keep the flame alight beneath the boiler.

I dread to think what would have happened if Grandfather had not looked out of the window when he did. There would not have been a shed left for a start. Nor would my steam engine have survived. It was as a result of the fire that several soldered engine pipe joints had to be re-soldered. Should those joints have held, the boiler would probably have exploded with a very loud bang !

*   *   *   *   *

TO MAKE A POINT

If you asked any young boy of that time what he would do with a long bamboo cane, the chances are he would suggest making a bow or a kite. But I had already made these and had some success with the former. The kites however were not so successful, mainly because the covering fabric was too heavy. I had a job getting the kites properly balanced too.

I well remember acquiring a six-foot bamboo cane, probably from Grandad's shed. I managed to get hold of a short length of mild steel piping. I intended using it to make a spear-head. Using a hammer I beat one end flat for a length of about six inches. The second layer of flattened steel was removed with a hacksaw, as were the two corners, which were sawn off at an angle. Then I filed the edges until some sharpness was achieved. All that was left for me to do was to jam the thicker end of the cane up the remaining end of the pipe.

I raced to the field near the end of our road and taking aim at the trunk of a large tree, hurled it as hard as I could. It was a resounding success but (there is always a `but`) it had embedded itself in the trunk so deeply I was unable to pull it out. This was not for want of trying. It just would not budge. In the end I tugged on the cane once too often and it suddenly came out of the spear-head. I decided to call my father to assist me. I ran home. He walked back to the tree with me and immediately freed the spearhead effortlessly. After I had forced the cane back into the spear-head, Father said he would like a throw. He hurled it at the tree-trunk. It again embedded itself in the trunk as before, but this time when my father freed it he suddenly turned to me and said,

"Look John, we have both thrown your spear and it works very effectively as a weapon. Therefore I think you should now leave it in Grandad's shed, because if you were tempted to throw it towards someone, you might easily injure or even kill them. I don't want the worry of it."

I was extremely upset at the time but on reflection I had to accept my father's opinion. He was only being cautious.

*   *   *   *   *

CHAPTER FIVE

ONE TO THE MIDRIFF AND ONE TO THE JAW

My father decided I should learn the art of self-defence. On Saturday mornings, after he had finished work in the cellar, he would take me to Affleck`s Gymnasium on the Fulham Road, between Fulham and Putney. Initially I was put in the boxing ring for one round with a lad much bigger and older than myself to gain experience. I was so thin my punches carried no weight and my reach did not match that of my opponent`s. We finished the round unscathed, but I suspected my adversary was holding his punches. After several such encounters, in which I often ended up with a bloody nose, my father decided he wanted me to make more use of the gym equipment. And so I had sessions on the punch ball, the punch bag, a rowing machine, dumb-bells, a chest expander and the Indian clubs. Most of all I enjoyed the punch ball and the rhythmic slaps I could get from it. Skipping was also encouraged, but up until then I had thought this was a pastime for girls. I soon learnt differently. All this energetic activity did not turn me into a boxer, but it did do heaps for my morale.

I had recently passed an exam at school. This meant that instead of leaving school at fourteen I would go on to Acton Technical College until I was sixteen. So the work in the gym was to stand me in good stead at the college.

* * * * *

EDUCATION , EDUCATION

During my first year at college I experienced what I can only describe as `growing pains`. This also happened when I had attended school at Greenford. Without warning a joint would suddenly lose strength. This weakness usually occurred in the knee or the wrist, but particularly in the knee when I was running. The knee would just give way and I would fall over. I often ended up with grazes, especially to my knees. This sensation of weakness only lasted for a few seconds but was very disconcerting while it lasted.

An incident happened at college when a lad picked on me. I cannot remember what it was about. He took a swipe at me. I reacted by hitting him in the face. He took another swipe so I hit him again. I was winning and I felt good ! Suddenly when I tried to continue the scrap, I had an awful weakness in my wrist and so could not defend myself properly. I knew at once that fight was over. I just sat down on the quadrangle step and wept with frustration.

The school gym instructor who happened to be passing had been watching the fight and realised something was wrong. He came onto the quadrangle and gave me some words of encouragement. That man had represented England in gymnastics in the 1908 Olympic Games held in London. It goes without saying that we all showed him great respect.

* * * * *

CHAPTER SIX

THE CON

In 1938, although we still lived with my grandfather, we were shortly destined to move to North Ealing, on the outskirts of London. Grandfather put the house on the market and there was a `FOR SALE` sign in the front garden. On that occasion I remember Grandfather answering a knock at the front door. Standing on the doorstep was a smartly dressed man, wearing a trilby hat. He asked if he could look round the house with a view to buying. Grandfather allowed him in and showed him round. Afterwards the man said he was very impressed with the house and wished to buy it. He reached into his coat breast pocket and produced a cheque-book.
"I will make out a cheque as a deposit. Will seventy-five pounds do?" he asked.
"That will be fine," Grandfather said. The man gave Grandfather the cheque and left.

To say that Grandfather was pleased would be an understatement. He could hardly believe his luck that he had sold the house so quickly. About an hour later, there was another knock on the door. It was the same man.
"Sorry to bother you but I am having trouble. I have run out of petrol and have left my wallet at home. This is very embarrassing," he said. "Do you think you could lend me a pound ? I will pay you back the next time I see you and anyway you have my cheque". Grandfather parted with a pound Needless to say he never saw the man again.

Grandfather learnt later that the man had worked the same confidence trick at several local addresses on the same day. Apparently he was well known to the Police. On that day the crook had netted several pounds. Quite a haul for one day`s `work`, bearing in mind it represented the equivalent of several weeks wages to the ordinary working man.

*   *   *   *   *

UP TO NO GOOD

The chemistry lab` at Acton Tech` overlooked the quadrangle. In 1939 during one lunch hour, another lad and I left the playground. We went upstairs to the Lab`, suitably armed with a few brown paper bags. We opened a window overlooking the quadrangle. Two bags were filled with water and leaning out of the window we selected a `target`. The target was any unfortunate boy who happened to be beneath us at the time. If our aim was good the bag would burst on some boy's head. Knowing that from then on our window would be observed, we just filled the rest of the bags as quickly as we could and without showing ourselves, lobbed them out of the window. This caused much panic and laughter in the playground, as potential victims dodged the `bombs`.

Suddenly, a prefect appeared in the `Lab` doorway. We were caught red-handed. Both of us were made to go round the school, to wash all the blank blackboards we could find. When this chore was completed, we had to report back to the prefect. We were then detailed to pick up all the soggy bags in the quadrangle. Further humiliation was heaped upon us. We were also ordered to stand still for five minutes in the middle of the quadrangle with the soggy paper in our hands where everyone could see us.

Many grinning faces leered at us from the surrounding corridors. We could hear ribald comments being aimed at us from several directions. We mutually agreed not to pull the bag stunt again.

*　　*　　*　　*　　*

THE `ROLLS ROYCE` OF BIKES

By 1939 we were living in Selby Road, North Ealing. My mother bought me a second-hand piano-accordion. For a short while I spent all my spare time encouraging not-too-well-played tunes from it. I am one of those fortunate people who can pick up a musical instrument for the first time and coax a tune from it, playing by ear of course.

Several months later the accordion was gathering dust at the top of my wardrobe. I had let it be known that I would like a racing bike for my next birthday. My plea had fallen not so much on deaf ears but on a parent who could not afford such a luxury at that time. However fate turned out kind to be cruel because in a short while one of my schoolmates wanted to swap his bike for my accordion. I asked my mother if she would mind my doing the swap. She had no objection. I was soon the proud owner of not just any old bike, but a Claud Butler racing bike. In those days they were considered to be the `Rolls Royce` of bikes. I was very lucky. Even today, bikes bearing the Claud Butler name are still highly regarded.

I cycled many miles - on one occasion as far as Swindon. And then disaster struck! I called into Woolworths in Ealing Broadway, standing my super-bike against the kerb. I was in the store for only three minutes, but in that short time my bike was stolen. Dejectedly I walked round to the police station. I was told by a sergeant that several bikes had gone missing in a very short space of time. He expressed his opinion that a cycle gang was involved and they must have gone through the town with a lorry, picking up the bikes as they progressed. Several angry victims called round to the police-station to report their loss.

Thieves really are a low form of life, especially those who prey on the working man and his family and on the elderly. There are of course different reasons for stealing. I have no sympathy for those who thieve for gain. I do however have sympathy for those who are starving and steal food to survive. Also, there are those who steal to feed their drug-habit. Who is to blame then ?

What epitaph shall I write for a mean thief who has passed on ? How about:-

Here lies a thief
His life was bent
Misery he sowed
Wherever he went
His joy was brief

*　　*　　*　　*　　*

CHAPTER SEVEN

THE OUTBREAK OF WAR

At the outbreak of the Second World War on 3rd September 1939, we were all on holiday on the South Coast at Lancing in Sussex. My parents were glued to the radio (then called a `wireless`), and we all heard Neville Chamberlain's famous broadcast bringing Britain to the aid of Poland against Germany. To my parents it must have been shattering news. To my father especially it would have brought back terrible visions of the trench warfare of WW1. The bad news did not exactly cheer my mother up either. She had experienced the air raids on London during that war and had witnessed on October 1st 1916, the shooting down in flames of Zeppelin L31, at Potter's Bar. I cannot speak for my sister Pat, because she was much younger than I, but to me in my ignorance, the news came as a new excitement. Being a lad of fourteen, I had little comprehension of war, other than what I had read in such boys' magazines as The Eagle, The Wizard and The Hotspur. Even in those, the stories were highly romanticized. They were all about the `Goodies` getting the better of the `Baddies`. They contained no gore.

At 11.30 am we heard the wail of an air raid siren. My father immediately marshalled us down to the beach. We all started to dig some sort of hollow or trench in the sand and then crouched in it, waiting with fear in our hearts. Father took some wet face flannels from the house. This reflected his Army training in dealing with a gas attack. We peered over the top of our `trench` across the sea towards the distant horizon, expecting to see waves of German bombers droning towards us at any moment. After a long wait, it turned out to be a false alarm and the `All Clear` was sounded. Father said we could return to our holiday home. The trench would have been of little use after that, as the tide or the weather would soon have obliterated it.

The next day my father decided to return to London to resume his work as a dental mechanic, but first he contacted the friend at Virginia Water who owned our holiday home. Permission was obtained for us to stay indefinitely, until the situation became clearer. The last thing my parents wanted was for us to go back to London, where everyone was expecting air raids. People had already heard what the Germans were doing in Poland and so my mother, Pat and myself stayed behind in Lancing.

To keep us company were the owner's wife and her three lovely daughters. I have vivid recollections of the two older sisters, who were both attractive, especially the younger of the two. She was beautifully tanned, tall, dark and lissom. I had a terrible crush on her but kept this to myself. Strange to say, she and her younger sister teased me about having a crush on the older sister. That wasn't true. What mixed up children we were! I was quite embarrassed by all this. My moment of discomfort soon passed and we became good playmates.

And so it was we settled down to a seemingly endless holiday. There is a very expansive sandy beach at Lancing, where one can wade out a long way when the tide is out. The beach is backed by a high ridge of shingle. The sea at high tide percolates through the shingle, to leave a long backwater. This was absolutely ideal for children to play in, as it was quite shallow. We spent many a happy hour rowing up and down this long stretch of water. I experimented, using some old sacking for a sail and with some success. On a windy day, I often managed to get the boat to sail from one end of the backwater to the other. I also tried my hand at building a raft from odd lengths of wood, lashed together in a most un-seamanlike fashion.

On one occasion I made an oar, comprising a broom handle with a flat piece of wood nailed to one end. This I assume, was brought into use because one of the proper oars was lost or broken. I used the makeshift oar straight away. As we made progress down the backwater I let Pat take over. She had on a spotless dress. She was not used to the makeshift oar, and after a struggle soon `caught a crab`, which promptly tipped her out of the boat. Pat emerged from the water gasping and spluttering and displaying a very muddied dress. We laughed after her initial shock, but now I knew I had some explaining to do. After all, I was supposed to be keeping a brotherly eye on her.

With the onset of winter our playmates and their mother returned to Virginia Water (their father ran a pub). Suddenly the house was very quiet and those idyllic, warm days were replaced by days of lower temperatures and cold, blustery winds.

*   *   *   *   *

A FRUITFUL DAY

A storm blew up during the night. A ship got into difficulties off Selsey Bill. Possibly her cargo had shifted. Whatever the cause, some of her cargo ended up in the foaming sea. I normally started each day early by walking westward along the beach. You could say I had become an experienced beachcomber. I know I had a very keen eye for spotting anything foreign to the beach.

On this stormy day I was watching the white horses rolling in towards the shore. It was not long before I spotted a large wooden box being rolled about by the crashing waves at the water`s edge. As I approached the box had begun to split open and oranges galore were spilling out onto the sandy beach. Looking along the beach I soon noticed more boxes had been washed up and there were many loose oranges rolling about. Gleefully I gathered and stuffed as many oranges as I could carry inside my shirt. I ran home as best I could. On the way I passed other people and told them what I had found. Soon there were many happy people down at the beach, gathering in the `harvest`. Although it was exciting to pick up all this free fruit, it was also quite risky. The breakers crashing onto the beach were big, but rows of sturdy timber breakwaters helped to diminish their force.

*   *   *   *   *

A SUSPICIOUS OBJECT

One of the events that took place at about this time involved my mother and has been a source of amusement in my family ever since. Lancing Police Station was situated almost opposite our holiday home. A notice was posted on the board outside the station, requiring all suspicious objects to be reported. This of course was a precaution in case enemy activity was involved. There was so much going on that affected civilians during the war, that most people were very conscientious about reading notices, including my mother.

Mother was strolling along the beach when she spotted a round object bobbing about on the waves. It was a green glass fisherman`s float, for supporting fishing nets (they are now plastic). It was the first time she had ever seen one. Mother suddenly got it into her head that this glistening ball must be a sea-mine ! You will gather from this that she had never seen a sea-mine. Being very public-spirited, she decided she must do something for her country. Mother waited until the object washed onto the beach. Bravely she picked it up and carried it over to the police station. She placed it on the counter and explained what she thought it was. The desk sergeant, in a rare moment for him, completely lost his self-control and bent backwards with laughter. Poor Mum; how embarrassing !

*   *   *   *   *

AN IRATE ALIEN

Another day dawned and I went for my usual early morning beachcombing expedition. I walked around the end of the backwater to head for the beach. To my right was a small pool. Two men using paddles were frantically beating at something on the ground. My curiosity aroused, I ran over to see what they were up to. To my amazement, I saw literally scores of large eels wriggling out of the pool and over the shingle towards the beach. It was an amazing sight and not often seen, not by me anyway. I was lucky enough to be in the right place at the right time, because when once this mass exodus starts, it does not take long for the entire eel population to vacate a pool.

My sister Pat recalls seeing a bald German man raging at people to leave the eels alone. He had suddenly appeared from nowhere. But one thing was certain. As far as we were concerned he was one of `them`, the enemy at war with us, so people contemptuously ignored his protestations. No doubt his activities were shortly to be curtailed. As I recall, all German and later Italian and Japanese nationals residing in Britain were interned for the duration of the war. They were generally referred to as `Aliens`

On first seeing the eels, I ran home to find a sack (no plastic bags in those days) and on my return to the pool, managed to catch two large eels. Shortly afterwards there were no eels to be seen and the two men and the German had gone. Presumably those eels that escaped the chopping paddles would have reached the sea and started their 3,000 mile journey to Bermuda to spawn .

*   *   *   *   *

ASPIRING ENTREPRENEURS

With my sister accompanying me we headed for home, carrying the two large eels. Mother was out. We went into the bathroom, where I filled the bath with cold water. After opening the sack, I tipped the eels into the water. They seemed quite at home, actively swimming about each other. After a while we tired of watching their antics and left the house to head for the beach. It wasn`t long before Mother was calling us. She had gone into the house and received a nasty shock when she discovered the eels.
"I don`t care what you do with them but they are not stopping in the house," she said. Mother could not bring herself to help me catch them. I was unable to grasp them as they were too slippery, so I pulled the plug to let the water out. I managed to push the eels back into the sack. I did not enjoy doing this and to make matters worse, they were now very smelly indeed.

I thought perhaps I could sell the eels, so Pat and I walked to a fishmonger`s in

Shoreham to find out if he would buy them. By the time I reached there I had broken out into a sweat as the eels weighed quite a bit.

"Let`s have a look at them," he said, but when we opened the sack he found they were dead. They smelt even stronger by now. He would have nothing to do with them, so we trudged home dejectedly with the poor `corpses`. I took them down to the beach and buried them in the sand. It was just another example of the sea claiming its own.

*   *   *   *   *

ACTIVITY AT SHOREHAM AIRPORT

Shortly after the outbreak of war, most civil airliners at Croydon were transferred to Shoreham aerodrome. This action was taken to reduce the risk of destruction from enemy air raids, to preserve our large Cross-Channel airliners. These might well be used as troop-carriers, or as air ambulances. This movement of aircraft brought me an additional interest during my extended holiday - plane spotting ! Shoreham aerodrome was only a mile up the coast road from Lancing. I found those strutted, silver-winged biplanes and triplanes quite fascinating. To anyone interested in the very early civil aircraft and coming to look across from the perimeter fence, it would have been like finding gold ! There were DeHavilland Dragons and Rapides, Imperial Airways Handley Page H.P.42s etc. Sometimes, I spent a whole afternoon watching and waiting for things to happen.

The decision to transfer our civil airline fleet to Shoreham was later proved to be well justified, as on the 15th August 1940, Croydon Airport was specifically attacked by some thirty Nazi dive-bombers. A hangar suffered hits. A number of houses in the area were destroyed as a result of the attack. As a point of interest, not one of the attacking bombers managed to return to base, thanks to the RAF.

London anti-aircraft batteries did not come into action until three days after this raid, the 18th of August.

*   *   *   *   *

AN EVACUATION

The war seriously disrupted my education. The authorities decided to transfer the entire staff and pupils of Acton Tech` to Wolverton Technical College, in Buckinghamshire. I knew my extended holiday would not last for ever and when it finally came to an end, I returned to London and was immediately made an evacuee. Mother and my sister stayed at Lancing for about six months and Pat went to school there. Then my sister was sent to stay with an uncle and aunt in Redbourne, Hertfordshire.

With my gas mask housed in a cardboard box hanging from a string around my neck and a name-tag tied to my lapel, I boarded a train with many other children. We were all being separated from our parents. Not many children cried. It was regarded as an adventure but even so, most children had a wan look on their faces, not knowing what to expect. We arrived at Wolverton Station and were soon allotted to our new addresses. I was billeted in the nearby village of Stony Stratford, on the A5.

My new `foster mum`, Mrs Millard was a widow with two grown-up sons. They both worked at the Wolverton Railway Carriage Works. I took to the family straight away. They were very kind and considerate. I was soon attending Wolverton Tech` but the classrooms were overcrowded and I think most of the evacuee-pupils felt very insecure.

Mrs Millard said I could borrow her bike, a large, sit-up-and-beg affair, with a ladies black frame, rod brakes and a carrier frame behind the saddle. There were no toys in the house, so I rode the bike at every opportunity. The winter of 1939 - 40 was a hard one. A large local pond became frozen over. I used to take the bike out onto the ice and ride slowly round the pond, trying hard not to skid or fall over. This was a dangerous thing to do, but then doing risky things like that prepared us for tougher adventures in the future. Like many other children, I did not fully appreciate the danger of `testing` the ice.

Food rationing was introduced in January 1940 and the national food situation did not finally return to normal until July 1954. I give here some idea of the food ration allowance for each person per week :-

Bacon or Ham	4 oz
Butter	2 oz
Cheese	1 oz
Cooking fat	2 oz
Margarine	4 oz
Meat	About 8 pence worth
Sugar	8 oz
Tea	2 oz

There was a points allowance for many foods. eg. Cereals 4, Baked Beans 4. Oranges were limited to expectant mothers.

Even with all these restrictions, Mrs Millard managed to feed me with some wholesome meals. I remember eating whale meat in late 1940. Actually it wasn`t too bad.

Each person, be they man, woman or child, was allocated a clothing allowance of sixty six coupons per year. Thanks to our merchant seamen and the endeavours of the Royal Navy, no one starved or went without clothing of some sort during the war.

I am told one in three merchant seamen were lost in that war. That sort of loss is hard to come to terms with. If a merchant ship was lost, a merchant seaman`s pay was immediately stopped and he did not start earning a wage again until he was signed on another ship. This seemed a very harsh way to treat brave men, who were continually risking the horrors of convoy war, to keep Britain fed and fighting.

*   *   *   *   *

THE DATE

At Wolverton Tech`, a school party was organised at the end of the Summer Term 1940, to which girls were invited. Nothing unusual in that you might think, but I have to emphasise, there were no girls attending Acton Tech`, so this was a `first` for us evacuee lads. We were paired off, boy with girl, and had to sit down at table to eat jelly and custard and a cake. Union Jacks were strung about overhead.

During the party I made the first proper date of my life with my partner for the evening. When the party had finished I walked her home. We stood on her doorstep and I was about to give her a goodnight kiss, when she suddenly spotted a tall lad walking up the garden path of the house opposite. She called out to him and ran across the road, saying "Goodnight" as she brushed past me. Now I knew what it meant to be given the brush-off ! I walked back to Stony Stratford feeling miserable, inferior and thoroughly inadequate. Life has so many lessons for us, especially when we are in our adolescence .

*　　*　　*　　*　　*

CHAPTER EIGHT

BAD NEWS

Whilst an evacuee, although separated from my parents I was reasonably happy. I was still receiving a good education, even if the classroom conditions were not ideal. One day the doorbell rang and Mrs Millard went to answer the door. I suddenly heard my mother's voice and rushed out into the hall. I sensed straight away that something was wrong. Mum looked ill and distraught. Mrs Millard left us alone in the sitting room and Mother told me to sit down.

" I am very sorry to tell you John, your father has left us," she said. I cannot fully put into words how I felt. It was a numbing shock and I can say now, it took years for me to get over it.

"You will have to come back to London with me John," my mother said. "The air raids are not too frequent and the RAF are shooting down more enemy planes now." And so I returned to London, to Selby Road, North Ealing, whilst London was now being bombed, not only at night but in the daytime as well.

From that time on I did not see my father for several years. He was very hesitant in paying my mother her maintenance money and so we were often nearly starving. Years later after my mother had died, a letter was discovered amongst her papers, which had been written by me as a lad, during our ordeal.(Page 37)

*   *   *   *   *

THE BLITZ AND AN UNUSUAL BOMB

As soon as I returned to London in 1940, the air raids seemed to become more frequent and more intense, but nothing compared to what the East End of London was getting, especially the Docks and around St. Paul's. That area was taking a terrible hammering but even so what we were experiencing in Ealing was still very unpleasant. The month of September was particularly bad. My mother was an Ambulance Attendant in the Auxiliary Ambulance Service and was often on duty.

With Mother being away on duty, my sister being away at Redbourne and my father abandoning us, I was left in the house on my own. When there was an air raid, the lady next door Mrs Phillips, would bang on the wall and shout,
"Are you on your own John?" If I replied in the affirmative, she would invite me round and we would both shelter in her stair cupboard until the danger had passed. As soon as the `All Clear` sounded I would return to my own home.

I remember one raid being in progress when I was under the stairs of the house next door. Suddenly, there was an almighty `Whoosh` and a ground-shaking thud. It was a near thing ! A bomb had hit a house in the very next street and immediately opposite to us, but this was no ordinary bomb. This was an oil-bomb. Flames were licking out of shattered windows and the unfortunate occupants were frantically trying to save what furniture they could, by passing or throwing it out of the blazing house. There was a sickly stench of crude oil. No one seemed to have heard of an oil bomb before. If it had been an HE bomb, the house would not have still been standing and

Dear Mum

Here is a pound which I obtain from (Shailer) (Senior) I told him we could not have any proper meals. I said as soon as Dad sent your money I would take the money back to him. Do not worry about me going over there. At any rate you can have a decent dinner.

Love John.

Page 37. The note to my mother, written when I was a young boy.

the occupants would probably have been killed. Possibly our house would have been destroyed, as well. To try and match the heavier bombs which were now being introduced by the RAF the Germans came up with the idea of chaining some of their bombs together in pairs. An instance of this was not far away at West Ealing, when a community hall, where a function was being held received a direct hit, killing nineteen of the guests.

In late January, or early February, 1941, not long after returning from Stony Stratford, I heard a great deal of aerial activity. Curiosity got the better of me and I ran out into the garden to see what all the noise was. There to my surprise, as it was broad daylight and I had not heard the sirens, were a large number of German bombers heading in a westerly direction. Two of our fighters were weaving in and out, trying to shoot them down. One enemy plane started to smoke. Suddenly, a damaged tail plane dropped off and fluttered down towards the Western Avenue. The enemy plane immediately went into a steep, erratic dive and crashed a couple of miles away. By now our fighters had left, presumably having run out of ammunition or being short of fuel.

Now the 4.2 inch AA battery opened up in Pitshanger Park, at the bottom of our road. I could see shell-bursts amongst the enemy. I did not observe any hits. Large pieces of shrapnel rained down, making peculiar whining noises and clunking onto roads, pavements and roofs, smashing through roof tiles in the process. If one of these large pieces had struck you, you would have a hole in you the size of an orange ! You will gather from this that my mother was not in, otherwise I certainly would not have been allowed outside while the air raid was in progress.

In this raid, I did not escape completely unscathed. As I was gazing skywards, I felt a sudden sharp pain in my left eye. It turned out to be a piece of cordite. When the raid was over and my mother eventually arrived home from ambulance service, she tried to remove the offending foreign body, without success. She hopefully took me to the local chemist, just up the road, but he said he dare not touch my eye and sent me to King Edward`s Hospital in Ealing. They could not deal with it either and sent me up to the eye hospital in Tottenham Court Road, London.

I walked into the busy Casualty Department, where a nurse soon came to my aid. "Open your eyes," she said. Then after a careful examination, "I will soon have that out." I was surprised I did not have to see a doctor. The nurse put some drops into the offending eye and shortly afterwards brought a needle towards it. `God, what is she going to do ?` I thought. I did not like the look of this at all, but when she got to work with the needle there was a slight pulling sensation, and no pain whatsoever. "That`s it !" she said, "I think I`ve got it all out." I felt so grateful. I went home on the Tube feeling enormously relieved. There was considerable blood staining left in my eye, but the nurse had assured me it would disperse within a few days.

I was due to report to the Royal Navy Recruiting Office in Leicester Square, at the end of the week. I hoped to become a Visual Signalman, so naturally my eye was giving me cause for concern.

*   *   *   *   *

CHAPTER NINE

THE NELSON TOUCH

One Friday I travelled to Leicester Square to the Naval Recruiting Office. I answered some simple questions, had my reflexes tested and was checked for ruptures. Then it was time for me to take the visual test. As far as I can remember, this consisted of three tests. The first was the usual eye test, reading letters from a wall chart, as conducted in any optician`s. Next, a large book was placed in front of me. Each page displayed numerous small coloured circular blobs, with letters and other shapes in different pale colours, cleverly intermingled. The test was to identify the letters and shapes from the confusing background of blobs. I managed this very well. The final test involved a black box, which emitted a pin-point of bright, white light. The room lights were switched off and the pin-point of white light shone on the wall behind me. The white light was changed to various colours, which I was told to identify as they appeared. This involved shutting one eye at a time I found it impossible with my stained eye and explained my problem. They waived the test on that eye. My ordeal was over. It was deemed I had passed all the tests.

I was summoned to report to HMS St.George, a boys` training establishment on the Isle of Man. Eventually I set off from home on 30th April 1941, for a new life in the Royal Navy. My mother shed buckets of tears.

Perhaps I should mention here that the only way for a lad as young as sixteen to join the Navy during WW11, was to sign on as a regular sailor. Otherwise it meant him waiting for conscription call-up at eighteen. I was not prepared to wait that long. Just before leaving college, I was offered a five-year apprenticeship with the Hoover Company, at their factory at Perivale, but my heart was already set on the Royal Navy and I wanted `to do my bit`, so I turned down the offer. I signed on for twelve years` service, but as I was only sixteen, and the twelve years` service would not commence until I was eighteen, that meant I would have to serve almost fourteen years regular service.

After serving a trial period of the first two weeks as a Boy Signalman 2nd Class, there was no turning back and in those days certainly no chance of buying myself out of the Navy if I found it was not for me. I sometimes wonder what my life would have been like if I had taken up the apprenticeship. Very different no doubt !

$$* \quad * \quad * \quad * \quad *$$

TRAINING FOR WAR

Life in any naval barracks or camp was organised into a shipboard routine, just as though the trainee sailors were actually on board ship. In a training establishment the training staff, mostly officers and NCOs, have usually had considerable sea-going experience. HMS St.George was situated on Onchan Head, near Douglas, Isle of Man. Howstrake Naval Camp as it was known, had previously been a holiday camp before WWII, when it was known as Cunningham`s Camp. I believe it was one of the very first holiday camps, certainly in Britain. It got its name however during WWI when rows of large, round white tents were erected to accommodate Germans,

Austrians and Turks.

There was a new intake of twenty one trainee signalmen in my class, but our lives from now on were going to be nothing like that of a holiday-maker. The class was designated Benbow 221v. There was also a new intake of thirty four trainee telegraphists designated as Benbow 221w. For much of our training the two classes combined. All classes in the camp bore the names of famous Admirals of the past.

The next day the 1st of May 1941, after our arrival we were all kitted up :-

2 pairs boots
2 pairs white shoes
1 pair brown shoes
2 navy jerseys
2 pairs navy serge bell-bottom trousers
1 black silk
1 woollen scarf.
1 white lanyard.
1 leather belt.
2 pairs underpants.
2 vests.
2 white canvas duck suits.
1 cap.
1 HMS St.George cap ribbon (All cap ribbons displaying a warship name were later replaced with ribbons bearing just the letters HMS. This was for reasons of security and the Navy did not revert to ship names until near the end of the war).
1 hatbox
1 housewife (a folded set of linen pockets to house needles, darning wool, threads, beeswax and buttons).
1 pair green gaiters
1 pair sports shorts
2 naval shirts
2 blue naval collars
1 Service gas-mask and holder
3 pairs navy blue socks
1 tin black shoe polish
1 tin white blanco
1 tin green blanco
1 pair swimming trunks
1 small brown case
1 kitbag
1 overcoat

Every item of clothing had to be identified with the name of the owner. Name-stamps were made by the `Chippie` out of wooden blocks and were used with black or white paint. Principle items of clothing had the name stitched over with chain stitch, using red embroidery thread. The stitching had to be done by the trainees. Those recruits with short names were considered the fortunate ones.

The Navy has a language of its own, so we were soon having to learn the meaning of strange slang words and expressions such as : The Andrew`, `rabbits`, `the Jaunty`, `Jimmy-the-One`. We also had quickly to learn customary pipes which came over the tannoy such as : `Belay the last pipe`, `Lights out`, `Liberty men fall in`, and so on. I could go on and on with these, there are so many naval words and phrases. Of course, it was essential to get the meaning of these quickly fixed in our heads, otherwise we would not understand the commands being given directly, or over the tannoy. Instructions coming via the tannoy were either by bosun`s pipe and voice, or by recognised bugle calls.

The medical and catering services in the Navy were excellent. Inoculations and vaccinations were rife. The food was certainly better than in Civvy Street, although we still had to use ration cards.

The day began with *reveille,* sounded by a bugler at 5.30 a.m. The order "Call the hands" belched forth from the loud-speakers and we turned out of our bunks. There was time for a wash before the order came at 6.00 a.m. "Hands fall in". The next hour would be spent in `cleaning ship`. In our case that meant cleaning out the huts. At 7 a.m. it was time for breakfast.

At 9.05 a.m. every morning we were obliged to muster on the parade-ground. A guard-of- honour would march on with rifles and bayonets fixed, accompanied by a Royal Marine band. The daily morning parade had begun. The guard would face the mast, the parade would be called to attention. The guard would then Present Arms, whilst the Colours, the White Ensign, would be ceremoniously hoisted to the masthead to the sound of a bugle, always played by a Royal Marine. The ranks of sailors would then be inspected. The order would be given to `March Off. The band would strike up with the tune `The March of Saint George` and the guard would march off, followed by the ranks of sailors. This daily weekday ceremony was called `Divisions`. As soon as we left the parade ground, Benbow 221 Class was formed from `columns of fours` into `column of threes`. Led by two naval drummers, we were marched about a mile to Ballakermeen High School for daily morning lessons. Our main subjects were Maths, English, History and Science. On the whole, the level of education was on a par with my lessons at Acton Tech`. It may seem odd in a way, that I was being taught the same things over again, but it should be borne in mind that many of the other young trainees had left school when they were only fourteen.

Our instructors in the afternoon sessions back at camp were all experts in their own field. In the early stages we were frequently being drilled on the parade-ground, wearing boots and gaiters and with bayonets fixed. I often seemed to be marching in my sleep!

No regular sailor of the Royal Navy was allowed to put to sea, unless he could swim. Consequently we all had to pass a swimming test. The test comprised swimming two lengths of the baths dressed in a canvas duck suit, diving to retrieve a house-brick from the bottom and swimming underneath a twenty feet long submerged net. Looking back when I think about it, there was considerable physical effort required of the trainees most of the time. Cross country-running, swimming, football, rugby, hockey, cricket and boxing were the main sports. But as part of our trade, we had to learn rope-climbing and rowing. The latter involved several sessions of rowing on the sea crewing a naval cutter in Douglas Bay. This training stood me in good stead several years later, off the coast of New South Wales. I will tell you about that later.

Whilst doing my training I was about six feet tall, but only weighed nine stone twelve pounds. A bean-pole ! Obviously I was not cut out for rugby. I only played one game and was not asked to play any more. However I did get involved in most of the other sports. As a junior sailor, I was very surprised and somewhat disappointed that our training did not include sailing.

Training to be a signalman involved daily lessons in communications, notably semaphore, both with mechanical arms and hand-flags. (The mechanical semaphore arms became obsolete on ships by the time I went to sea in 1942). The hand-flags (small flags on sticks) were used to visually transmit letters of the alphabet and numerals 0 to 9. Much of the semaphore practice was accompanied by music. A sea of arms, flailing to the tune of `TEDDY BEARS` PICNIC`, could be seen on any weekday by passing onlookers, much to our embarrassment. I have to say it was the only tune ever played and that was on a scratchy record. It nearly drove us all round the bend.

We were obliged to learn the Morse Code. We had to practise transmitting the code by using a single hand-flag, by Aldis lamp(a hand-held, pistol-operated, flashing lamp, which had an internal tilting mirror), by a 10" lamp (operated by depressing a mechanical lever/shutter handle) and finally by a 20" lamp, using a similar mechanical shutter assembly. The latter was virtually a searchlight with high candlepower, generated by an electric arc between two automatically fed carbon rods.

We were also taught how to hoist flags. Sounds simple, but again these complied with a recognition code and were controlled by a strict procedure. Naval flags are made of bunting (naval slang for a signalman is `bunting tosser`) and are stored in steel lockers - flag lockers. The lockers are made up of a number of pigeon-holes, one for each flag. Flags are hoisted on halyards. A special coupling cleat is attached to the halyard ends. Likewise a similar cleat is permanently attached to the top and bottom of each flag. By `bending on` (clipping on) the Inglefield clips/cleats of the flags to those of the halyard, one or more flags can be hoisted up the mast or yardarm in quick succession. A lot of physical effort went into this, especially if the flags were wet. When they were hauled down and uncleated, it was imperative that the right flags were stowed in the correct pigeon-holes, otherwise the next time there was a flag-hoist, chaos would reign.

Going back to the Morse Code. A boy signaller also had to learn how to transmit and receive Morse whilst wearing ear-phones and using a Morse key. This was primarily the job of a telegraphist. A signalman was not expected to read and transmit Morse at the high speeds required of a telegraphist. This was mainly because it was impossible to transmit with signalling lamps at 125 w.p.m(words per minute). A flashing light would also be impossible to be read by the human eye at that speed.

We were taught to shoot. This was conducted on a small range. The weapons used in training were a .22" rifle, a .303" Lee-Enfield rifle and pistol shooting, using a Webley 0.38" revolver. We were also shown a Very pistol for firing a Very light but we were not asked to fire it, possibly because they were worried about the trainees setting themselves or the place on fire. Seriously though, they were used for illumination purposes, or for firing a Very flare at sea as a signal of distress.

My mother was anxious that I be confirmed in the Christian Faith before I went to sea. Consequently on 16th November 1941, I was confirmed in St Ninian`s, Douglas, Isle of Man, by The Lord Bishop of Sodar and Man.

Supper was normally at 7 p.m. We were allowed to turn in at 7.45 p.m. if we so wished, but most of us were busy either writing letters home or spit and polishing our boots, ready for the next day. The First Post was sounded at 8.45 p.m. and the Last Post at 9 p.m.

*   *   *   *   *

FIGHTING FOR GLORY

Initially we were not allowed to pick and choose which sports we wanted to participate in. We had to try them all and so by a process of elimination we ended up being involved in those sports for which we showed the most aptitude. There were however one or two sports which were compulsory. Boxing was one of them.

Because in Civvy Street I had already been in the ring several times at Affleck`s gymnasium and had done reasonably well, I thought I stood a good chance at welterweight. This was not to be. In my first fight I was matched with a slim, fair-haired bloke with an engaging smile. The bout started and in twenty seconds I went down. This man was a `natural`. I didn`t realise I had been knocked out as I didn`t feel a thing. In fact when I came round shortly afterwards, I wouldn`t accept that I had been KO`d. The PTI said that if I felt like that, I had better go another round. I stayed in the ring with the same bloke and was promptly knocked out again.

I decided after that that I wasn`t cut out to be a boxer, although I have been in one or two scraps in the Navy since. In one fight in Ceylon (Sri Lanka) I was to suffer a badly bruised cheek-bone. Until the swelling subsided, any slight pressure on the area caused a strange bubbling sound in my right ear. I remember the Medical Officer asking me how I had done it. I told him I had fallen down a monsoon ditch ! By the look on his face I could tell that he didn`t believe me.

* * * * *

THE INCINERATORS

We were allowed shore-leave twice a week. Spending money was practically non-existent as we were only paid for a fortnight, one shilling the first week and one shilling-and-sixpence the second week. This was not as bad as it seems, because fifteen shillings a week was set aside for us until completion of our training, but it still meant there was little ready money available to us.

Smoking was not allowed in the camp. This led to a black market racket in cigarettes, run by two Irish lads from Belfast. One lad would go on shore-leave into Douglas and purchase a large quantity of cigarettes. His `oppo` would remain in the camp. At a prearranged time the `oppo` would wait at a certain spot, close to the camp perimeter wall. The `buyer` would then give an agreed signal (a whistle) and the lad inside the camp would respond, to indicate he was waiting there. A small sack containing the cigarettes was then heaved over the wall into waiting arms. Having caught the sack, the `receiver` would quickly melt back into the shrubbery.

The smuggled cigarettes were sold at a grossly inflated price, not necessarily by the packet but singly as well. Because of the exorbitant price, I used to stick a pin in the stub to make them last longer. I have since learned the foolishness of my ways, because the nicotine-tar collects in the stub-end and over a period of time becomes a health hazard. We knew very little then about the dangers of smoking.

One day we had to go on parade unusually early. Many of us were not properly dressed. Because I was pushed for time, I shoved a fag (with a pin stuck through it) under my pillow. Whilst we were all on the parade ground, the Master-at-Arms entered the huts and inspected our lockers and beds. When he reached my bed he pulled back the covers and lifted my pillow. The incriminating evidence was revealed. I was put on `Captain`s Defaulters`. Standing in front of the Captain the following day, came the order, "Off caps." I removed my hat smartly down to my side. The Master-at-Arms read out the charge.

"Have you anything to say Shailer?" said the Captain.

"No Sir," I replied. Well what else could I say ? They had the evidence. For such a minor misdemeanour the punishment was harsh. No shore-leave and fourteen days `jankers`. This involved one hour of my spare time each evening, doing rifle drill on the parade ground. But these were not the usual drills. Every drill was carried out at the double. Some of the movements must have been devised by a sadistic gunners-mate ! As an example; crouch down, put the rifle horizontally across your shoulders. Then hold the rifle up with arms half outstretched and remaining crouched, hop across the parade ground. If I had wanted to join the French Foreign Legion I would have said so ! Several lads had been caught, so I had others to accompany me. When our punishment finally ended, most of us continued to smoke furtively, but with much more cunning when it came to disposing of our fag-ends.

The Irishmen`s racket in cigarettes came to an abrupt end when the Master-at-Arms discovered the signal for passing them over the perimeter wall. He apprehended one lad within the camp, when his `oppo` had gone ashore. Then, waiting by the wall for the call from outside the camp, he gave the appropriate response signal and confiscated the fags as they dropped over the wall. He then ran to the quarter-deck and arrested the other lad as he came through the gate.

*   *   *   *   *

PAIN AND TLC

I developed an in-growing toenail on my left big toe over which grew a fleshy lump, which the M.O. described as `superfluous flesh`. He decided the toenail had to be extracted. I was very pleased that something was going to be done as it was really painful and was preventing me from swimming etc. Also I was starting to limp.

It was decided to send me to hospital. There I had the toenail pulled out. For the first couple of days, having it dressed was extremely sore. However the situation in which I found myself had its compensations. I was put in a wheelchair and pushed around the hospital grounds by a pretty nurse. As my toe improved and I became more mobile, I used to help this young nurse make the beds, just for something to do. She was very appreciative (you can read into that whatever you like !) and when it was time for me to leave the hospital I remember her standing in the entrance and waving me farewell. I had been in there one week.

I returned to the camp to the daily routine, but fervently wished I could develop another in-growing toenail ! No such luck !

*   *   *   *   *

FAREWELL TO HMS ST.GEORGE

In 1942 our training was drawing to completion. Tragically we were hearing rumours of the class before ours being torpedoed in the Atlantic. Some said they had all been lost. The trouble was, during the war, any news of a demoralising nature was suppressed for obvious reasons. We never did find out officially what really happened to them.

Late in our training volunteers were called for to form a small choir. We sang sea-shanties. There were several practices. Eventually we were transported into Douglas and dropped off outside the Marina on the seafront road. We took part in a concert for the public. It was well received, although I do not think we gave a very good performance. However we received thunderous applause, probably because we were members of the Armed Forces. Anyone in uniform during WWII was held in high regard by the civilians. Looking down the promenade we could see all the holiday hotels surrounded by barbed-wire. These buildings housed people classified as aliens (Italians etc).

We participated in a military exercise with the army that year. We were obliged to wear tin helmets and carry rifles and gasmasks. There was a mock battle. They had us running up and down a small mountain - Snaefell (2036 feet). The army overran our positions which I must confess didn`t surprise me. We were so cold we were glad to get it over with.

There was a passing-out parade and then we were sent on leave, with instructions to report to the Communications Barracks, HMS Mercury, in Petersfield, Hampshire, at the end of our leave. This was to be my home base for the majority of my naval service, although I was hardly ever there. The base trained adult communications personnel (signalmen and telegraphists) to a very high standard. Most of these men were conscripted into the Navy for the duration of hostilities. They were referred to as HOs (Hostilities Only). Also there were a few members of the Womens Royal Naval Service present, fondly referred to as `Wrens`. They were instructed by WRNS officers and Petty Officers of the Regular Service. More and more HOs were needed. This came about as the Royal Navy rapidly expanded to meet the ever increasing demands placed upon it. It was now mid-September 1942. At HMS St. George I had learned much that was necessary and useful for my new life at sea. I left the Isle of Man feeling fitter and much more confident and capable than when I had first arrived the previous year.

* * * * *

CHAPTER TEN

SCAPA AND THE FAR NORTH

My leave seemed to be over before it had begun. Training class Benbow 221 was no more. The young sailors were now being dispersed to various ships of the Fleet all over the world. I hoped to be sent to warmer climes. I had a mental vision of South Sea islands, dusky girls in grass skirts and waving palm trees. It wasn`t to be ! I was sent with a lorry-load of young sailors to Victoria Barracks, Portsmouth, where we were all issued with extra warm clothing, such as long woolly underpants and sea-boot stockings. Of what use in the South Seas were these very thick-knit `long johns` or in naval jargon `Scapa panties`? Disappointingly none whatsoever! They were though to be very much appreciated in the Far North, which we guessed was where we were now heading. I was given to understand all the thick woollen clothing had been knitted on very large needles, by patriotic elderly ladies in Civvy Street. They had also knitted magnificent, thick sea-boot stockings.

The next day at HMS Mercury, we mustered in the gymnasium. A Regulating Petty Officer informed us he was in charge of our draft to Scapa Flow, in the Orkney Isles - the main base of the Home Fleet. He would accompany us all the way. For security reasons we were not informed at this stage on which ship we were to serve. After the briefing we returned to the huts to pack our kit. Nothing was to be left in the lockers and the huts had to be spotless, ready for the next draft intake. We slept at Portsmouth overnight.

In the morning we boarded a train at Portsmouth Station. Our kitbags and lashed hammocks were stored in a separate wagon. We rattled north towards London. The journey from Portsmouth to Thurso, North Scotland, was anything but straightforward. It took nearly two days for the draft to reach their ships. Our draft was kept together when we reached Waterloo and when crossing London on the Underground to Euston. It wasn`t easy to carry a large kitbag, lashed hammock and gas mask, especially in the confines of a Tube train and on the escalator. It was with a sigh of relief that we unburdened ourselves at Euston, on the next stage of our journey. All our bulky kit was stowed in a goods wagon. The train was crammed with service personnel from many branches of the Armed Forces. Our compartment seated five sailors of the Communications Branch and one woman, a member of the Women`s Royal Auxiliary Air Force {WRAAFs).

This leg of the journey took us to Preston, which we reached in five hours, just as it was beginning to get dark. After blacking out the compartment we were allowed off the train for three hours. Most headed for the pubs of the town. There I quaffed my very first pint of beer. It made me feel quite light-headed. I began to feel unsteady and decided to make my way back to the train. I flopped down in my seat and soon fell asleep. Perhaps I should mention that during my time as a boy trainee at HMS St. George, we were not allowed to consume alcoholic drinks, hence the effect one pint of beer had on me. Our train eventually departed for Carlisle and from there to Perth. There was a very dim light in each compartment. With nothing to see and with such poor lighting, it was impossible to read. Added to this was the fact that

Page 47. An aerial view of the battleship King George the Fifth.

alcohol of one sort or another had been consumed. There was only one thing for it, to get our heads down !

After a short while the WRAAF woke up and nudged me awake.

"Are you going to Scapa ?" she asked. "We are heading North," I replied. She was silent for a short while. Suddenly she turned to me and asked,

"Which one of you is the youngest ?" I pointed to the young sailor sitting the other side of her. Surprisingly she woke him up.

"Can you come outside with me ?" she asked. He looked bemused and followed her into the corridor.

"What on earth was going on ?" I asked myself !

Some fifteen minutes elapsed before they both returned. He looked very red-faced and winked at me. As the train reached Perth Station she got ready to alight. When she left the compartment she wished us all a safe voyage. Then the young sailor told us they had made love in the toilet. Of course after she left there was many a ribald comment in the compartment. Her behaviour was something of a shock to me. I thought it was the male of the species that did the pursuing. How times were changing.

We were allowed off the train at Perth for another `leg-stretcher` of about an hour-and-a-half. Upon our return we were told to unload our kit and load it onto yet another train. That train chugged north through Scotland on what seemed to be an endless single-line track. When once dawn broke and it got light, up went the blackout blinds. We gazed out at the beautiful scenery of Scotland - heathers, firs and craggy hills. Eventually we arrived at Thurso. We transferred our kit to a waiting lorry. We were led to a hotel, where we were given our first cooked meal since leaving Portsmouth the previous day. Up until then we had been living off sandwich packs - corned beef, spam and the like. Feeling a lot better for having partaken of `proper grub`, we loaded our kit onto the Stromness ferry and proceeded across the Pentland Firth. This is a notorious stretch of water, but on that occasion we had a calm crossing. It was fortunate because most of us had never been to sea, or in my case only on my journey from Australia as a very small boy, so that didn`t count.

As we approached Stromness many sailors were first disembarked at Lynness, for the destroyers, frigates and submarines, etc. We could see several warships in the distance- mostly destroyers. Surprising as it may seem, this was the first time I had ever seen a warship. I know we had set out from Portsmouth, but we never went near the dockyard, where there would have been plenty of warships. From this moment on we were about to be dispersed, to be finally taken to our individual ships. We wished each other `Good Luck`.

Capital ships, such as battleships, aircraft carriers and cruisers were each allocated a MFV (Motor Fishing Vessel) or drifter, for use as a ship-to-shore transport facility, for personnel, stores and mail. Also as a liberty boat, to take the sailors on shore-leave (Liberty Men) to the large NAAFI canteen on the island of Flotta. I should imagine that during the entire duration of the war there was enough beer consumed in that canteen to replace all the water in Scapa Flow !

The Regulating Petty Officer who had been in charge of the draft since we left Portsmouth, produced his draft list for the last time and called out our names. We were then told the name of our ships, and were required to board that ship`s MFV with our kit. Each MFV displayed the name of the warship it was attached to. This helped to avoid any confusion. My ship was the King George the Fifth (one of a class of four battleships) 35,000 tons displacement, main armament - ten 14" guns, secondary armament - sixteen 5.25" guns in twin turrets. She was now to be my new home. I say `home` but a ship is a honeycomb of metal watertight compartments. It requires a special mental attitude to live successfully in the cramped conditions of a ship. The wrong attitude could make it your prison. Several of my draft boarded the MFV so I wasn`t amongst complete strangers.

When once we rounded the headland a breathtaking sight greeted us. Many warships were at anchor in Scapa Flow. Most were painted battleship-grey, but there were one or two camouflaged with light patches for Mediterranean service. I was awestruck by the sheer size of the KGV. (Page 47). There was a constant traffic of ships in the Flow. As some arrived, others departed on various operations and sadly, some never to return ! If Scapa Flow was bereft of warships, you could bet your life something big was afoot.

As the MFV approached and went alongside the huge battleship, the sea had become choppy. The MFV rose and fell quite alarmingly. I was feeling apprehensive about getting myself and my heavy kit safely onto the companionway. It was with some relief that we saw our kit hoisted by derrick and rope sling and dumped unceremoniously on the upper deck. When I jumped onto the bottom platform of the huge companionway, I felt I had managed to make myself appear quite seamanlike. I realised it was all a matter of timing. Get it wrong and you could easily end up in the `drink`. Worse still, while in the sea, you might be struck by the MFV as it wallowed alongside the ship. A Petty Officer warned us to salute when we stepped from the top of the gangway onto the upper deck. We already knew this, as naval traditions and customs had already been drummed into us back on the Isle of Man.

I was met by a killick and shown below decks to my mess. After being introduced to the Communications staff I was told to stow my hammock in a hammock rack. In the evening it was time to sling our hammocks from the overhead hammock-rails and turn in. I learned there was a preordained allocation of spaces on the rails. The best positions were considered to be those nearest a matelot`s personal kit-locker. Being the most junior rating present and because I had only just joined the ship that day, I had to wait until everyone had slung their hammocks in their customary places.

The mess consisted of a long wooden table secured to the deck. An equally long wooden bench-type seat was positioned on either side of the table. During daily cleaning the mess table and seats were thoroughly scrubbed. After this the table was suspended out of the way, until the deck had been scrubbed, mopped and dried. Looking round the mess I observed ventilation trunking, overhead cables supported by perforated metal trays, bulkheads, bulkhead doors, bulkhead clips, portholes and a metal deck, partially covered by a brown, tough, non-slip coating.

There was a constant hum of machinery from pumps and generators, which provided ventilation and light. The rushing air in the ventilator outlets was particularly audible. There was also emergency lighting, which came on automatically if there was an interruption to the generator electricity supply. The whole ship was like a small town. Although the crew numbered well over 1,500, I doubt if I knew more than thirty to forty other sailors by the time I had to crew another ship.

It didn`t take me long to fit into this new pattern of life and to be accepted by my messmates. In a mess space is at a premium. One of the things we all had to learn was tolerance. Anyone with a good sense of humour easily fitted into the life of a matelot. Let`s face it, life was going to be tough on this ship for a mere boy signalman, with no seagoing experience and certainly no experience of the rough and extremely cold conditions of the North Sea and the Arctic. A signalman has one of the most exposed jobs on a ship. There is no hiding from whatever Nature has to throw at him. Aboard a battleship, he works on the exposed flag-deck, high up in the superstructure. When he observes a hoist of flags or a flashing signal he must respond immediately. Flag signals are normally read through a hand-held telescope. Speed and accuracy are vital. A lookout at sea might spot a periscope or an approaching ship or aircraft. It is essential to get that information over to the flagship immediately.

The Commander-in-Chief Home Fleet, Admiral, Sir John Tovey, KBE was flying his flag in the KGV at the time I joined her. He had distinguished himself as a destroyer captain in the Battle of Jutland. The safe passage of convoys to Russia was now his responsibility. In 1941 he oversaw the destruction of the German battleship Bismarck, which earned him his KBE. As this was the flagship, the Communications Branch, understandably had to handle a far greater volume of signal traffic than any other ship in the fleet. When in Scapa Flow the KGV was also dealing with signal traffic from the island of Flotta signal station.

When receiving a flashing-lamp signal, the signalman reading the message shouted out each letter, as he mentally converted it from Morse code to plain language. A colleague wrote down each letter on an official signal pad. The message was handed to the Yeoman-of-the-Watch, who would hand it to the addressee, or to the most senior officer on the bridge - usually the Captain, or the Officer-of-the-Watch. Messages for personnel not on the bridge were delivered by bridge messenger. Messages were graded into different levels of priority and confidentiality. The originator decided the appropriate priority and signified this in his message. Messages were filed in chronological order. You can imagine the difficulties encountered, while trying to do this job efficiently. The main problem was the weather. Howling winds, driving rain or snow, poor visibility and whilst at sea, also trying to contend with the rolling and pitching of the ship. The latter can prove very tiring. Surprisingly very few signalling mistakes occurred under those conditions.

When signalmen were not in the process of transmitting or receiving signals, they had to be constantly on the lookout for the appearance of other ships or approaching aircraft and nearer, the tiny wake of a periscope. Floating mines were another hazard to look out for. Invariably the wayward mine had broken free from its securing cable, probably during a storm. I recall seeing many of these mines in the North Sea. Seamen were detailed to shoot at them with rifles. They had limited success, as a capital ship would not stop just to sink a floating mine. I can only remember seeing one actually explode as a result of taking such action, but I assumed, if they were well riddled, a lot of them would subsequently sink. Smaller ships are better adapted to dealing with floating mines. When there were `white horses` on the sea, floating mines were difficult to spot and at night they were unseen messengers of death.

Part of a signalman`s duties was to raise or haul down the White Ensign. These ceremonies were known as `Colours` and `Sunset` and were accompanied by a full Royal Marine band in harbour or by a RM bugler at sea. The signalman had to control the speed of hoisting the flag halyard, so that the ensign reached the top of the staff at the precise moment the music finished. The same applied to `Sunset`, but in reverse.

Should a landing party be required a signalman would accompany it, drawing a revolver from the armoury.

On 5th October 1942, I was promoted to Ordinary Signalman. It was at this time I was informed I was being placed on the C-in-C Home Fleet staff (a small cog in a very large wheel). This meant that on whatever ship the C-in-C flew his flag, that was the ship I would serve on. Altogether I served on C-in-C`s staff on five different ships at Scapa - King George V , Duke of York , Iron Duke and Rodney - all battleships and because I spoke a smattering of schoolboy French, I also served as a member of the liaison staff on the FFS. Richelieu, a powerful French battleship, but I was retained on the Duke of York`s books.

Naval watches, of which there are seven , were :-

WATCH	TIME	NUMBER OF BELLS
Afternoon	Noon to 16.00	1 to 8
First Dog	16.00 to 18.00	1 , 2 , 3 , 4
Last Dog	18.00 to 20.00	1 , 2 , 3 , 8
First	20.00 to Midnight	1 to 8
Middle	Midnight to 04.00	1 to 8
Morning	04.00 to 08.00	1 to 8
Forenoon	08.00 to Noon	1 to 8

A roster was automatically established amongst the crew so that every man changed the time of his watch, from day to day.

* * * * *

A DRUNKEN SAILOR

Scapa Flow is a vast ten-mile by eight-mile stretch of water, surrounded by barren, windswept, hilly islands which form a natural harbour. There are no trees to be seen. It is one of the largest anchorages in the world. From our position we could just make out the town of Kirkwall in the far distance. At nearly any time of day, `cats` paws` could be observed scudding across the dark surface of the water. The seven channels between islands, which led to the open sea, were blocked off by permanent anti-submarine netting, stretching from shore to shore or by concreted block ships. Where anti-submarine netting was employed, a `gate` was secured to and operated by a boom defence vessel. BDVs were manoeuvred to open a gate to allow the passage of ships to and from the open sea. There were two such gates - Hoxa for use by the capital ships and Switha for use by the destroyers etc.

It was through a narrow gap between two of the islands that Gunther Prien, captain of U-boat U47, undetected during darkness, entered the Flow on October 14th 1939 and managed to sink the battleship Royal Oak. Many lives were lost. Many of the sailors, swimming in those cold waters and lost in the darkness, became disorientated. They swam away from the shore and were drowned.

When I first went to sea I felt seasick for the first half an hour. After that I just felt slightly giddy with the motion of the ship but was never actually sick. This applied to every voyage I did, throughout my service. It was something you got used to. A few men were seasick on every voyage and had my sympathy.

On very rare occasions, KGV left Scapa and steamed south, for refitting and repairs. As we approached the boom defence, we passed the sad sight of the top masts of the Royal Oak poking above the surface, denoting her location. Of a crew of approximately 1,400 men and boys, 833 went to their deaths. Nowadays all that can be seen to mark this important war grave is a large green marker buoy.

51

We steamed south and proceeded up the Firth of Forth, passing beneath the mighty Forth Bridge, to dock at Rosyth just beyond. This was a time for some shore-leave and relaxation, when the sailors were able to visit the pubs in Rosyth, Dunfermline or Edinburgh and perhaps meet a girl. There was a very good ice-rink at Dunfermline.

Most young people do something stupid or outrageous before they reach adulthood, especially when in drink. I was no exception ! It was at this time that I drank several pints of beer - well above what I was used to. I ended up extremely drunk and my senses deserted me. Normally a drink made me cheerful and the world seemed a good place. On this occasion I suddenly became aggressive. I got it into my muzzy head that the American servicemen thereabouts were Nazi officers. The truth of the matter was what I can only describe as `national jealousy`. They were stealing our women ! Let`s face it, both the Americans and the Germans had very flashy uniforms and when it came to attracting the girls, British servicemen were at a disadvantage - little money and uniforms that could hardly be described as `dashing`. There were a few exceptions of course. Anyway to call any member of our brave allies a Nazi, was the ultimate insult and is behaviour of which I am particularly ashamed. I vaguely remember a very irate and extremely large American sergeant sending me to the floor. I lay in the gutter. A woman attending a milk bar came out and helped me inside. She gave me a coffee, made from Camp coffee essence, I believe.

I was aware of nothing else until I found myself sobering up in a police cell, dressed only in my singlet and underpants. I was cold and had no idea of the time. In my drink-sodden state, it wasn`t long before I was again asleep.

I was awoken early in the morning by the sound of a policeman unlocking the cell door. He shouted,
"Here are your clothes." My head felt as though it had been in collision with a train !
"Where is this place ?" I asked.
"Edinburgh," he replied unhelpfully. I got dressed and was told to report to the desk. Collecting my watch, service pass, wallet and what little change I had left, I stepped out into the dim street.

I was in luck. Just at that moment, three young women came by. They laughed and waved and asked me if I was going back to my ship.
"Yes, I must get to Waverley Station. Will you direct me ?"
"We will do better than that Jack. We will take you there." To miss one`s ship is a misdemeanour the Royal Navy regards very seriously and will not tolerate. I thought those cheerful girls were marvellous, especially as on the way to the station, I learned they had just spent the night working in a munitions factory. They were on their way home when I first spoke to them. They must have felt tired, going out of their way like that. Finally they pointed out the station.
"Good luck Jack," they shouted cheerfully. I was soon able to board a train for Rosyth, which trundled over the Forth Bridge - quite an experience. I thought, `Thank God for British girls.` I`d soon changed my tune about girls ! After that I really kept my drinking at a sensible level. Well most of the time anyway.

*   *   *   *   *

CONVOY DISTANT COVER TO THE FAR NORTH

While I served aboard the KGV, she provided distant cover to four Russian convoys :-

CONVOY	SAILED	ARRIVED	KGV COVERING FORCE		
			SAILED	COVERED TO	CONVOY ATTACKS
JW51A	15/12/42 Loch Ewe	25/12/42 Kola Inlet	19/12/42 Scapa	22/12/42	None
RA51	30/12/42 Kola Inlet	11/01/43 Loch Ewe	04/01/43 Scapa	10/01/43	None
JW53	15/02/43 Loch Ewe	27/02/43 Kola Inlet	21/02/43 Scapa	26/02/43	High Level
RA53	01/03/43 Kola Inlet	14/03/43 Loch Ewe	02/03/43 Scapa	09/03/43	U-boats

Up until December 1942 Russian Convoy identification was prefixed :-
PQ = Outward-bound .
QP = Homeward-bound .
From December 1942 Russian Convoy identification was prefixed :-
JW = Outward-bound .
RA = Homeward-bound .

CONVOY JW51A

This convoy was the first to sail to Russia under the new identification prefix. It also initiated the use of Loch Ewe in Scotland, as the assembly terminal for the merchant ships and their close naval escorts. It took several days to gather together 27 ships. Three more ships joined the convoy the day after sailing.
The convoy was made up of merchant ships, as follows :-
11 British, 10 American, 3 Russian, 1 Polish, 1 Panamanian and 1 Dutch.
42 warships gave convoy escort or cover, but not all at the same time. The KGV, the cruiser Berwick and destroyers Musketeer, Quadrant and Raider gave distant cover. Arriving at Kola Inlet on Christmas Day 1942 the convoy had managed to remain undetected by the enemy.

The time the distant covering force gave convoy cover depended very much on the location of enemy capital ships and destroyers in the Norwegian fiords. The force had to be in a favourable position, relative to the convoy, should enemy ships such as the Scharnhorst or Tirpitz for example, leave their lair. At the same time, the distant covering force needed to avoid placing itself in a vulnerable position for attacks by enemy aircraft, from airfields based along the north western Norwegian coast.

CONVOY JW53

I give a detailed breakdown of this convoy, not just because I was involved with it, but because it had to endure what was considered to be one of the worst storms, if not <u>the</u> worst storm experienced by any Russian Convoy - possibly the worst storm of World War II, at sea. Also, I wish to emphasise the huge scale of the logistical problems that had to be overcome to make these convoys operationally successful.

Western Local Escort on sailing out of Loch Ewe -

HMS Hazard (Minesweeper), Bryony, Lord Middleton and Dianella (Corvettes) up to 17 February 1943.

Meynell, Middleton and Pytchley (Destroyers) up to 21 February.

Halcyon (Minesweeper) up to 22 February.

Bergamot and Poppy (Corvettes) and Lord Austin (Trawler) were escorts for the entire Kola Run.

Camellia and Bluebell (Corvettes) joined from 20 to 27 February.

Boadicea, Faulknor, Obdurate, Opportune, Orwell, Obedient, Milne and Inglefield (Destroyers) joined from 19 to 27 February.

Scylla (Light Cruiser) together with Fury, Eclipse, Intrepid, Impulsive and Orkan (Destroyers) reinforced Convoy JW53 from 21 to 27 February.

The cruisers Norfolk, Cumberland and Belfast gave additional heavy cover to the north of the convoy from 21 to 26 February.

Distant cover was provided by KGV and Howe (Battleships) and Berwick (Cruiser), screened by destroyers Icarus, Meteor, Musketeer, Offa, Onslaught and Piorun (Polish), from 24 to 26 February.

EASTERN LOCAL ESCORT, comprising Russian destroyers Gromki, Grozni, Kuibyshev, Uritski, Uragan and Britomart (Minesweeper) joined from 26 to 27 February.

In addition, HMS Sheffield (Cruiser) and HMS Dasher (Escort Carrier) set out with the distant covering force on 24 February but suffered severe storm damage. The hurricane blew for four days. During its height, wind speeds went off the Beaufort Scale. Waves were approximately 40ft to 100ft high. I can confirm the latter height, as I took three photographs with a box camera of those monumental seas, from the flag deck of the KGV at an eye level of some 78ft above sea level (Pages 55, 56 and 57). The Jack-staff tripod support stand, measuring about 9 feet in height, can clearly be seen at the extreme end of the bow. This allows for a good scale comparison of the height of the mountainous waves.

Ships of the destroyer screen were seen very infrequently, hidden by giant seas and poor visibility. We rarely saw the cruiser Norfolk either, even though she had tall masts and was sometimes in line abreast with us on our port beam. Visual signalling was almost impossible during much of the storm.

The convoy was scattered over a very wide area. Many ships suffered severe damage. The King George the Fifth lost her forecastle breakwater which was swept away by the force of the enormous waves. Some of her 5.25" twin-turrets on the port side were cracked and flooded. The Walrus aircraft catapult was torn away. Substantial steel companionway ladders were twisted like bits of rope by the force of the water.

Page 55. The battleship HMS King George the Fifth, covering Convoy JW53, facing an oncoming giant wave with an estimated height of 90 feet, on the journey from Scapa Flow to Akureyri, Iceland. The jack staff tripod at the extreme bow is 9 feet high.

Page 56. HMS King George the Fifth riding a giant wave in the great storm.

Page 57. HMS King George the Fifth in the great storm, dropping from the crest of a
giant wave.

For me, as a boy sailor, and probably for the more hardened salts, the most frightening incident occurred when the battleship had to heave to for a short while to sort out a problem in the engine-room. KGV quickly swung round to present her port beam to the full force of the wind and the mountainous waves. She was designed with a maximum safe list of thirty five degrees, which she exceeded. Struck by a huge wave, she rapidly listed at such an acute angle her starboard gunwale and guard-rail were submerged. Up on the flag deck I was looking over the starboard side (more sheltered) when, whereas I normally looked out across a vast expanse of sea from a lofty height, it suddenly seemed as though the surface of the sea was right in my face. Alarmingly KGV seemed to be suspended at that extreme list. It was only for a few seconds she hung there shuddering, but it seemed an age. I thought she was never going to right herself ! Then slowly she recovered. There was a terrific cacophony of noise from below decks. Everything not attached either fell or slid, with much banging and crashing. It was with a sigh of relief that I realised her screws were turning again. Her bow slowly came round to thrust at the oncoming waves. The constant violent movement of the ship had a very tiring effect on the sailors.

KGV, together with other capital ships, made for the shelter of Akureyri on the north coast of Iceland - virtually on the Arctic Circle. The town is situated at the head of a fjord which, with hills on either side, provides excellent shelter. In the entrance to the fjord and for some way up we experienced strong cross winds, which made things difficult, but as we neared Akureyri the wind died and the water took on an almost glassy appearance. After the harsh conditions of the storm, it was a wonderful feeling to steam up the fjord in the dark, to see the many bright lights of the town reflected in the water. After experiencing years of blackout back in Britain, to me the lights here seemed to twinkle ever more brightly in the cold air. With snow lying on the ground and the surrounding hills, it seemed just like a Christmas card.

Shortly after KGV had listed so dangerously, my relief arrived and I went off watch. I made sure I descended the battered and bent ladders on the lee side of the ship. To have attempted the weather side would have been sheer suicide. When I reached my mess I could not believe the havoc the storm had wrought. Swishing water in the mess was at least a foot deep. The hot food my watch had been looking forward to was slopping about in the water. Kit-lockers were wet and of course the dry clothes we were expecting to change into were also sodden. The bulk of the water was pouring into the mess from the overhead ventilation shafts.
"Why on earth had I volunteered for this life," I asked myself ?

As KGV had approached Akureyri she had overtaken the escort carrier HMS Dasher. Her flight deck had suffered severe storm damage. Sailors from her crew later described the damage, saying the flight deck had split and as she battled through the extreme waves, the fault in the flight deck was widening and narrowing. How alarming! She returned to Scotland shortly afterwards, for repairs. Sadly on 27 March 1943, whilst in the Firth of Clyde, off Arran, she was destroyed by an accidental aviation fuel explosion. Out of a crew of 528, 379 sailors lost their lives. As far as I am aware, there has never been a full explanation regarding the aviation fuel spillage. As this disaster struck so soon after the great storm, I ask myself, was it possible that the explosion stemmed from some unknown storm damage to the internal aviation fuel feed pipes or storage tanks ?

The next day those of us who were `off watch` were allowed ashore in Akureyri. The Icelanders were playfully skiing. One or two of us were offered skis, to try our hand at the sport. I soon found out that you cannot learn this skill in five minutes, but we enjoyed the fun while it lasted.

Now we were back on board, KGV made her way a short distance down the fjord and dropped anchor. An RFA (Royal Fleet Auxiliary) oiler came alongside and refuelled her. Then she again made for the open sea.

Earlier, I made mention of HMS Sheffield having been damaged in the great storm. She actually had a third of her `A` gun turret opened up, as though by a giant tin-opener. I am talking about one and three quarter inch thick armoured steel, which was ruptured by the pressure of water exerted upon the turret. There were 27 turret crew members inside when it happened. Three of those were injured, including one who suffered a broken jaw. Sheffield withdrew south and was replaced by HMS Glasgow (a cruiser of the same class). Cross winds caused Glasgow to run aground, but she was later re-floated.

Apart from the ever present threat of an enemy attack, especially to ships heading further north, and the prevalence of foul weather and extreme cold, there was always the problem of refuelling. In southern reaches where the weather is on the whole calmer, ships are able to refuel at sea without much trouble. But in Arctic conditions this is not so easy. Hoses can freeze at the drop of a hat and the sheltered fjords of Norway were not accessible to us (enemy occupied). It must have been a constant logistical nightmare.

After the storm abated, that wasn`t the end of trouble for Convoy JW53. By mid-February there were now seven hours of daylight, ample time for the coastal-based Luftwaffe to do its dirty work. JU88s carried out two high level bombing attacks, before the convoy split into two groups. One group reached Archangel and the other Murmansk on 27 February. Unluckily whilst at anchor, they were attacked by JU87 aircraft. Ocean Freedom sank and British Governor, Ocean Kinsman and Dover Hill were damaged.

There was considerable U-boat activity after the convoy had reached a position north-west of Iceland. Homing signals were picked up by HF/DF apparatus , deemed to come from U-boats. These transmissions gave away their position. The immediate response from convoy escorts was to illuminate the area with star shell. Any echo within range was attacked with depth charges. This kept the U-boats at bay. Two destroyers were attacked by U255, but her torpedoes missed their target.

Having refuelled, KGV and her destroyer escort left Akureyri and proceeded north, in preparation for giving cover to the returning convoy, RA53. That convoy left the Kola Inlet on March 1st. The Arctic ice edge extended unusually far south that year. As a consequence, KGV soon reached the edge of the floating pack ice, which her bow easily parted. To me, a `nautical greenhorn`, the first sight of the ice was exciting. At first it looked like a thin white line extending along the horizon. I suddenly spotted a long dark object moving amidst the ice and immediately thought of U-boats. I informed the Yeoman-of-Signals. I need not have worried. It turned out to be a narwhal which, before that day I had never even heard of, let alone seen.

Before the ship reached the edge of the ice field she had experienced a build up of freezing sea spray, which tended to settle on all external surfaces of the ship, eg upper decks, guns, guardrails, ventilator cowls, cables, mast rigging etc.
The ice had to be removed by the use of steam hoses, or by chipping. If allowed to remain untouched the ice would soon build up into a thick layer, weighing many tons. In the past it had been known to cause smaller ships to capsize completely, owing to the accumulation of tons of ice interfering with their stability. An example of this was the armed whaler Shera, which capsized and sank for that reason on 9th March 1942.

Hence the necessity of removing the frozen spray. Because of extremely cold conditions, it was drummed into us not to touch any metal surfaces without wearing gloves. To ignore this instruction was asking for trouble. Skin frozen to metal is no fun. It happens very quickly and there is the risk of frostbite (Page 61).

CONVOY RA53

This returning convoy ran into heavy weather, which again scattered the merchantmen, allowing U-boats to penetrate the escort screen. U255 torpedoed Richard Bland and Executive on March 5th. Richard Bland failed to sink but was given the *coup de grace* by the same U-boat five days later. Executive however, sank immediately. On 7th March J. L. M. Curry foundered through storm damage. On 9th March Puerto Rican was sunk by U586. The destroyer Opportune prevented the loss of John H. B. Latrobe, which had broken down, by giving her a tow into Seidisfjord, Iceland.

During the passage of RA53 the Scharnhorst left Gdynia, after repairs and after her daring famous Channel dash. She was now heading north for Norway. This put a different complexion on the current disposition of the ships of the Home Fleet. Scharnhorst might attack Convoy RA53. As a result, their disposition was quickly altered. Two aircraft carriers on the Clyde were put on stand-by - HMS Indomitable and HMS Furious. The battleship HMS Anson (same class as KGV) was despatched to Seidisfjord. Anti-breakout patrols in the Denmark Strait and in the Iceland - Faeroes Gap were strengthened, hopefully to stop Scharnhorst should she try and break out into the Atlantic.

Convoy RA53 eventually arrived at Loch Ewe on 14th March. In the meantime Tirpitz, Scharnhorst and Lutzow arrived at Altenfjord Norway on 24th March, where they remained.

Russian Convoys were suspended from mid - March until Winter 1943.

* * * * *

Page 61. Iced up forecastle behind the breakwater of the King George the Fifth, on an
earlier occasion.

EXERCISING AT SEA

When the KGV was not engaged on naval operations she was anchored in Scapa Flow, `swinging round the buoy`. These were in the main long periods of stultifying boredom, sprinkled with occasional periods of relief. The ship would proceed out into the Pentland Firth and beyond. Then the crew would be called to `ACTION STATIONS`. These periods of exercising all aspects of the ship`s defence and attack systems were intended to keep everyone `up to scratch`, in such things as gunnery, damage control, radar and communications, etc. To leave Scapa, KGV, like all capital ships leaving the Flow, had to make her way past the sunken Royal Oak and through the opened Hoxa gate of the anti-submarine boom net. The boom gate entrance was immediately closed behind her.

As KGV headed out to the open sea to exercise, all watertight bulkhead doors were closed. When not on watch we had to make our way to a specific watertight compartment. The hatch cover above us was clamped and screwed down by men of the damage control team, to seal it. We were now completely shut in. There was no way of getting out until someone came to release the hatch clips, when the ship`s company was stood down from `Action Stations`.

If a compartment below the water-line should be holed by the enemy, say by a torpedo, there was only a slim chance you would survive the explosion. Then your only unlikely chance of escape would be when the compartment filled with the incoming rush of seawater. You might be able to swim out through the large jagged hole in the ship`s side. To open the hatch at such a time would cause the compartment to flood completely and allow a huge and rapid ingress of seawater to reach vital parts of the ship. That is why it was necessary to seal the hatch down with clips. The Navy was prepared to sacrifice the sailors trapped in a watertight compartment, for the sake of saving the ship and the rest of her crew. Most of the sailors in that compartment would probably be dead already anyway.

If the 14-inch main armament guns fired when we were shut in a sealed compartment, all we felt was a shudder and we heard a loud metallic noise. It was very claustrophobic. During a gunnery exercise I much preferred to be on watch on the flag deck. Then anti-flash gear (for head and hands) and ear-plugs or ear-muffs were worn . They were certainly needed. If you were on the flag deck and the 14-inch guns fired, a great belch of flame billowed out from the muzzles, accompanied by a terrific noise together with shock waves to your chest as though you were being thumped by some unseen hand. A smell of cordite pervaded the air and a rushing, swishing sound assailed the ears, as the huge projectiles cleaved their way to the target. At two or three miles away, it was possible to see a projectile travelling away from the ship at great speed. A 14-inch British naval shell weighed about 1560 lbs. The range of a 14-inch gun (the maximum distance a shell can be fired) was 28,000 yards. That is about sixteen miles. Such heavy guns could only be loaded by hydraulic means. The speed a 14-inch shell left the gun was about 2000 mph.

Long range naval gunnery is a complicated business and is beset with difficulties. A visual sighting of the target is necessary. Visibility can be spoilt by gun smoke, funnel smoke, mist or other unfavourable weather conditions, the target`s alteration of course, your alteration of course or your roll, owing to rough seas.

Heavy guns were rarely operated at distances over fifteen miles, but the chances of a successful hit increase with a reduction in range. A ten-mile range was considered the most practical. Even so only about one in ten shells or fewer would reach the target.

In gunnery practice the target was usually a narrow, floating, welded steel hull, above which was an odd-looking structure of vertical wooden poles and canvas sheeting. The whole target assembly was towed by tug, which for obvious reasons, played it out astern for some considerable distance. There was a joke doing its rounds in the Fleet concerning HMS Howe (same class of battleship as KGV). She was taking part in a gunnery exercise, using her main armament on such a target. Her first shot straddled the tug instead of the target. With a wonderfully witty and instant rebuke the tug-master signalled to the Howe,
" I am pulling not pushing ! "
I have heard from another source that the RAF claimed the joke stemmed from them. Their version claimed that the target was a drogue sleeve being towed by one of their aircraft. We shall never know the truth now shall we ?

In that region when a towed target could not be used, KGV would direct her main armament at a large, bare rock protruding from the sea - Stack Skerry. Firing of the battleships` 14-inch guns guaranteed that when we returned to the mess we would find everywhere covered in a layer of sooty smuts. The vibration and pressure waves caused by such gunfire would loosen the build up of dirt in the ventilation shafts, which was then blown into the mess. I do not recall KGV firing a full broadside during gunnery practice. She did on occasions fire two guns simultaneously from a single turret. Plates would groan and rivets would pop. On top of that the cost must have been enormous, although in wartime expense seemed of little concern to the Ministry.

*   *   *   *   *

SOME THOUGHTS ON CONVOY DISTANT COVER

In my opinion, provision of a convoy distant covering force by the Home Fleet was fully justified for the following reasons :-

1. The reluctance of the German capital ships to show themselves, when there was a high possibility of coming into contact with our battleships, cruisers and destroyers. This meant they were always a threat to our convoys by just lurking in some Norwegian fjord. I am not insinuating that they were not a brave adversary, far from it, but the *Kriegsmarine* was relatively thin on the ground. They were anxious to preserve what warships they possessed. At the same time, they tended to come out of their lair to sink convoy shipping whenever circumstances were right for them. Their very presence tied up a huge Allied naval fleet of warships that was desperately needed elsewhere. This pressure on our fleet persisted until finally the Tirpitz was sunk by the RAF.

2. Protection from our capital ships to convoy escorts and merchantmen .(Proved necessary by the sinking of the Scharnhorst which, if she had got amongst our convoys, would have sunk ships at will).

3. The locating of scattered merchant ships by the use of powerful battleship HF/DF radar.

4. Lessons learned from the PQ17 convoy debacle. This was a monumental cock-up by the Admiralty, compounded by Admiral of the Fleet Sir Dudley Pound. An order was given instructing the withdrawal of escorts and heavier units and telling ships of the convoy to scatter ! This virtually allowed German air and naval forces to attack and sink at will. Of a convoy of thirty nine ships which set out from North Scotland at

the outset, PQ17 lost twenty four ships.

Sailors ending up in those extremely cold seas were given only a few minutes, before they were expected to succumb. It wasn`t only the cold they had to contend with. There were heavy seas, gale-force winds, freezing fog and ice and sometimes after being hit, blankets of oil on the surface, often ablaze. Most sailors lost in WW11 were drowned, but some were burnt and then drowned. Those on torpedoed or bombed ammunition ships stood no chance, as those ships invariably were blown to smithereens or sank quickly.

*   *   *   *   *

ARCTIC CONVOY DATA from 21st June 1941 to 8th May 1945

<u>British and Allied Warship Losses</u>

Cruisers	2
Destroyers	7
Sloops	3
Frigates	1
Corvettes	3
Minesweepers	4
Submarines	1
Armed Whaler	1
Total	22

<u>German Warship Losses</u>

Battlecruisers	1
Destroyers	2
Escorts	2
Submarines	31
Total	36

<u>Merchant Ship Losses</u>

From aircraft attack	41
From U-boat attack	51
From destroyer attack	4
From mines	6
Wrecked	1
Foundered	1
Total	104

The fact that 31 German U-boats were lost gives some idea of the volume of U-boat activity and of the considerable risk British and Allied ships took in getting cargoes of tanks, aircraft, locomotives and other war supplies to Russia. In addition the Germans had several coastal military airfields in northern Norway, from which they launched attacks on our convoys at every opportunity.

It is estimated that nearly four million tons of equipment was successfully convoyed to the Soviets during the war.

*   *   *   *   *

64

FOLLOWING THE ADMIRAL

On the 8th May 1943, Sir John Tovey struck his flag on the KGV. He was relieved by Admiral Sir Bruce Fraser who, on his appointment as C.-in- C. Home Fleet, hoisted his flag on the KGV class battleship, HMS Duke of York. This meant that his staff had to be transferred to that ship. I joined her on 15th April, along with other staff. On the same day I was promoted to a fully fledged Signalman. Admiral Fraser had played a leading role in the development of the 14-inch gun - the main armament of the four KGV Class battleships.

While I served on board HMS Duke of York, she took part in the following naval operations :-

OPERATION	FROM
FH	31st May `43  to  13th June `43
CAMERA	7th July `43  to  9th  July `43
GOVERNOR	27th July `43  to  29th July `43
LEADER	2nd October `43  to  6th  October `43
CONVOY JW58 and TUNGSTEN	30th March `44 to 3rd April `44
CONVOY RA58	3rd April `44
BRAWN and PROTEUS	29th May `44 "
MASCOT	14th July `44 to 19th July `44
VICTUAL and GOODWOOD	18th August `44 to 3rd September `44

The Duke of York gave cover for Operation `FH` (Allied reliefs for Spitzbergen), leaving Scapa for Hvalfiord on 31st May 1943, returning to Scapa on 13th June.

OPERATION `CAMERA`   Just prior to the Allied landings in Sicily (Operation Huskey) which took place on 10th July 1943, a diversionary dummy invasion fleet was assembled at Scapa . By making the dummy fleet obvious to the Germans it was hoped they would react by diverting some of their forces north, away from the Mediterranean theatre of operations. The Duke of York (C-in-C aboard), together with other capital ships of the Home Fleet and a motley fleet of small craft - MFVs, trawlers, drifters, tugs etc., left Scapa on 7th July 1943 and sailed due east, towards Stavanger, Norway. Every effort was made for the fleet to be spotted by the enemy. A

JU88 followed us for a short while before disappearing . Ships endeavoured to belch out more smoke than usual.

Eventually a German BV138 reconnaissance seaplane was spotted, just above the horizon at a great distance. It was not fired on because Admiral Fraser wanted it to have the opportunity to radio a sighting of the fleet. After allowing sufficient time for the enemy plane to report back our approach, two Martlet aircraft, piloted by Lt-Commander (A) Bird and Sub-Lt (A) Lindsay, RNVR, were launched from HMS Furious (one of the Royal Navy`s first aircraft carriers). They shot the German plane down. A destroyer was sent to the spot, but only wreckage was found.

The battle fleet steered an easterly zig - zag course for hour after hour to within 100 miles of Norway, but there was no response from the enemy. As one disgruntled Chief gunner`s mate was heard to exclaim, "Not a sausage!"

The fleet turned back, then turned towards Norway a second time. Still no enemy response so we made for home, arriving back at Scapa on 9th July.

It was at about this stage of the war that RN communication personnel had to be `re-educated` into the ways of the US Navy. A good example of this was the adoption of the USN phonetic alphabet (ABLE, BAKER, CHARLIE etc). This proved to be a judicious step, especially later, in 1945, when the British Pacific Fleet was to come under the operational command of the US Navy in that theatre of war.

OPERATION `GOVERNOR` This was a similar operation to `Camera`, but uneventful. The Duke of York (C-in-C aboard) left Scapa on 27th July and returned on 29th July.

OPERATION LEADER The flagship left Scapa (C - in - C aboard) on 2nd October `43, to accompany American carrier USS Ranger for an attack by her aircraft on enemy shipping off the Norwegian coast and on Bodo iron workings. Carried out on the 4th, the operation was considered a success. We returned to Scapa on the 6th.

*   *   *   *   *

CHAPTER ELEVEN

RED WINE INSTEAD OF `PUSSERS`

While I was serving in the Duke of York, a notice appeared on the board in November, calling on those men of the Communications Branch who could speak French, to volunteer for liaison staff duties on board the Free French battleship Richelieu. This powerful ship had an equivalent displacement to our KGV Class battleships . Her armament was impressive - 8 x 380mm(15-inch guns), 9 x 152mm(6-inch) guns, 12 x 100mm(3.9-inch) A.A.guns, 56 x 40mm Bofors A.A. guns and 50 x 20mm Oerlikon. I would not have liked to meet her on a dark night ! She was due to arrive at Scapa Flow to join the Home Fleet on 20 November 1943, after an Atlantic crossing from Brooklyn Navy Yard, U.S.A, where she had just been refitted. Her refit included the replacement of a 15-inch gun barrel in her `B` turret, which had previously been damaged by a 380mm defective shell, during a gunnery exchange between HMS Barham and HMS Resolution at Dakar (Page 68) . Numerous additional 40mm Bofors had also been installed on all available upper deck space, especially on her forecastle. She was to come under the command of Admiral Sir Bruce Fraser, C-in-C, Home Fleet.

I put my name forward as a volunteer for this liaison work, although I remembered only a little French from my schooldays. Soon I was ordered to report to the Signal Officer, a Lieutenant.
"Why do you want to serve on the Richelieu ?" he asked.
"Because I would like a change. This will be a new experience for me sir, " I replied . Then he said, "Say something to me in French." I thought for a moment and then replied, "Il fume la pipe." This was the only coherent sentence I knew.
"You'll do," he said and soon, as she anchored in the Flow, I was transferred to the FFS Richelieu, along with several other Communication ratings from the Duke of York. We were a mixed bunch of signalmen and wireless telegraphists, with a Petty Officer telegraphist in charge.

On Christmas Day 1943, the Richelieu lay at anchor in the Flow. The only other ship at anchor was the county class heavy cruiser HMS Kent. While I was on watch on the bridge, keeping an eye on the Kent in case she signalled, I suddenly saw something being hoisted to her yardarm. At first, training my telescope, I had difficulty in making out the object. Then as a slight breeze took it, I was amazed to make out a pair of `Scapa panties`, (Those thick, woollen, long, knitted pants, for protecting vital parts from the Arctic cold!). I took this to be some sort of Christmas Day tradition, which I found amusing. I promptly nipped down to the mess and fetching one of my own pair, tied them to a halyard and hoisted them. Some time later a livid French officer stormed onto the bridge and demanded that I haul down the offending article of clothing immediately. This I did, but under my breath I was very uncomplimentary about his poor sense of humour.

The very next day up in the Arctic, the Home Fleet was playing a very different game of cat and mouse with the Scharnhorst, which was finally sunk that Boxing

Page 68. The Free French battleship Richelieu on her arrival in America, with a 15 inch gun barrel missing.

Day, with our ship HMS Duke of York playing a major role in the battle. Those of us who had volunteered for the job on the Richelieu had missed this action by the skin of our teeth, much to our chagrin. Apparently during the battle, an 11-inch shell struck a leg of the Duke of York`s tripod mast, but failed to explode. If we had not volunteered for this duty, we could well have been standing on the flag deck very near to the point of impact. Knowing my luck the shell would have exploded !
Later it was a solemn moment to see the cruiser HMS Norfolk entering Scapa Flow with the bodies of eight dead sailors from the Scharnhorst battle wrapped in sail-cloth and respectfully laid out on her upper deck.

Two months later at Scapa, I was on watch on the bridge just before dawn when the alarm for `Action Stations` sounded. Many sleepy French gunners poured out onto the upper deck from below, like ants from a disturbed nest, to man the Bofors and Oerlikon guns. Meanwhile a bevy of officers and other ranks reported to the bridge. All eyes gazed skywards. At first it was not realised that anything was amiss. Eventually however, when no enemy put in an appearance, questions started to be asked. Nobody could be found who had given the initial order to activate the alarm. Suddenly the same officer appeared on the bridge, who had made all the fuss about the `Scapa pants`. He made a beeline for me and accused me of sounding the alarm. Needless to say I was quite taken aback. It turned out that there were several locations on the Richelieu from where the alarm could have been activated.

The alarm activator consisted of a brass swivel arm bearing a brass knob, which could only be depressed in the `ACTIVATE` position. Normally however, the brass arm was set to the left, in the `DEACTIVATE` position. Being on watch at night could be very boring. Our only respite from the boredom was if a signal was flashed to us, or if we brewed ourselves a drink. Then we would lean against the instrumentation at the back of the bridge, with `cuppa` in hand. If the alarm lever had not been swung over to the deactivated position from a previous alarm-sounding, the alarm could easily be sounded by applying pressure to the knob. So under those circumstances I could well have set it off. However because I felt I was innocent, I refused to admit to anything. `Napoleon` (my nick-name for him) eventually calmed down. Because there were so many other alarm positions in the ship, this French officer knew he could not prove that I was the culprit. Personally I considered the real culprit to be the person who had last used the lever on the bridge and neglected to deactivate it. Anyway I thought that this unfortunate event did the entire crew of nearly 2,000 French matelots a favour, as they had not held an `Action Station` exercise since we British had joined their ship.

Amongst the British liaison staff was a Welshman, whose mother was French and whose father was Welsh. He spoke French fluently. It was interesting to note that those French sailors who came from Brittany could well understand many words spoken by our Welsh shipmate, when he spoke his own language. Unlike men of the Royal Navy, who had three meals a day and the option of a tot of rum, the Free French Navy had two meals a day, and drank a tumbler of rough red wine with each meal. The liaison staff were obliged to have the same as the French. As a result we all seemed to suffer from hunger, sleepiness and the occasional headache.

On the Richelieu the storage tanks for storing red wine were reputed to be of a larger capacity than those for storing fresh water. They were expecting a vessel to arrive within the next ten days from North Africa to replenish her with wine, but in the event it was torpedoed. So it looked as though the French would have to forego their wine. This was as disastrous to them as it would be to RN sailors if our

69

supply of rum ran out. Making something of a diplomatic gesture, Admiral Fraser ordered that the Richelieu should have Navy rum in place of their wine. Royal Navy rum takes some getting used to. Very soon Richelieu was full of tipsy French matelots. This was a source of much amusement to the liaison staff but, of course this state of affairs could not be allowed to continue. The order was very quickly rescinded.

The size and structure of the Richelieu was impressive. For a start there were so many decks in her superstructure that the French Navy had had an automatic crew-lift installed (like being in Selfridges !) The ship was divided into many small watertight compartments, along the lines of the German battleship Tirpitz. Her bows had the `Italian look`- beautifully streamlined, for cleaving through the water.

Eventually on the 9th February 1944, Richelieu tied up at Rosyth. Passing under the Forth Bridge made a huge impression on the French sailors, as it did on me. We were granted shore-leave. Two of their sailors asked if they could accompany me ashore. I had no problem with that and escorted them onto a train for Edinburgh. We met up with some Scottish girls. I think it was the red pom-poms on the Frenchmen`s hats that attracted them. I cannot remember much about that `run ashore` except that we all paired up with those girls. I was quite shy then, believe it or not, and when we came to part, I asked my partner if I could kiss her goodnight. In her broad Scottish accent she said, "In Scotland we don`t ask we just take !" I could not have had a better invitation than that could I ?

Soon we sailed north, back to Scapa. The Richelieu with a few ships of the Home Fleet, headed out into the Pentland Firth for a short exercise. After nearly five months on board the Richelieu, we were all back on the Duke of York. Before I left, some of the French signalmen presented me with an enamelled crest of the Richelieu, which I still have.

Strange to relate, nowhere on my Service documents can I find any mention of my having served on board the Richelieu. This I assume is because I was still on the Duke of York books. If a historian examined my papers, it would appear I was aboard the Duke of York during her battle with the Scharnhorst. I was not, but it wasn`t for the want of trying .

*   *   *   *   *

CHAPTER TWELVE

CONTINUATION OF OPERATIONS WITH HMS DUKE of YORK

CONVOY JW58 and OPERATION `TUNGSTEN`.(attack on TIRPITZ)

Force 1 left Scapa on 30th March 1944 and comprised Duke of York, Victorious, Anson, a cruiser and five destroyers. This force provided heavy cover up to 1st April for CONVOY JW58.

Subsequently on 2nd April 1944, Force 1 and Force 2 combined for OPERATION `TUNGSTEN` - an attack on the German battleship Tirpitz, which was lying in Altenfjord.

Duke of York moved to a position north west of Bear Island (well up in the Arctic). At the same time oilers and 2 destroyers made for a point 300 miles north west of North Cape.

After much warming of engines, 61 carrier aircraft took off at 0437 on the 3rd of April. The aircraft were divided into two strikes. The first strike of 21 Barracudas carried seven 1,600 lb armour-piercing bombs, twenty four 500 lb semi AP bombs, twelve 500 lb bombs and four 600 lb bombs (for surface or underwater blast effect). The planes flew low to minimise detection. At twenty five miles from the Norwegian coast they climbed to 10,000 ft and made landfall at 0508 . (Page 73). Our incoming aircraft were detected by German radar at 0505. Their warning did not reach Tirpitz until 0524, only four minutes before our attack commenced. Sadly, one Barracuda was lost from each strike. So what did `TUNGSTEN` achieve ? To answer this question I have tabulated the damage accredited to each attack wave.
FIRST WAVE ATTACK :-

ARMAMENT	AIRCRAFT	DAMAGE
1,600 lb AP bomb	Barracuda	Reached armoured deck above Port engine. Exploded. Started fire fed by ruptured petrol refuelling pipes.
1,600 lb AP bomb	Barracuda	Through roof `S1` 150 mm turret, deflected on penetrating the upper deck. Exploded at base of funnel. Caused large fire.
1,600 lb AP bomb	Barracuda	Under-water hit, below lower belt. Exploded outside protected bulkhead, which dished inwards for 15ft. Wing compartments flooded. Hole 3ft wide x 18 ins deep in outer plating.
5 x 500 lb bombs	Barracuda	1 penetrated quarterdeck abreast D turret. Caused serious fire in mess deck. 1 passed through boat at foot of mainmast.Exploded in wardroom. Caused large fire. 3 exploded on hitting 2 inch armour.
600 lb bomb	Barracuda	Burst in the air on hitting funnel. Port side of funnel crushed. Blew in Port hangar roof, causing a fire.
600 lb bomb	Barracuda	Exploded 10ft from starboard side and 30ft

below belt armour. Extensive damage to frames and starboard bilge keel. 50ft length of hull split along weld. Damage to boiler room at inboard end of sea-water inlet pipe.

Hellcats	Sank patrol boat Vp 6103.	
Hellcats	Strafed a net layer.	
Hellcats	Strafed a cargo steamer.	
Hellcats	Strafed heavy repair ship C.A.Larsen.	
Wildcats	Put flak directors out of action.	
Hellcats	Strafed ground based AA batteries.	

SECOND WAVE ATTACK :-

ARMAMENT	AIRCRAFT	DAMAGE
1,600 lb AP bomb	Barracuda	Penetrated forecastle. Failed to explode.
2 x 500 lb bombs	Barracuda	Exploded on upper deck.
500 lb SAP bomb	Barracuda	Penetrated starboard hangar. Exploded near `S1` 150 mm turret .
500 lb SAP bomb	Barracuda	Exploded, passing through the upper deck. Caused large fire below `P1` 150 mm turret. Turret damaged.
?	Barracuda	Near miss abreast starboard propeller bracket. Caused minor splits in hull. Dishing around the bracket and some flooding.
	Hellcats	Damaged anti-submarine craft UJ1212 and UJ1218.

Page 73.   Barracuda aircraft flying over Norway on their way to attack the German battleship Tirpitz.

The Duke of York had a threefold responsibility with the joint task of providing protection for Convoy JW58, for the carriers taking part in Operation `TUNGSTEN` and for the returning Convoy RA58. However owing to the damage inflicted on Tirpitz, it was not considered necessary to provide heavy cover for Convoy RA58. After all Scharnhorst was no more ! A major threat from U-boats to the Arctic convoys still existed. From January 1944, Germany still had 21 U-boats in that area of warfare and there was still the possibility of air attack, although what remained of the Luftwaffe was now badly overstretched. The U- boats were now having a hard time of it from the Allied fleet, owing to improved countermeasures in weaponry and logistics. As an example I here set out the naval escort protection given to Convoy JW58 and the punishment dished out to its attackers.

The convoy comprised fifty merchantmen - a large convoy , which sailed from Loch Ewe on 27th March 1944 . The Navy ships were :-

USS. Milwaukee (to be handed over to the Russian Northern Fleet)
MAIN ESCORTS :- Diadem (Light cruiser), Activity and Tracker (Escort carriers) and Destroyers Impulsive, Inconstant, Obedient, Offa, Onslow, Opportune, Oribi, Orwell, Saumarez, Serapis, Scorpion, Venus and Stord. The Diadem, Activity and Tracker joined on 29th March to 4th April. The destroyers joined from 27th March. Also present :-
WESTERN APPROACHES 2nd ESCORT GROUP :- SO - Capt F.J.Walker in Starling, Magpie, Wild Goose, Wren, Whimbrel (all Sloops) and Destroyers Beagle, Boadicea, Keppel and Walker. Joined 29th March to 4th April.
DISTANT COVER:- The Home Fleet was engaged at the same time in Operation `TUNGSTEN` .
LOCAL ESCORTS :-Rhododendron, Starwort (Corvettes), Rattlesnake, Onyx, Orestes (Minesweepers), 27th March to 29th March.
CLOSE A/S ESCORTS:- Westcott, Whitehall, Wrestler (Destroyers) and Bluebell, Honeysuckle and Lotus (Corvettes). 27th March to 4th April 1944.

Six long range German shadowing aircraft were shot down by Fleet Air Arm fighters. The enemy set up a line of sixteen U-boats to attack the convoy. They were heavily attacked by A/S aircraft and surface escort vessels. As a result, on 29th March, U961 was sunk by Starling. On 31st March U355 was sunk by aircraft from the Escort Carrier Tracker and by the depth-charges of Beagle. On the 2nd April the Destroyer Keppel sank U360 with Hedgehog. On the 3rd April a FAA Swordfish spotted U288 and called up an Avenger A/S aircraft and a Wildcat fighter. By their combined efforts they were able to sink U288.
Convoy JW58 arrived at Kola Inlet unscathed, on the 4th April 1944.

Convoy RA58 sailed from Kola Inlet on the 7th April, at least knowing they were safe from any attack by the Tirpitz, thanks to the damage inflicted on her by the Home Fleet (Operation `TUNGSTEN`).

Convoy RA58 arrived at Loch Ewe unscathed, on 14th April, after the U-boats failed to locate it.

* * * * *

OPERATIONS `BRAWN` and `PROTEUS`
The Home Fleet, with the C - in - C on board Duke of York, left Scapa on 29th May 1944 for a further air strike on the Tirpitz. Plans were thwarted when the weather

rapidly deteriorated.

Operations `BRAWN` and `PROTEUS` were cancelled and the Fleet returned to Scapa.

The invasion of Europe (D-Day) took place on 6th June 1944, but we saw none of that vast action.

On the 11th June 1944, Duke of York arrived at Rosyth where we were able to have a reasonable spell of shore-leave. On the 14th June, Admiral Sir Bruce Fraser struck his flag and was relieved by Admiral Sir Henry Moore. Shortly afterwards on 17th June, Duke of York returned to Scapa.

*   *   *   *   *

OPERATION `MASCOT`

The Home Fleet, with the new C - in -C on board Duke of York, left Scapa on the 14th July 1944 for a further naval air attack on Tirpitz. This attack proved unsuccessful and the Fleet was ordered back to Scapa arriving on the 19th July.

*   *   *   *   *

OPERATIONS `GOODWOOD` and `VICTUAL`

On the 18th August 1944 Duke of York as flagship, left Scapa with the rest of the Home Fleet to cover Russian convoy JW59 and returning convoy RA59A. This duty was labelled OPERATION `VICTUAL`. It was run concurrently with OPERATION `GOODWOOD`, an air strike on the Tirpitz. The attacking Navy fleet comprised : three Fleet carriers, Duke of York, 3 cruisers, a destroyer screen escort, plus one other screen escort - a frigate, HMS Bickerton. In addition, HMS Nabob, upgraded from escort carrier to strike carrier, participated in the attack.

We steamed into the Barents Sea. Nabob`s four Wildcats flew CAPs (combat air patrols). Her Avengers flew anti-submarine patrols (A/S). Bad weather fouled the operation, but three squadrons of Barracudas scored hits on the Tirpitz. Sadly, eleven Barracudas were lost.

On the 22nd August, whilst preparing for a second attack, the escort /strike carriers laid out their fuel hoses to replenish the destroyers. I was looking directly at the Nabob from the flag deck, when it happened. Suddenly without warning, a huge white plume shot in the air, starboard side aft of her. "NABOB has been hit !" I exclaimed. The Yeoman shouted up the voice pipe to the bridge. Immediately the Duke of York was steaming away from the area, hell for leather, quickly followed by all the other capital ships and most of the destroyer screen.

Battleships don`t normally drop depth-charges. That is a job for the escorts, but they are usually only dropped when an echo gets louder and is considered within vulnerable range. It is vital for the capital ships to get out of enemy torpedo range as soon as possible. There could well be a T5 acoustic torpedo being fired at any moment. We didn`t wish to meet one. These sensitive weapons homed in on the noise generated by a ship`s propellers, but they often exploded prematurely in the wake of a ship before making contact with the target. Minutes went by but nothing happened to us. We were very fortunate !

Nabob meanwhile was down about 15 degrees by the stern. She had been hit by a FEDERAPPARAT (FATS) spread, a zig - zagging torpedo ; what you might call a hit-and-miss weapon. Bickerton manoeuvred to go alongside her, but eight minutes after the first torpedo, the same submarine (U354) fired a T5 torpedo at Nabob to finish her off. Because Bickerton was in the immediate proximity, she was struck instead. Eventually the destroyer Vigilant went alongside and took off the injured and about 200 survivors. Then as the Bickerton could not be saved, the destroyer Vigilant sank her. The very next day the Navy wreaked retribution on U354, when HMS Mermaid sank her.

Meanwhile Nabob`s damage control party (her crew were Canadians) were doing a heroic timber-shoring job to the engine-room bulkheads, which were bulging ominously. Her main engines had to be shut down. Nabob had sustained a fifty foot gash below the waterline. Eventually Captain Lay managed to work his ship up to ten knots and slowly headed south back to Scapa. After all that effort, in which the damage control parties had risked their lives, the authorities decided she was not worth saving because of more pressing priorities. She lay moored in Scapa for a while, her hull broken into two parts.

Eventually the two parts of what was left of Nabob were towed away to a dockyard for scrapping. But firstly because she had suffered 21 dead and missing, the bodies from her Canadian crew had to be recovered. The dockyard mateys refused to undertake this gruesome task, perhaps because some women worked as dockyard mateys too. It fell upon the shoulders of the Canadian sailors to manhandle the bodies of their dead shipmates up from down below, deck by deck. I cannot think of a sadder or more unpleasant task. Finally they managed to recover a total of fourteen bodies.

The Duke of York finally arrived back in Scapa on 3rd September 1944.

* * * * *

CHAPTER THIRTEEN

MOVES AFOOT

Now that the Scharnhorst was at the bottom of the sea and the Tirpitz was disabled, many capital ships of the Home Fleet could be released for operational duties in other theatres of war, such as Operation Overlord (the invasion of Europe) and to the Pacific in support of the Americans against the Japanese. Scapa Flow began to look quite bereft of warships.

Duke of York was shortly destined for refitting and modernisation at Liverpool. Her communications staff were distributed to various destinations, but the Navy was not going to let me escape from Scapa to warmer climes just yet. Shortly after our return from Operation `Victual` I was transferred to HMS Iron Duke (a WWI battleship) which had been the flagship of Admiral Sir John Jellicoe at the Battle of Jutland in 1916. She was being used as a base at Scapa and had suffered the indignity of being tucked out of sight of the main Flow and cemented to the sea bed. My first impression of the old lady was the sheer size of everything. Everywhere one looked, much brass work, vast companion-ways and robust metal fittings. I was stuck on the Iron Duke for a fortnight, but still retained on the Duke of York books. Strange to relate, at the western end of the Flow was the hull of a German battleship from WWI, the Derfflinger. As a final indignity to the Germans, the British had erected a couple of contractor huts on her whale-like upturned hull.

I spent the first two weeks of September in London on leave. On 9 September, I decided to call on Mrs Phillips who, when I was fifteen you will remember, gave me shelter in her stair cupboard during the Blitz. She was pleased to see me. After a long conversation I left. As I walked up the road there was a huge rumbling explosion, followed by a strange rushing sound. It seemed to come from the direction of Chiswick. Mercifully that was the only V2 rocket terror-weapon I was to experience.

On 17 September 1944 I was transferred to HMS Furious, one of the Navy`s early carriers. She had started her service as a cruiser, but was converted to an aircraft carrier well before the war. I only served on her for three weeks. I do remember giving my head an awful crack on one of her bulkheads in the after flats. It fetched me to my knees.

* * * * *

THINGS ARE WARMING UP

On 11 October I joined the battleship, HMS Rodney. With so many transfers, I was beginning to think the Navy did not know what to do with me. I was wrong. All I remember of the ship was the fact that there was hardly any room to sleep. I was issued with a camp bed as there was not enough rail-space for all of us to sling our hammocks. The truth of the matter was that all ships had been fitted with extra AA guns. Extra guns meant extra guns-crews so ships` crews were increasing, but the accommodation space was not. Before Duke of York sailed for Liverpool on 18 September she discharged most of her crew. Where do you put some 1,700 sailors ? You send them on leave and then into barracks, from where they will be drafted to other ships and shore establishments.

Thankfully I left the Rodney on 1st November 1944 and made my way south to my shore-base HMS Mercury, from where I was sent on embarkation leave, prior to service in the Pacific.

*   *   *   *   *

TROOPSHIP TO THE ANTIPODES

My new draft was bussed from HMS Mercury to HMS Collingwood in Hampshire. There we were prepared for overseas service. We had lectures on several personal health aspects of living in the tropics : the avoidance of sunburn, salt intake, daily intake of lime juice to compensate for the lack of fresh fruit and vegetables, warnings on sexual diseases, sweat rash (*prickly heat*) and athlete's foot.

Sailors don't have baths, they have showers. But whereas in the UK the showers are of fresh water, in the tropics they are of salt water. This is very beneficial for skin diseases, but not so good for comfort. One's skin feels slightly sticky and hair is difficult to comb. Other talks were on the military side, such as on the silhouettes of Japanese warships. Strangely we were not given any aircraft recognition instruction on aircraft of the Japanese Air Force. We were warned about our behaviour when on shore-leave in a foreign country. Having got all that off their chests, the instructors reverted to signal exercises. There were innumerable kit inspections, held at Morning Rounds, when we had to stand to attention by our beds.

We had been at Collingwood nearly one week. In the early morning prior to Sunday Divisions which incorporated a religious service, the parade ground was cloaked in thick fog. The drill sheds around the perimeter were shrouded in gloom. Slowly the fog lifted to reveal the body of a sailor, hanging by his neck from a rope, which had been slung over a cross-beam in one of the sheds. We were told he was the second man to die in that way in a fortnight. We were likely to be away from our loved ones for up to two years, perhaps even more. Sadly this prospect drove a few men right over the edge.

We were kitted out for the tropics. This included the issue of a lightweight camp-bed, which could be very quickly assembled or dismantled. In tropical latitudes a ship can become unbearably hot below decks. Later on this little camp-bed would prove a godsend. It could be assembled on the upper deck during calm seas, allowing one to lie and gaze up at the myriad of stars before dropping off to sleep.

After a few more days we were bussed to Portsmouth Barracks. The following morning we were lined up in the gymnasium for various injections. Several sick berth attendants were administering the jabs from both sides of a long queue. They were dealing with several hundred men a day. Each attendant used a separate table to carry their needles. Most injections were in the arms, but further down the queue we had to have one in the backside. It was an unusual sight to see a row of bare bottoms. The whole organisation was rather like the conveyor belt system in a factory. A certain Irishman, having just had an injection in his left arm, remained standing on the same spot while talking over his shoulder to the man behind. The attendant on the opposite side of the queue turned round from his table and promptly gave the Irishman another injection in his right arm by mistake. There was quite a panic but I did not hear of the outcome. I found the jab against yellow fever to be the most painful.

During the late morning we were all paid six weeks pay in advance. This was to cover us for the six to seven week journey from Liverpool to Sydney Australia, via the Panama Canal. We were allowed shore-leave that afternoon. I made my way to a small funfair and had several goes on the dodgem cars. Afterwards I made for a milk bar, where I soon discovered to my horror that my wallet was missing. I rushed back to the dodgems but failed to find it and the attendant pleaded complete ignorance. I had lost £14 - not to be sneezed at in those days. With sore arms, a sore backside and now, apart from a few coins, empty pockets, I dragged myself back to barracks. Down in the dumps is not an adequate description of how I felt.

Next day my draft was put on a train for Liverpool. There we boarded the troop-ship Athlone Castle. We were each allocated a bunk - not as comfortable as a hammock but not too bad. The ship soon filled with a cross-section of the Services, including a large contingent of WRNS (the first contingent of `Wrens` to be sent to Australia).

The ship sailed that night. It wasn`t long before we had a lifeboat drill. After that it was `heads down` until dawn. The servicemen were soon fraternising with the Wrens , including me, but when they found out I had no money most of them disappeared as if by magic. However one felt sorry for me, but although I responded in a friendly manner I was not attracted to her.

The weather was cold and those who braved the upper decks wrapped themselves in blankets. At least this was better than being cooped up below. What can be done to pass the time on a troopship ? Well for a start you can lean on the guard-rail and watch the naval escort vessels accompanying you. You can lean on the guard-rail astern and gaze at the ship`s wake as though mesmerised. Then, if the visibility is good, you can gaze at the horizon. Or you can gaze at the sky, looking out for unusual cloud formations. Then perhaps you could look out for periscopes or aircraft, play cards or tombolla, squat on the deck and chat up the women as they walked by, or pace the deck yourself or join in physical jerks. It was wise to try and avoid the funnel smoke and to be especially on your guard against any approaching figure of authority, who looked as though they might wish to detail someone for some demeaning chore or other. Of course you could always nip down to the NAAFI to purchase a packet of `carbohydrates` if you had the money, which I had not.

Occasionally whilst squatting on the upper deck looking out to sea, I would suddenly feel something landing in my lap, such as a small packet of biscuits, some sweets or a cigarette. Word about my plight had got around. It was all very embarrassing. I felt like a squatting beggar. After six or seven weeks in this predicament they would be taking me away !

To relieve the general boredom which was plaguing the ship, those in charge organised a concert. Anyone who could do anything in the way of entertainment was encouraged to volunteer. I put my name forward to play the harmonica - the type which has a chromatic scale (operated by a button at the side). At last something to do - something to aim for. This meant I had to practise. I could often be heard on the upper deck going through my repertoire. At first this attracted quite an audience, but after hearing `Brazil` and other popular tunes of the day for the umpteenth time, they drifted away. After the third day out our escorts left us. We were now alone in the vast Atlantic Ocean, at the mercy of God knows what.

Soon we were in sunnier climes, being entertained by flying fish and dolphins crossing our bow. Men started stripping to the waist to sunbathe. Warnings were put out over the Tannoy about the dangers of sunbathing. Many ignored the warnings and paid later for their foolhardiness. Some lay in the sun and fell asleep. I always remember seeing one man being carted off to the sick bay, with his stomach one enormous blister. Those men who suffered such serious sunburn were disciplined.

Being fair skinned, I avoided the sun as much as possible for most of the journey. Even so, by the time I reached Australia I had acquired a reasonable tan. That is, except for my nose, which continued to peel for the next two years.

One day we sensed we were near land. You could smell it in the air. More birds started to appear and strands of seaweed and pieces of wood floated by. Then suddenly there ahead of us was land. Everyone excitedly crowded the guardrails. We slowly eased into the Panama Canal, through the Gatan Locks. The canal held everyone`s interest, especially the sight of the small locomotives, which were the work-horses to pull us through the locks. The canal is just 47 miles long and some 25 metres above sea level. It is in the midst of some 500 square miles of rain forest, which continuously tops up the canal. Nowadays the canal carries some 14,000 ships a year. We made our way through a tranquil lake. I was fascinated by a particularly high, sheer-sided plateau on the port side, crowned with thick jungle growing from a flat peak. It made me think of Conan Doyle`s `The Lost World`.

From the time the ship finally turned its back on Panama and the canal, and steamed out into the Pacific, we did not sight land or see any other vessel until we reached Australia.

On the 8th January 1945 as we crossed the Equator, a `Crossing - the - Line` ceremony was held and much fun was had by all. Demon barbers with shaving brushes and much soapy lather did their devilish work, with a certainty that the victims, as they vainly tried to stay on a greased pole, would receive a ducking in the water below. Certificates were handed out to each individual who had willingly, or unwillingly, gone through the ordeal.

A few days from Sydney we were joined by an albatross, which stayed with us for nearly all the rest of the journey. As we sailed into Sydney harbour and were manoeuvred to the quay, one couldn`t help but notice the famous Sydney Bridge. You couldn`t miss it. It was enormous, casting a long, dark shadow over the harbour. We had expected glorious sunshine, but instead it was overcast and drizzling.

A steady stream of passengers started to disembark, leaving the stuffy and cramped conditions of the Athlone Castle for the severe heat of an Australian summer. These included repatriated RAAF personnel, the contingent of WRNS, men of the Royal Navy for ships of the new British Pacific Fleet, a contingent of Dutch troops, Voluntary Aid Detachment personnel and finally, a few government civilians. My draft was crammed into double-decker buses, not unlike the London buses and driven to Wynyard Station Sydney. There we boarded a dusty train for Warwick Farm, which is some fifteen miles out from Sydney. Our spirits rose when we realised we would easily be able to reach Sydney for shore leave. I was shortly to be paid at last, so things were looking up.

We soon found ourselves billeted in a camp on Warwick Farm Racecourse that had recently been vacated by the American Army. They had left their tents behind when they moved far north, to recapture various Pacific islands from the Japanese. With the Royal Navy now in occupation, the camp was renamed HMS Golden Hind. The Navy was not wasting any time. Long corrugated iron huts were already being erected on the opposite side of the road. There were several galleys, which were basic wooden huts. There was a daily mail call, which everyone looked forward to.

I spent several weeks under canvas, awaiting the arrival of my destroyer HMS Wager. At the time there were many ships of all kinds making for the Antipodes. When finally mustered they would become the biggest fleet ever assembled in the history of the Royal Navy - the British Pacific Fleet (BPF).

The worst part of living in this hot and dusty environment was the sand-flies. They were a persistent nuisance and got into everything : food, clothes, hair, sweat and bedding. They could also bite ! Many sailors contracted what was generally spoken of as `sand-fly fever`. For a couple of days it left you feeling nauseous and as though all the energy had been sapped out of you. There was plenty of shore leave and naturally most sailors made for the bright lights of Sydney, using the dusty trains to get there. Because of the intense dry heat, the train doors were usually left open. We would stand by the open doorways to try and catch some cooling draft. There was no blackout out there. So in general for a few weeks we were having a pretty good life, what with the wonderful Australian hospitality, their fabulous beaches, beautiful girls, good food (including fresh fruit) and schooners of beer.

There was plenty of accommodation for British servicemen in Sydney. This included THE BRITISH CENTRE, set up by the Australian Comforts Fund. Good on you Aussies ! You did us British proud. Thank you so much.

*   *   *   *   *

A HOME FROM HOME

On my first run ashore in Australia, I made a point of going to see an elderly great aunt (Auntie Minnie, my grandfather`s sister) who lived in North Sydney - a district over the other side of the harbour from Circular Quay. I had never met her before. She turned out to be a very pleasant lady and we got on extremely well. She had three grown-up children; Len, Stan and Valerie. Apart from her own family she had an adopted daughter, Helen, the daughter of an Australian Army officer. Helen`s father had died in Singapore, as a prisoner of the Japanese.

Shore leave expired at 08.00hrs, so my aunt gave me a spare bedroom. What bliss to be lying on a soft mattress between clean sheets, after all the discomforts of the troop-ship and the intense heat of the camp. The war seemed very far away. This was a proper home-from-home. My aunt always made me feel welcome. We used to have interesting conversations about `the Old Country`. She produced a photograph of her son Len. He looked very much like my grandfather (the artist), when he was young. In fact Len was himself very artistic. I remember seeing his striking low-relief carvings of animals. They were impressive.

One incident I never forgot was one evening when I was ashore at my aunt`s. As she was quite an old lady, I used to turn in fairly early. On this particular evening, I entered my bedroom and was shocked to find it reeking of perfume. Helen had been up to her tricks. As I turned to leave the bedroom, to jokingly complain to Auntie, I spotted Helen peeping round her bedroom door. She was trying to stifle her laughter. We both sat on the side of the bed and talked. Although a practical joker, Helen was highly intelligent and could be very serious at times. She was studying to be a doctor. Suddenly she made a statement which really shocked me.
"I am going to be a doctor, but when I reach the age of sixty five I intend to take my own life." I could not come to terms with her way of thinking and it troubled me. But having said that, we say and do some stupid and awful things when we are young. Helen did achieve her ambition to become a doctor, but we lost touch. Now in the evening of my life, I often wonder if Helen carried out her threat. I sincerely hope not ! From experience I know there is plenty of enjoyment to be had out of our retiring

years, as long as we have the right mental attitude and are comparatively healthy. There is a lot of truth in the old sayings, `Life is what you make it` and `There`s life in the old dog yet`. Perhaps I should add a third. `There`s many a good tune played on an old fiddle`.

Helen had a college friend called Lillian, a Jewish girl. She was fairly plain but had a warm personality. She came from a wealthy refugee family, which had fled from Poland to Australia to escape the Nazis. Her father had owned a steel works. Also living in Sydney was an uncle who was a jeweller. Lillian`s parents were divorced but they still went out together as friends - an unusual arrangement but it seemed to work. Understandably there were many broken marriages during the war. It might be worthwhile pointing out that during WWII, Britain had the lowest birth rate ever recorded. I was often invited to wine and dine in Sydney by Lillian`s parents. I felt slightly uncomfortable about this, when I thought of my countrymen in other parts of the world fighting and perhaps dying, while I was there in a land of plenty enjoying myself. Then again I would think about life being a lottery of highs and lows. It was my turn to be on a high. Fate could take a nasty turn at any time now.

Helen, Lillian and I would often take a tram to Cronulla beach. Lillian`s family had a holiday chalet there. It was much quieter than the Bondi or Manley beaches.

Eventually HMS Wager, part of the 27th Destroyer Flotilla, arrived in Sydney and I soon bade farewell to Warwick Farm, its dry withering heat, its dust and sand flies. I joined this destroyer on 16th February 1945. Soon I was settling into my new `home`, Mess 4. This mess was right in the bow of the ship - the roughest part in foul weather. Just before the BPF sailed to join action with the Japanese, I read in a newspaper about a particularly bad storm, with surf so powerful it had swept away the entire Cronulla beach. It was as though `our` beach had been taken away to coincide with the dissolution of our little discussion group.

*   *   *   *   *

CHAPTER FOURTEEN

OPERATION `ICEBERG` - THE ASSAULT ON OKINAWA

The British Pacific Fleet left Sydney on 28th February 1945 and sailed for Manus, Admiralty Islands. There it languished in the steamy heat, waiting for operational orders from the American Navy. Their navy was many times larger than ours, especially in aircraft carrier numbers, so they called the tune. Eventually the BPF was ordered to make for Ulithi Atoll in the Caroline Islands. The Fleet left Manus on 18th March 1945 and headed north for this new destination, arriving 22nd March.

At Ulithi the BPF was designated by the Americans as Task Force 57 and assigned to the U.S. Fifth Fleet. When the Fleet arrived at Ulithi there were ships stationed in every direction as far as the eye could see, in readiness for the invasion of Okinawa. A truly breathtaking sight.

On the very next day, 23rd March at 0630, TF57 left Ulithi Atoll to commence the first phase of Operation `ICEBERG`. We headed north for objectives in the Sakishima Gunto Islands, which are situated southwest of Japan between Okinawa and the Japanese mainland. Approximately one month after leaving Sydney the British Pacific Fleet was in striking distance of the enemy.

TF57, at that time, consisted of the following warships : -

Battleships	King George the Fifth - flagship (Commander of TF57 - Vice Admiral Sir Bernard Rawlings), Howe .
Aircraft Carriers	Victorious, Illustrious, Indefatigable, Indomitable .
Cruisers	Swiftsure, Gambia, Black Prince, Euryalus.
Destroyers	Grenville, Quickmatch, Quiberon, Queensborough, Quality, Ulster, Undaunted, Undine, Urania, Whelp and Wager.

Other ships continued to arrive.

A Replenishment Group consisting chiefly of oilers and supply ships, of one sort or another, had to be available to keep this task force at sea.

On 25th March the Fleet refuelled from the Replenishment Group, under bad weather conditions - strong winds and a heavy swell. The American system of oiling at sea was for the warship to be positioned abeam of the tanker. This proved to be a better method than that employed by the British. The British method of trailing a buoyant hose astern of the tanker was slow and fraught with difficulty, especially in heavy seas. In those conditions pumping was slow and hoses easily parted. Ships of the Fleet Train (supply ships) were based at Leyte, but obtained their stores from Australia.

Sakishima Gunto is made up of two principal islands, Ishigaki and Miyako.

Three airstrips had been laid on Ishigaki - Miyara, Hegina and Ishigaki. On Miyako the Japanese had built Nobara, Hirara and Sukhama.

The first fly off, at 0605 on 26th March, took place 100 miles due south of Miyako Island .

The carriers` order of battle was :-

Indomitable	29 Hellcats 15 Avengers
Victorious	37 Corsairs 14 Avengers 2 Walrus (`Shagbats`)
Indefatigable	40 Seafires 20 Avengers 9 Fireflies
Illustrious	36 Corsairs 16 Avengers

The brief was to strafe parked aircraft and defences, to crater the runways and to maintain a permanent Combat Air Patrol (CAP) over the enemy airfields, to prevent staging of their aircraft from other enemy islands or from the Japanese mainland. It would take our planes about one-and-a-half hours to return after take-off.

At 0615 a CAP of four Corsairs was launched from Victorious. At 0630 Victorious launched 15 Corsairs to Ramrod attack the airfields of Hirara and Nobara. Leading the attack was Lieutenant Commander (A) C.C.Tomkinson, CO of 1836 Squadron. He stated :-
"The form-up took longer than usual as the aircraft had not been ranged on deck in the correct order and several went unserviceable."
Not a good start, especially as pilots revealed later that airfields attacked so far only had dummy aircraft or aircraft grounded from some previous raid. Sadly Lieutenant Commander (A) Tomkinson RNVR, who had only one kidney, was hit by AA fire and forced to ditch in the sea. He was seen wearing his lifejacket by another pilot but was never found.

At 0920 a combined force of forty aircraft was launched. These were mostly Avengers, each armed with four 500-pound MC bombs, to bomb and strafe the Sakishima Gunto airfields.

Enemy runways were of crushed coral. The islands were formed partly of coral, so it was easy for the Japanese to obtain this material to fill in the bomb craters overnight. In any case the craters created were comparatively small.

On 27th March four major strikes, each of forty aircraft, were made using mostly Avengers, but Hellcat and Corsair sorties were interspersed with these. After two days of attacking the enemy, twelve Japanese aircraft were destroyed on the ground, plus a further twenty eight shot down over their own airfields. This was for the loss of nineteen Fleet Air Arm planes.

The Fleet was aware that during the hours of darkness enemy reconnaissance planes were active. Our flyers emphasised the need on our side for a radar-equipped night fighter. No such luck !

As the huge American landings on Okinawa were to take place on 1st April, this meant the 31st March to 2nd April was a critical period for the British Pacific Fleet if we were to give the Americans effective and telling support.

More attacks had been planned for the BPF to repeat the strikes on the airfields of Sakishima Gunto on 28th March, but a typhoon warning put paid to that. Admiral Rawlings wisely cancelled those planned air strikes and utilised the time for replenishment. At 0730 TF57 met the Replenishment Group to refuel, replace lost or damaged aircraft, take on stores, provisions and replacement aircrew. Because of strong winds and rough seas, these conditions made the replenishment at sea (RAS) a hazardous and lengthy process.

At 2008 HMS Wager, having transferred a large number of drop tanks to the Victorious, made to get back on station. Instead of passing astern of her Captain Watkin chose to cut across her bows. A collision was only just averted through Victorious going full speed astern. It was a near miss! There were a couple of terse signals I believe, not recorded in the signal log. When the Fleet met up with the Fleet Train (the supply ships), Wager, together with one or two other destroyers, was like a Jack-of-all-trades. She would steam hither and thither amongst ships of the Fleet, with precious stores, replacement spares (including aircraft drop tanks) but most important of all and most hoped for, with mail from loved ones at home.

By 1430 on the afternoon of 30th March replenishment was completed. Task Force 57 again proceeded to the combat zone at some 22 knots.

On 31st March Wager and the newly joined light cruiser Argonaut took up radar picket stations halfway between the Sakishima Gunto Islands and the Fleet. We were well aware of our vulnerability positioned so close to the enemy and felt we might be attacked when it became light, but nothing materialised.

At 0600, our first fighter sweep of the day of 8 Hellcats and 16 Corsairs reported no change to the enemy airfields since the last time they paid the Japanese a visit, four days earlier. Patrols of four fighters were flown off in succession during the day. Some carried bombs which they dropped on the airfields. Two bomber strikes of eleven Avengers each took off at 1215 and 1515 respectively. Both flights had a small fighter escort. An attack was made on Ishigaki Airfield and the installations. The enemy replied with flak. Buildings and runways sustained more damage.

April 1st 1945 was the day of the massive American assault by 50,000 U.S. soldiers and marines on Okinawa, only 300 miles south of Japan and the last major Japanese stronghold to be recaptured before reaching the mainland of Japan. To defend Okinawa, the Japanese had 70,000 troops, plus in support an additional 30,000 naval and garrison personnel. The enemy air strength was estimated at nearly 6,000 aircraft of their 5th Air Fleet and 6th Air Army, based on the Japanese mainland and Okinawa. Nearly two thirds of these comprised the newly formed Special Attack Units of kamikaze squadrons. By the time Okinawa fell to the Allies, 2,000 to 4,000 suicide aircraft had been destroyed. The British Pacific Fleet covered the southern flank of the American assault (Operations `Iceberg` and `Oolong`).

At 0643, TF57 launched fighter Ramrods against the airfields of Ishigaki. The radar picket detected a group of enemy aircraft some 75 miles to the westward and approaching TF57 at 8,000 feet. Defensive fighters were launched from Victorious and the fighter Ramrods were recalled to assist. The raiders split up some forty miles from the Fleet. The first interception was made by Corsairs from Victorious and one Zeke was shot down. The bogeys were first detected by our own aircraft at 12,000 feet but later the enemy changed to 19,000 feet.
All our squadrons climbed. Next the bogeys were down to sea level and our planes dived down on them and followed them right onto the guns of the Fleet.
Aircraft recognition became difficult, as there were similarities between aircraft of both sides. The Japanese knew their planes could be detected by our radar. To avoid detection they would often try and intermingle with our returning bombers. Then as our planes were landing, they would launch an attack.

At 0727 a Zeke machine-gunned the battleship KGV. Then the same plane made a feint diving attack on the Indefatigable from the port quarter. Within seconds the Zeke struck the carrier abreast the forward barrier, at the junction of the flight deck and the island. Its 500-pound bomb shattered the flight deck sick bay, briefing room and both flight deck barriers, killing eight men outright and wounding sixteen, including the Lieutenant Commander Flying, an Air Engineer Officer and half the Operations Room crew. The blast bent the flight deck armour to a depth of some three inches. Splinters caused much superficial damage. The blast also started a small fire in the roof of `B` hangar, which was put out in four minutes.

At 0816, just thirty-eight-and-a-half minutes after the attack, the first range of Seafires was landed on.

While all this mess was being cleared up, a second Zeke scored a near miss on the destroyer Ulster, causing serious damage. She was unable to steam and had to be towed by the cruiser Gambia to Leyte for repairs.

At 1715 Wager and Argonaut rejoined the Fleet. Prior to this Wager had plucked a fortunate or unfortunate (depending on how you look at it) pilot from the sea. The Wager was soon back on station, but hardly had she positioned herself on the destroyer screen when there was another kamikaze attack at 1730 . A kamikaze aircraft hedgehopped over the destroyer escort at 500 feet, climbed and then dived at the Victorious, which did not use her AA guns until the very last moment. The `Vic` was already turning to starboard and as the kamikaze was already approaching the starboard quarter, it found it more and more difficult to maintain such a tight turn. He roared in. His starboard wing struck the port edge of the flight deck, causing his plane to cartwheel into the sea on the port side. His bomb (probably a 500-pounder) detonated underwater some 80 feet from the side, sending tons of water, fuel, aircraft fragments and body parts onto the flight deck. We on the Wager had a first-hand view of this attack, but on reflection many of us felt a chill in our hearts, as we witnessed a determined and fanatical pilot deliberately sacrificing his life in this way.

At noon on the 2nd April, TF57 retired to the refuelling area. Wager took on board numerous drop tanks from the Fleet Train and transferred them to Victorious. Bad weather delayed replenishment, which was still incomplete when TF57 headed back for the operational area on Thursday 5th April. At dusk Victorious had taken the opportunity on the 4th April to ditch three deck-accident damaged Avengers. Useable parts had been stripped. Such planes were dropped unceremoniously over the side by crane.

Later on the 5th, TF57 relieved an American Task Group in the operational area to return to the frustrating and sometimes heartbreaking task of neutralising the enemy airfields. Raids were launched on Hirara, Miyara, Nobara and Sukhama airfields. The Illustrious was attacked at dusk by a single kamikaze. Slight damage was inflicted to the carrier when the suicide plane`s wing tip caught the island and ended up in the `drink`. The ship had to reduce her speed to 19 knots. On 6th and 7th April attacks from our aircraft continued on runways and targets of opportunity on the Sakishima Gunto airfields.

By now, although the Americans were slowly beating very fierce resistance on Okinawa, the rate of shipping losses from hundreds of kamikaze attacks was proving unacceptable. These attacks came in waves and are thought to have originated from the staging airfields of Shinchiku and Matsuyama, in the northern part of Formosa (now called Taiwan). It is worth pointing out that total American shipping losses by the end of the Okinawa campaign were 36 ships sunk and 368 damaged. This rate of death and destruction had to be curtailed. On 9th April, Admiral Spruance, USN, (the Commander US 5th Fleet) asked TF57 to strike at these enemy airfields in Formosa, on the 11th and 12th April, to try and relieve the pressure on the Americans.

Operation `Oolong` was set up to meet the American request, but on the 11th bad weather put paid to any flying. On the 12th however weather conditions had improved. It was a day of success for our aircraft. It was also quite an eventful day for Wager too.

While it was still dark the carriers of TF57 launched a force of twenty-four bombers, escorted by fighters, to attack Shinchiku airfield on northern Formosa. A similar force was launched to attack Matsuyama airfield. Just prior to this, a TBS (Talk Between Ships) R/T message was received from Victorious over the bridge speakers, by all destroyers of the escort screen - `My chickens are about to depart`. This was a precautionary measure to warn any trigger-happy gunners that these aircraft, flying in the dark, were ours. The destroyer screen was positioned in roughly a wide circle about the capital ships. The distance from one side of the screen to the other varied between approximately six to ten miles. In the dark our aircraft, flying within the escort screen area, were obliged to display two recognition lights of pre-planned colours. The colour combination was changed religiously every twelve hours. In conjunction with these lights was a double-letter code. If challenged our aircraft were expected to transmit this Morse letter-code by Aldis lamp back to the challenger.

On board Wager the sound of aircraft engines came out of the darkness from the direction of the carriers. Soon our planes roared off, each displaying the correct recognition light combination, which they switched off as soon as they flew outside the destroyer screen perimeter. The drone of our aircraft fading into the distance could be heard for a short while as they headed for Formosa. After the sky fell silent and only the familiar swish of the ship making way could be heard, the Fleet altered course and awaited the return of our brave airmen. It was at this time, as it began to get light, that the Fleet was most vulnerable to air attack. To conserve fuel the Fleet speed was reduced to less than aircraft launching speed. At 0705 a CAP of Seafires intercepted four Zekes and shot one down. Should a visual attack on the Fleet develop, speed would be increased to assist in taking avoiding action. Violent alterations of course were needed to try and make it difficult for the kamikaze to hit their target.

On the Wager Captain Watkin and I were on the bridge. Everyone else was at action stations. It was just getting light. Suddenly we heard the drone of a plane approaching with engine at high rev`s. It was difficult to spot in the half light but then I saw it skimming over the sea, at an angle to the destroyer screen .
"What`s that plane?" the captain barked. I managed to train my binoculars on it and saw it was displaying the correct recognition lights and its wheels were down.
"Can`t tell sir. It has its undercarriage down and is showing the correct lights. It might be a Hellcat," I replied. The captain snatched the binoculars from me and after a brief look, he agreed with me and handed them back. I raised my glasses again and realised (too late) it was not a Hellcat but a Japanese, possibly a `Val` dive bomber ! All I could see was this aircraft turning in towards us, at virtually zero altitude and now larger than life. He was so low in fact, it was as though we on the bridge were above him. I could see the Japanese roundel on his port wing, he was that close. Mentally it was as though I was watching a slow-motion film. I thought, "This is it !" I had a mental flash of my loved ones. `He will machine-gun the bridge or just keep coming and smash into us` I thought, but luckily he was after bigger fish - the carriers.

Suddenly he banked slightly and hedge-hopped over our stern. It had all happened in a few seconds. There was an instant feeling of relief. We had been spared. He made for the Illustrious. Now he was inside the destroyer screen we could not fire at him. It was now up to the carrier's gunners. Illustrious opened fire when the Japanese was almost on her. The kamikaze seemed to be level with her flight deck, forward end and crashed into the sea very close to her side. Rumour had it that the plane released a bomb, which bounced off the flight deck and failed to explode. Personally I don't believe that, but we were never told the details.

This was a failed kamikaze attack, even though the pilot was astute enough to trick us into thinking he was one of ours. He must have observed our planes setting off for their mission and showing their two-colour recognition lights. How else could he have known the correct colours to display ?

Another aspect of this incident occurred immediately after the Japanese hedge-hopped our stern. A blond, curly-haired gunner suddenly appeared on the bridge from his port Oerlikon gun. He was very young - a Cockney.
"That was a bloody Jap," he screamed, his voice shrill with anger and frustration. "Get back to your gun," Captain Watkin bellowed. The curly mop withdrew in silence. I felt sorry for him for he had missed his moment of glory, but then so had the captain and so had I. We had been tricked, good and proper. Had his months of training been for nothing, or the Captain's, or mine come to that ? Personally I do not think so. In that poor light there had been a considerable element of doubt as to whether the plane was friend or foe. I suppose the maxim should have been : `If in doubt, shoot`, but then there was the trick with the recognition lights. If we had fired and scored a hit and the plane had turned out to be one of ours, we would have had to try and live with that burden for the rest of our lives.

Meanwhile Operation `Oolong` was continuing. The bomber force that made for Matsuyama ran into bad weather, so a diverted attack was made on Kirrun Harbour. Two Fairy Fireflies from Indefatigable shot down four Japanese `Sonia` light bombers, in as many minutes. Attacks on the enemy continued, alternating with replenishments from the Fleet Train.

On 13th April (the day American President Roosevelt died) more strikes were made against Shinchiku and Matsuyama airfields. A factory was bombed by an Avenger. A passenger train was strafed in a tunnel entrance. One twin-engine plane on the ground at Giran was strafed. AA fire was described as `uncomfortable`. And so TF57 carried on with this task until finally it withdrew to Leyte in the Phillipines for a long replenishment, aided by good weather on 23rd April, (exactly thirty two days after Ulithi). There was no shore leave because of the lack of sufficient small boats and the long distances involved to reach shore.

On 30th April (a black day for the Americans) their ships were attacked by waves of kamikazes, mostly from Shinchiku and Matsuyama airfields. Twenty US ships were sunk and 157 damaged. I wonder what the result would have been if TF57 had not been replenishing at Leyte ?

The British Pacific Fleet sailed from Leyte at 0630 on 1st May 1945. The carrier Illustrious was replaced by HMS Formidable and Wager and Whelp were detached to escort Illustrious to Sydney.

I must at this point in the tale, express my respect and admiration for all our Fleet Air Arm pilots, for their guts and determination in carrying out their low-level attacks on an enemy, who invariably retaliated with withering AA fire from the ground. Besides being pilots they were also sailors, suffering the same discomforts of the tropics as the rest of us. It is worth noting that during `Operation Iceberg` every carrier of the BPF was damaged in some way by kamikaze attacks, but in each attack the damaged carrier was very quickly brought back to an operational state. This made a very big impression on the Americans.

*　*　*　*

FIREWORKS

The aircraft carrier Illustrious, escorted by destroyers Whelp and Wager left the operational area of TF57 round about 1st May. After ten weeks at sea, living in cramped and stifling conditions and closed up at action stations for lengthy periods in a high state of readiness, everyone was in need of a break. No member of the Wager's crew had set foot ashore for over two-and-a-half months. These two destroyers had steamed 25,000 miles or more and needed dockyard attention. The fact that none of the ships of the BPF had broken down during Operation `Iceberg` and had covered such vast distances, was proof of the efficiency of the engine room crews. Consider also that they were working in the hottest part of their ships. Some of the credit must also go to our ship builders.

As we steamed south east there was no point in returning to Ulithi en route. This atoll had only been used as a vast natural staging point for ships of the Okinawa invasion fleet. Instead our group of three ships wasted no time in heading for Manus, where they refuelled. Now steaming south east again, we headed through the Bismarck Sea and approached the strait between Papua New Guinea and the island of New Britain.

On the 8th May 1945 we passed very close to the New Guinea coast, on our starboard side. It was VE-DAY and there was much to celebrate. At last our families far away in Britain were safe from the Nazi bombers, buzz-bombs and V2 rockets.

Looking across at the vast forested island, it was realised that in the midst of that steamy green jungle were Australian soldiers, still seeking out their Japanese opponents - a dangerous and thankless task. It was decided to lay on a spectacular pyrotechnic display, for the benefit of any Allied jungle fighters who might be able to see the ships from beneath their green canopy, or from the shore.

At a given signal, Illustrious opened fire with her 4.5 inch all-purpose guns pointing skywards. She used star shells. At the same time her Bofors and 20mm guns fired tracers. Wager and Whelp fired their 4.7 inch guns, also using star shells. Their Bofors and Oerlikons also fired tracers. Even a Very pistol was fired from Wager's bridge. It must have been a heart-warming display to those in the jungle. To round off our VE-Day celebrations `Splice the Main Brace `(an extra tot of rum) was ordered.

We eventually arrived in Sydney about the 15th May. On that day determined attacks were still being carried out by TF57 against the Sakishima Gunto airfields, in order to protect the American's southern flank of Okinawa.

*　*　*　*　*

A MYSTERY PIE

During the last replenishment of TF57, the NAAFI on board Wager was unable to obtain replacement tinned foods. Consequently the stock on board soon ran out. This was particularly worrying for me as I was the mess caterer. Let me explain. Destroyers such as the Wager had a very small galley, which was quite adequate for cooking the food but had minuscule space in which to prepare it. For that reason, each mess of the Lower Deck crew had one man who was designated as Mess Caterer.

This man would normally hold this task for about one month (I did it for two) during which time he was expected to prepare the food for the whole mess. He received a monthly catering allowance to buy food from the NAAFI shop. This normally came in tins, so there was tinned fruit, tinned vegetables and tinned meat, including spam and corned beef (the latter being referred to as `corned dog`). He was also able to purchase flour and so it was possible to make pastry. Luckily, I remembered a tip my mother had given me about making good pastry. `The less handling, the lighter the pastry`. I never forgot that advice and tried to apply this pearl of wisdom to my catering, but it didn`t always prove successful.

The mess caterer was expected to come up with a good cooked meal every day. He would spend some time in the mess, preparing it himself. Then having taken it along to the galley, he would collect it at meal time, properly cooked. If he managed to pull off a savoury culinary miracle, voices of approval would echo round the mess, not only because the meal was enjoyable but to encourage a repeat performance. However woe betide the unfortunate mess caterer who served up something unsavoury. There would be howls of disapproval, caustic comments, sarcasm and threatening physical gestures. The worst reaction was for him to see, under his very nose, half empty plates being scraped into the gash bucket. The most popular caterer was the one who could achieve culinary excellence, but also manage to show a surplus from the catering allowance at the end of the month, as this money would be shared out equally to all members of the mess.

It was my lot to be mess caterer during the two months that the BPF ran the gauntlet of kamikaze attacks. At first everything went smoothly, except for the odd occasion when the pastry was somewhat hard. (If ever Wager ran out of ammo` that was something to fall back on !). As Operation `Iceberg` progressed into its second month, the job of mess caterer became increasingly difficult. The varying duties of Wager often meant the NAAFI. shop had insufficient opportunity to restock. Consequently what stock it did have started to run out. This put a great restriction on me as to the choice of food I could prepare. Eventually there was nothing left in the NAAFI but flour, lard and tins of peas. I decided to put a brave face on it and bought the peas. Then while the mess was empty I quickly made pastry, rolling it out and laying it in a baking tin. Next I drained the fluid from several tins of peas and tipped them onto the pastry. Finally I rolled out a pastry lid which I placed over the tin and then trimmed the edges. It looked a very presentable pie. Now that the peas were out of sight I felt much calmer.

When the time arrived for the meal I fetched the `peas pie` from the galley and placed it in the middle of the mess table. With a knife I drew section lines on the pastry and invited the men to help themselves. Imagine their faces when the first cut through the crust was made and a green liquid oozed out.
"What`s that ?" they groaned, sounding offended and with facial expressions to match . "It`s peas pie," I said apprehensively, but at the same time trying to make my voice sound as though peas pie was the most normal and tastiest dish in the world. There was a chorus of moans, but funnily enough they all ate it without further complaint. In fact some started to laugh about it. The thought of that incident still brings a smile to my face even now. We were not smiling the next day however. We were eating hard tack biscuits. That was my only time in the Navy when I had to eat these. You needed good teeth. They were rock-hard, almost tasteless and certainly a challenge to one`s alimentary canal.

*   *   *   *   *

90

A PAIR OF NEW SHOES

As soon as the two destroyers had discharged their duties to Illustrious they went their separate ways. Wager proceeded to Auckland on the North Island of New Zealand.

There was plenty of opportunity for shore leave while Wager was being refitted in dry dock at Auckland. Friendships soon blossomed between the crew and local girls. The ship`s company was invited to an evening buffet and dance in the town hall, so in the afternoon we got to know the town, service men`s clubs, the shops and much later at opening time, the pubs. While browsing round the shops my `oppo` got into conversation with two girls. Naturally we ended up with a girl each to take to the dance in the evening. Shipmates don`t always stay shipmates when they have a girl on their arm, so on this occasion we split up.

Elaine, the girl with me, was not much of a talker but she was pleasant enough. She had fair hair but looked dowdy. She suggested we look in the shop windows, which proved to me straight away that women have the higher intelligence ! I could not fail to notice that this young woman was badly in need of a decent pair of shoes. I decided to take her into a shoe shop. We came out with Elaine all smiles carrying a new pair of shoes and I felt good about it too.
"These will be okay for the dance tonight," she said.

After leaving the shops we reached the park and sat on the steps of the bandstand. Elaine became more talkative and there was some kissing and cuddling. Sailors desperately need female company. Their mode of life means they live in a streamlined metal box - a virtual prison from which there is no escape whilst at sea. Their isolation makes it easy for them to lose touch with the outside world.

In the evening we attended the dance which was enjoyable, as was the food. The only snag was that my feet did not understand the messages being sent to them by my brain so, apart from a couple of waltzes, I did nothing to impress Elaine with my dancing. However Nobby my `oppo` was a real `twinkle toes`. He would occasionally leave his girl sitting with me while he took Elaine round the floor. So she did get to have a few dances and I had some conversation, which I preferred.

When we left the dance we made our way back to the same bandstand. I produced my harmonica and entertained Elaine with a few tunes. I was prepared to play as long as she was prepared to listen. Soon I became aware of other couples sitting round the bandstand, including several sailors from my own ship, accompanied by their newfound girl friends. Suddenly Elaine said abruptly,
"I must go." We left the park and walked through the town. We reached a particular street and Elaine said,
"I live up here." When I went to accompany her she said,
"No you needn`t come any further John." I insisted, but she was adamant I should say goodnight there and then. I kissed her goodnight and she walked up the road. She had been so insistent that I sensed something was not quite right. I saw her enter a house a short way up the street, outside of which hung a brightly lit sign. I followed in her footsteps until I could read it. It read, `HOME for UNMARRIED MOTHERS`!
Needless to say I made no more dates with Elaine and ruefully put it down to one of life`s experiences. I am one of those who tend to laugh at life`s setbacks and even at myself Whatever else service life does for you, it certainly teaches you how to take the rough with the smooth. Tolerance is the name of the game. When I told my messmates what had happened there was much chauvinistic sarcasm.

Days later one of the signalmen approached me and asked, "Can you tell me where I can buy a good pair of shoes?" I took it in good part. He was a lot bigger than me.

The next day, because the dockyard mateys needed to work on Wager, we were sent on ten days 'rehabilitation' leave. I and two other sailors were sent to stay on a farm at Whangarei. We tried to behave as useful farm hands at every opportunity, humping sacks, feeding stock and riding on tractor and trailer. A day had been set aside for us to spend with a Maori family. They were really nice people and made us very welcome.

The farm overlooked the sea and was very hilly. North Island is beautiful country. Where we stayed the grass was green and kept short by the many sheep. In whatever direction we faced we were greeted with a scenic panorama of great beauty - not unlike some parts of rural Britain. The farmer was a devout Christian. I think he originated from Europe, possibly Czechoslovakia. I can remember him castigating us for swearing. We were expected to say grace at the meal table. He had two grown up sons who helped him on the farm.

Arrangements were made for us to attend a dance. One of the sons drove us to a village hall near Dargaville. There was no bar. Apparently New Zealand law forbade the sale of any alcoholic drink within half a mile of a dance hall and so we were stuck with soft drinks and tea. I got friendly with a girl who turned out to be a dental nurse. We finished up cuddling in the back of her car. I suddenly felt a sharp pain in my arm and discovered she was trying to remove one of my badges as a souvenir, using nothing but a pair of nail-scissors. I was not pleased, especially as I had shown much patience in diligently sewing the badge (crossed flags) onto my uniform, way back in the UK. After a few angry words I went back into the hall to rejoin my shipmates.

Before setting off to return to Auckland we thanked our hosts for their kind hospitality. It had been a very pleasant experience and a complete contrast to shipboard life. Soon Wager was once again afloat and fully manned. She sailed out of Auckland harbour for sea trials in the open sea. Accompanying her on the bridge were the Commander of the Dockyard and a brigadier of the New Zealand Army (Pages 93, 94 and 95).

Wager was put through her paces with speed trials, testing of close-range weapons and the dropping of depth charges. After this she hove to to pick up the resulting dead fish. These were destined for the galley.

On our return to harbour, shore leave was granted. I stayed on board however, because I was a member of the ship's hockey team and we were down to play a N.Z. team the next day at Pukekohe. When we arrived there, horror of horrors, we were taken to a school playing field to play against a women's team ! I can't remember the score but I know they beat us ! We never lived it down.

* * * * *

Page 93. An overhead view of HMS Wager`s bridge during sea trials with New
        Zealand officials on board.

Page 94. HMS Wager testing a new type of depth charge during New Zealand sea
    trials.

Page 95. Speed trials. HMS Wager altering course to starboard at full revolutions.

THE JERVIS BAY INCIDENTS

After waving goodbye to New Zealand and the girls we left behind, we set course for Sydney. There we were joined by HMS Whelp, our sister destroyer.
She had on board as a serving naval officer Prince Philip of Greece. He was a Lieutenant and was First Lieutenant (Jimmy-the-One) and second in command of the Whelp. After shore leave both ships proceeded to Jervis Bay, some thirty three miles south of Sydney. This is a coastal exercise area used by the Royal Australian Navy.

Although both ships had passed their sea trials and were now seaworthy and fit for action, their crews were not. So now both destroyers had to carry out a working-up exercise, in which new members of the crew would familiarise themselves with the ship and its equipment. The exercise included target firing of 4.7" main armament guns, using live shells and the firing of a torpedo fitted with a dummy warhead. Asdic / Sonar sweeps were also carried out. The gunnery target was the usual wood and canvas structure, supported by a watertight metal hull. This one had been left secured to a buoy by the Royal Australian Navy.

We were about ten miles from the coast of New South Wales in hazy sunshine. There was no wind and the sea was glassy. A torpedo bearing a dummy warhead was launched. After it had expended its run, it assumed a vertical stance. The red dummy warhead could clearly be seen rising and falling in the heavy swell, which was coming up from the south east. I judged the swell to be from six to eight feet high. The torpedo (an expensive weapon) had to be recovered. Our whaler was crewed by a midshipman (coxswain), a signalman as bow oar (me) and four seamen, one of whom was a torpedo man.

We donned lifejackets and climbed into the boat, which was then winched jerkily over the side. As soon as the whaler was fully in the water the rope was slipped and we drifted down the port side of the ship. When we were clear we rowed a steady stroke and headed for the torpedo.
"Blimey," I thought, "this is not going to be easy by any means." As we neared the torpedo the torpedo man shipped his oar and clambered over us, taking with him a stout rope. That could not have been easy, the way the whaler was behaving in the heavy swell. He leant over the bow and after several attempts, managed to feed the rope through an eye on the nose of the torpedo. He heaved. Then he endeavoured to passed the rope through the same ring again but, before he had a chance to play out some slack, a particularly large swell caused the whaler to collide with the torpedo. The whaler was immediately swamped. We now found ourselves trying to sit on water, which for obvious reasons didn't work. We ended up floundering in the sea ; a jumble of sailors, sixteen foot oars, rope and the torpedo.

Navy whalers do not normally sink, even when full of water to the gunwales. Instead they lie completely submerged just beneath the surface. Knowing that these coastal waters are infested with man-eating Tiger sharks, I instantly became aware of my feet and legs dangling below, like some inviting bait. Yes alright, I was bloody scared ! The midshipman did not have much of a clue. I did not hear him give a single instruction, when once we were in the water. "Grab the oars," someone shouted, but we weren't going anywhere. I thought the safest thing to do, as did the others, was to stay with the whaler so we all positioned ourselves over it as best we could. At least it gave some minor protection from any lurking sharks which might be in the vicinity.

The captain watched this incident from the bridge with, I suspect, a certain amount of concern. He must have ordered `dead slow ahead` then gently eased Wager towards us, until we were to the lee side of the ship - a masterly display of seamanship on his part in those conditions. It was with extreme relief that we clambered safely aboard, up the precarious ladders that had been hung over the side. Eventually both the torpedo and the whaler were recovered. The latter was winched up very slowly to allow time for bailing and for the water to drain out. If this is not done there is a good chance of the whaler breaking up from the weight of the water trapped within it.

The next day an even more serious incident occurred. It was the last day of our `work up` and gunnery practice was to be carried out for most of the morning. After that Wager and Whelp were to make for Sydney, hopefully in time for shore leave - for those off watch that is. The Whelp towed the target farther out to sea and played it out astern for some distance. `Action Stations` was sounded . Wager`s officers and men reported to their respective posts. This only left Captain Watkin and myself on the bridge. I reported to the captain that Whelp had just hoisted a red flag to her yardarm. This was the signal for firing to commence. Wager directed her 4.7 inch guns towards the target and one gun opened fire. A white plume of water rose just beyond the target. That was good shooting. And so the exercise progressed for a while and then Whelp hauled down her red flag. Firing ceased.

Now it was the turn of Whelp to exercise her guns. Wager relieved Whelp of the target by taking it in tow. Captain Watkin shouted, "Hoist the red flag." I ran down to the flag locker and hoisted the flag. Shortly afterwards Whelp opened fire. A shell exploded somewhat short of the target. Then an unpredictable thing happened. Without warning a sea fog rapidly descended between and about both ships. It was very thick but patchy. I can honestly say I have never seen a fog appear so quickly, before or since. Visibility was alternating between extremely poor to completely clear.

Suddenly Whelp was firing at us and not the target ! We quickly became aware of this when a shell exploded a few feet from our port side amidships, sending up a shower of spray. "Get that bloody flag down," bellowed the captain. I couldn`t have moved any faster if I had tried. I hauled the red flag down but left it bent on the halyard. I quickly returned to the bridge. Almost at once another shell landed near to us again on the port side. Whelp had not seen the flag come down ! "Oh My God !" exclaimed the captain. Owing to the fog she was still mistaking us for the target. I reacted instinctively. The adrenaline was running high. I expected another shell to land any time now. I clambered up to the 20-inch signal lamp (cum searchlight) and switched on. We hoped that the enormous candlepower of this arc-lamp would do the trick. It took a few unbearable seconds to arc then it came on with a splutter. As soon as the light reflected from its parabolic mirror I directed the extremely powerful beam in the general direction of Whelp. There was an anxious wait, which seemed to last an age but was only about twenty seconds ."Thank God. She has stopped firing sir," I shouted. All Captain Watkin said was, "Good." Upon reflection this incident could have had very serious consequences. We were thankful this one ended without tragedy. I really felt I had done the Navy proud that day.

We all had a great respect for Captain `Basher` Watkin. A destroyer man through and through, he had an exemplary naval career. Powerfully built, with black beard and gruff voice, he came across as an ominous figure. Not the sort of man you would want to pick an argument with. He was a very fair officer and always managed to get the best out of his men. My most vivid memory of him was when he was on the bridge. When things were quiet, he would spend as much as an hour hugging the compass binnacle and rocking from one foot to the other, staring ahead with his back to me. I could probably recognise him as much by his shorts-clad backside as by his face.

Owing to the poor weather conditions it was decided to abandon the exercise and Wager and Whelp steamed back to Sydney.

$$* \quad * \quad * \quad * \quad *$$

STEAMING TO VICTORY

After a quick run ashore Wager and Whelp steamed north for the Admiralty Islands, passing Papua New Guinea to port and New Caledonia to starboard. The two destroyers reached Manus about one week after leaving Sydney. They refuelled there and made good speed to rejoin Task Force 57 in the operational area.

By 21st June 1945, the battle for Okinawa had been won. The Americans continued to sustain some kamikaze attacks on a diminished scale, but there were no further such attacks on the British Pacific Fleet. The bloodiest fighting of the Pacific War had come to an end. The enemy commander, Lieutenant General Mitsuri Ushijama, came out from his bunker and committed hari-kiri in front of his staff. 110,000 Japanese were killed in the battle. 12,000 Americans were killed, including their commander Lt General Simon Buckner.

After the fall of Okinawa there was much reorganisation of the naval fleets. Initially many ships were assembled at Leyte to refuel and replenish stores. By the 16th July a powerful RN task force TF38, which included KGV and the carrier Formidable, was joined with the US Third Fleet (commanded by Admiral William Halsey) for dawn raids on Tokyo and the surrounding area. This was reckoned to be the most powerful Allied fleet ever assembled in the Pacific. Naval power was now being used to hit the Japanese mainland. Heavy shelling was directed at Murorau and four other cities.

Like most of us, I assumed that the Japanese would fight for every inch of their homeland, resulting in huge numbers of casualties on both sides. But on the 26th July at Potsdam, the Allies gave Japan an ultimatum. *SURRENDER or FACE SWIFT and COMPLETE DESTRUCTION.* There was no immediate response to this.

On August 6th an atomic bomb, the most destructive weapon yet devised by Man, was released by an American B29 Super-Fortress (`Enola Gay`) on the large Japanese city of Hiroshima. The city was completely destroyed. Loss of life from that one atomic bomb is conservatively estimated at 100,000. Many succumbed later to radiation sickness.

Meanwhile Duke of York, Wager and Whelp were detached from the Fleet and made for Guam, the Americans` main Pacific base, which we reached on 9th August, for a two day visit. The purpose of the visit was to allow Admiral Sir Bruce Fraser, C in C, British Pacific Fleet to bestow the Knight`s Grand Cross of the Order of the Bath on American Admiral Chester W. Nimitz, C in C, Allied Naval Forces in the Pacific. This was the first and only time, as far as I am aware, that this ancient order was ever bestowed by a commoner. The ceremony is normally conducted personally by the Sovereign.

There was a bonus from this visit. Officers and men were invited ashore as guests of the American Navy. They certainly did us proud! (Page 100}. I was only off duty for one afternoon, but even so it was an enjoyable experience for all that. When it came to making a comparison between the two navies, the Royal Navy was very much the poorer cousin of the American Navy. At Guam they seemed to have just about everything to maintain a higher standard of living. Their sports facilities were exceptional and the food was excellent. We had not tasted such good food since we left Australia.

On the same day as we arrived at Guam, we heard news of the release of a second atomic bomb, on the ship-building city of Nagasaki. This resulted in an estimated 70,000 deaths .(Pages 101 and 102).

On 11th August the three British ships left Guam to rejoin TF38. We realised later that we were at Guam when an American B29 Super-Fortress was actually on the runway on Tinian, loaded with the second atom bomb (codenamed `Fatman`) that was to end World War Two.

The bulk of the Allied fleet comprised American Navy ships, particularly carriers, but most of the British Pacific Fleet also formed part of this massive fleet.

Even after the unleashing of two atomic bombs and contrary to Allied expectations, the Japanese did not succumb to an inevitable defeat immediately. In order to persuade the Japanese that further military resistance was futile, TF38 cruised up and down the coast near Tokyo, to demonstrate the sheer power of the Allies. Eventually the order was given to fly off every available carrier-borne aircraft. It took about twenty minutes for well over one thousand planes to become airborne. The aircraft all circled the Fleet in a clockwise direction, forming themselves into flights . The sky seemed dark with aircraft and the continual drone of their engines was nerve-shattering. They streamed off towards Tokyo.

An uncanny silence fell upon the huge fleet, while we waited for the planes to return. Presently a distant drone was heard, which soon became a crescendo. The whole fleet altered course into the wind. The sky was busy. Wherever one looked there seemed to be aircraft approaching, circling or descending to land. On the whole this huge operation appeared to be working like a well-oiled machine. Sadly however, I observed a mid-air collision only about five cables from Wager. Two aircraft, possibly a Seafire and a Hellcat or Corsair, collided head on. There was an explosion, which did not seem loud, because of the noise of the vast number of aircraft circling the Fleet. A large ball of black smoke was created, which rained flying debris into the sea. I had witnessed the end of two of our gallant pilots, who, by a sad twist of fate did not survive and so near to the end of the war too. They must have been some of the very last flyers to give their lives in World War II.

On August 14th 1945, Japan finally surrendered unconditionally to the Allies, who, in the case of Britain, had suffered six years of war with an enemy. The news was hard to take in. Of course we were all overjoyed, but I think we were also a very tired body of sailors. It was hard to get used to the fact that we no longer needed to look out for enemy aircraft or periscopes. We would of course have to look out for

HMS DUKE OF YORK – HMS WHELP – HMS WAGER

WELCOME TO ✰✰ GUAM ✰✰

The officers and men of the United States Pacific Fleet and shore activities on Guam take pleasure in extending a hearty welcome to the officers and ships' companies of HMS DUKE OF YORK, HMS WHELP, and HMS WAGER.

It is our desire that your stay in Guam may afford the fullest opportunity for rest and recreation, and the facilities of the Island are at your disposal. It is our further hope that your visit will provide opportunities for friendly companionship between personnel of the two navies, so closely linked in the common cause.

C.W. Nimitz

Fleet Admiral, United States Navy
Commander in Chief, U. S. Pacific Fleet and
Pacific Ocean Area

9 August 1945

Page 100.   United States Navy hospitality itinerary for Royal Navy ships at Guam.

Page 101.   Atom bombed Nagasaki, Japan.

Page 102.   An atom bombed European style church, Nagasaki, Japan.

wayward floating mines, which would continue to break lose from their moorings for many years to come. Coincidentally my captain, Captain Watkin was put in charge of mine clearance around Britain after the war. Later he went on to become an ADC. to Her Majesty Queen Elizabeth.

On board the Wager I was given an official general signal to pin up on the notice board. The signal summarised the contribution made by the British Pacific Fleet in Operation `ICEBERG`, towards the defeat of the Japanese at Okinawa, by covering the American forces` southern flank. When the time came for me to remove the signal, I would normally have scrapped it as it was only a carbon copy, but I decided to keep it to show my folks back in England

The signal read :-

GENERAL ....From FOCA

ICEBERG.

(1)   The object set the BPF was to prevent the Japanese Air Force using the 5 airfields in the SAKISHIMA Islands to stage aircraft through from FORMOSA to attack the US Forces at Okinawa.
(2) COMMENT:-
No aircraft staged through by day. It is believed 1 or 2 occasionally got through at night using an air strip hastily repaired after our force had withdrawn. For total neutralisation we needed a night carrier whose planes would have kept the crater filling parties alerted during dark hours. We hope to have one soon.   NOTE:- With the best will in the world, a carrier cannot strike all day and then through the night also.
(3) The operation cost us many valuable lives and to enemy action, 54 aircraft. Against this we have to send,
(A) Enemy losses, 57 shot down, 113 destroyed or damaged on the ground.
(B) The damage inflicted on airfields, towns, airfield installations, small coastal vessels, barges, boats, RADAR stations, barracks, camps, Japanese soldiery and motor transport by 875 tons of bombs and 850 rockets and more than half a million rounds from front gun and cannon.
(C) The damage and casualties inflicted by the heavy bombardment by our battleships and cruisers.
(D) The assistance rendered to the OKINAWA forces by our presence and assault on SAKISHIMA GUNTO.
COMMENT:- It is agreed that the figures of enemy air losses against our own are disappointing. It is maintained however, that this is largely the fault of the Japanese in not presenting themselves more often for treatment, either in the air or on the airfields.
(4) 4,852 sorties were flown off carriers. This is an all time high in the history of the RN Air Arm and has imposed long flying hours on our airmen and very long hours maintaining aircraft by the repair and maintenance crews.
(5) A history not hitherto surpassed in the history of our navy has been established by the mileage steamed in 2 months by a considerable force taking part in the operation . (25,000 miles).
COMMENT:- No ship has broken down. It has to be remembered in considering these figures that the engines and the associated machinery and the

armament, electrical, RADAR and communications equipments of all kinds have been kept going by men both working and living in conditions of heat and discomfort, in ships which were not designed for this unremitting type of work, in this type of climate. Such steaming and running maintenance could only have been achieved in such conditions by men imbued with the spirit *TO TAKE IT*, to see the job through and confound the KING`S enemies = 270200 (end of message)

*　　*　　*　　*　　*

SURRENDER AT TOKYO BAY

The approaches to Tokyo Bay and the bay itself were heavily mined. Australian and American minesweepers had been busy for several days clearing these waters. An official surrender ceremony on board the battleship USS Missouri, was planned to be held in the bay for 2nd September 1945.

On 1st September, the Missouri and her two escorting destroyers together with the battleship HMS Duke of York and her escorting destroyers HMS Wager and HMS Whelp, anchored for the night in Sagami Bay. This bay is adjacent to Tokyo Bay. Many other warships also dropped anchor there.

Next day at first light, a Japanese destroyer with her guns depressed rounded the headland from the direction of Tokyo. The vessel was flying an exceptionally large Rising Sun flag. It had come to lead the Allied Fleet into Tokyo Bay.

The Fleet got under way and followed the destroyer - one of the very last surviving vessels of the Japanese Imperial Navy. USS Missouri with her escorts headed the Allied Fleet, followed by HMS Duke of York and her escorts.The rest of the fleet followed. We were feeling very wary of treachery, but our fears turned out to be groundless. As we entered Tokyo Bay we passed Yokosuka base on the port side. The runway there bore one or two wrecked planes. Occasionally the sickening sight of a bloated, floating corpse drifting amid the ships met our gaze. These bodies were not dressed in military garb. Wrecked enemy ships lay uselessly about the bay. The Fleet anchored. Wager anchored on the starboard quarter of the Duke of York.

When the time came for the surrender ceremony I used my binoculars. I could see the Japanese emissaries boarding the Missouri. The ceremony conducted by General Douglas MacArthur seemed very brief, considering the enormity of what had happened since the time of Pearl Harbour. I quote almost his final words :
"It is my earnest hope and indeed the hope of all mankind, that from this solemn occasion a better world shall emerge out of the blood and carnage of the past."
Although the bay held many ships, very few of their crews were able to witness the actual signing ceremony at such close proximity.

Jubilation in America was marred by the news that the heavy cruiser USS Indianapolis had been sunk by the enemy in the Philippine region, with the loss of most of her crew. It was revealed that her last mission was to convey atomic bomb material to Guam, the American base that had recently hosted us.

*　　*　　*　　*　　*

SALVATION

As soon as the Japanese party had departed, Tokyo Bay began to buzz with activity. Military personnel had been sent deep into Japan to find and release prisoners-of-war. On the inner harbour shore at Yokohama, an ever-swelling gathering of POWs could be seen, some hysterically cheering, waving or weeping, hardly daring to believe that this was the day of their salvation; the first day of many, to bathe them, feed them, heal and clothe them. To heal their minds was going to take a lot longer.

Strangely there were few aircraft carriers to be seen, but we learned later that for many of them their flying days were numbered. They were being hastily adapted to troop-carrying duties. The war was over yes, but now there was the huge logistical problem of repatriating thousands of POWs, internees and serving men and women from around the world, back to their home countries. Six years of war had put Britain in debt. Consequently there was an urgent need to set demobilisation in motion, so that our industry could receive the manpower it most desperately needed to get on the road to recovery.

Many of the POWs I saw had been handed out items of American uniform, as most of them were found in rags. A copy of another official signal was handed to me to pin on the notice-board. I resolved to keep it as a souvenir, when the time came to take it down. Rather than quote passages from the signal, I feel it is worthwhile to repeat the signal in its entirety :-

LIBERATION OF PRISONERS OF WAR AND INTERNEES.

SIGNAL SENT TO ADMIRALTY ON 14th SEPTEMBER 1945.

1. The liberation and evacuation of prisoners-of-war during this last few days has witnessed scenes which will live long in the memory of those of the British Pacific Fleet who are here in TOKYO BAY. In the absence of any representative of the British press the following account is sent in order that the public at home may have some idea of how British Commonwealth prisoners-of-war are being repatriated from the Japanese mainland.

2. This is an American theatre and the American Forces are responsible for the collection and evacuation of all Allied prisoners-of-war. The White Ensign however has offered all available ships to assist in the evacuation and, which matters most, is doing everything within its power to ensure that contact between British prisoners-of-war and their fellow countrymen shall be established as early as possible and maintained.

3. The British Task Force, which was operating as part of the American Third Fleet at the time when hostilities ceased, is now spread about the coasts of Japan and China, including Hong Kong, Shanghai and Formosa and only a part is available to assist in the repatriation from the Japanese homeland.

4. Among the ships in TOKYO BAY off Yokohama which have lent a hand in the evacuation are HM Ships KING GEORGE V, DUKE OF YORK, INDEFATIGABLE, SPEAKER, RULER, NEWFOUNDLAND, ARIADNE, APOLLO, TROUBRIDGE, TERMAGANT, TENACIOUS, WRANGLER, WAKEFUL, WIZARD, WAGER, WHELP, WESSEX, QUALITY, TEAZER, TERPSICHORE, ERNE, HMA. Ships SHROPSHIRE, HOBART, NAPIER,

NIZAM, NEPAL, QUICKMATCH, WARRAMUNGA, BATAAN, HMNZS
GAMBIA, Hospital Ships TJITJALENGKA, VASNA, Storeships CITY OF DIEPPE,
FORT WRANGLER, Oilers DINGLEDALE, CARELIA, SERBOL and WAVE
KING.

5. The first stage has been the identification of prisoner-of-war camps. Much
was known from information given by the International Red Cross and the Japanese
themselves. Further searches by aircraft from the Third Fleet carriers (including
INDEFATIGABLE) and of the United States Army have not only revealed additional
prisoner-of-war camps, but have enabled them to be supplied from the air during the
early stages. Today in the hospital ships there are unfortunately some prisoners-of-war
with broken limbs, because in their enthusiasm, they allowed the food containers
falling by parachute to strike them.

6. When the Allied Fleet anchored outside TOKYO BAY the first Allied
prisoners-of-war to be repatriated were a Royal Marine and a British soldier, who
escaped and attempted to swim out to the Fleet and were picked up by an American
patrol boat. When units of the Fleet entered TOKYO BAY and advanced landing
parties of American sailors and British sailors and Royal Marines were landed to
occupy strategic advanced posts, they were in many instances met by prisoners-of-war
who had broken camp and received them enthusiastically on the beaches.

7. Naturally those men came off in the landing craft which had taken the landing
parties ashore. Before the British and American Navies had even anchored, the
evacuation of former prisoners-of-war had in fact started.

8. Wherever camps were known to exist, parties of American , British and
Australian soldiers and sailors were sent off as `contact teams`. These teams have
gone into the depths of Japan, have found the camps, and with the assistance of the
Allied Commanders of those camps have organised the initial journey to Yokohama.

9. That journey was, in the case of the camps close by, made on foot or by motor
car, while in the more distant cases trains have been arranged, or where near the coast,
destroyers have been sent out to fetch the parties in.

10. Naval hospital ships were rushed into Yokohama and into Tokyo itself and
all former prisoners are first received on board these hospital ships, where they are
examined medically, given baths and clothes, fed, and where particulars are taken of
every man. Telegrams are sent to next of kin.

11. Those who owing to malnutrition or other causes are seriously sick are
retained on board. Those who are reasonably fit are sent to ships for immediate
evacuation. What has been perhaps more noticeable than anything else is the longing
of every man to shake off the dust of Japan once and for all at the very earliest
opportunity.

12. HMS SPEAKER was quickly converted into an evacuation ship and within
12 hours of being warned for this duty she was filled to capacity with over 450 British
Commonwealth men whose imprisonment in many cases dated from the fall of
Singapore, or the sinking of HMS EXETER.

13. Next day she sailed for the south and as she steamed through the British
anchorage the ships` companies of all the British ships gave her a send off which all
those who saw it will never forget. The sight of this small aircraft carrier with her
ship`s company fallen in for leaving harbour in accordance with naval custom, but
with in addition, those hundreds of ex prisoners-of-war ranged on the flight deck
cheering like mad and being cheered, brought tears to the eyes and the realisation of
what the presence of the great Fleet in TOKYO BAY meant to those men.

14. As the camps in the immediate neighbourhood of TOKYO BAY were cleared, ships went further afield. The TENACIOUS to Hamamatsu, where the KING GEORGE V, in company with American battleships, had carried out a naval bombardment only a few weeks before. WIZARD to Hamamatsu and later to Sendai . BARFLEUR to Hokkaido. WAKEFUL to Sendai. GAMBIA and NIZAM further west.

15. The resources of the Fleet, limited as they are after two months away from any base, have been used to fill each of these ships with blankets, beds, cigarettes, chocolates and other stores necessary for a sea passage.

16. Lately each evening one or more of these destroyers has come back, arriving at Yokohama just as, seen from the British ships at anchor, the sun has set over the Mountain of Fujiyama. But it is a different picture from the usual Japanese drawings. It has been a scene which in some ways has reminded one of Dunkirk ; destroyers carrying many hundreds of passengers, in all sorts of clothing, crowding all over the upper decks and receiving the tumultuous cheers of all HM Ships as they went by into the inner harbour of Yokohama, where the hospital ships are lying.

17. The United States air evacuation is now in full swing and over a thousand men are being evacuated daily from the TOKYO airport. A number continue to be sent by sea in order to maintain the maximum flow of evacuation.

18. Tomorrow HMS RULER, another escort carrier, leaves with over four hundred officers and men, including on this occasion a number of civilians and children. They include citizens of all the nations of the British Commonwealth and of many of the Colonies. The ship is very changed from the warship she was. The flight deck has been marked out for every kind of game and this evening a Royal Marine dance band was playing outside the island structure. Forward and aft a few rather disconsolate aircraft are made fast and serve as a reminder of what naval air power has done in achieving that for which the Navy stands.

19. Down below the ship has been transformed as far as possible into a passenger liner and as the Captain remarked, "I have never before heard the hangar called a fairyland." The change may perhaps best be summed up in the `pipe` which was broadcast at 1800; "Children to supper."

20. The hospital ship TJITJALENGKA with her American sister ships, the USS BENEVOLENCE and MARIGOLD, has been doing magnificent work in looking after the really sick and in strengthening those who would soon be fit for air or sea travel. There is however always a certain number who have to be kept behind and on Sunday next the TJITJALENGKA will be sailing for Australia with over four hundred cot cases.

21. Every effort has been made to enable men of HM Ships to mix with and help these returning victims of the war, who have not seen a new white face for years and to whom in many cases, the events at home since 1942 are a closed book. Many too are anxious to tell of their experiences and so ease their minds. As may be expected they have found a very sympathetic audience in the British sailor.

22. And so the repatriation goes on. It is estimated that already a third of the total number of Allied prisoners-of-war on the Japanese mainland has left Japan and it will only be a matter of days before the evacuation of Northern Honshu, including TOKYO, has been completed. It will be as much the privilege of some of the harbours of the British Commonwealth to welcome these men, as it has been of the White Ensign to start them on their journey home.

= end of message.

Sadly an Australian POW on shore succumbed before he could be taken to the hospital ship. Men from Wager were sent ashore to provide a firing party for his funeral. What a cruel fate for him to go at the time of his rescue, after all he must have endured. Shortly afterwards the Duke of York, with Admiral Sir Bruce Fraser on board and escorting destroyers Wager and Whelp, left Tokyo Bay and sailed for Hong Kong. There was also to be a surrender ceremony there, on the carrier HMS Glory.

After a couple of days, whilst still in the Pacific on a calm sea, the order was given to "Stop engines." The three ships wallowed in a gentle swell, while "Hands to bathe," was piped. This was the first time our crew was allowed to swim in the sea since the start of Operation `Iceberg`, although I do believe other crews were allowed to swim over the side whilst awaiting orders at Manus. After living all those months in the stifling intense heat with only salt water showers to sooth the prickly heat, plunging into the sea would be sheer bliss. The trouble was I was on watch on the bridge. I watched the sailors already in the cooling sea with considerable envy.

Suddenly and to my pleasant surprise, the Officer-of-the-Watch told me I could leave the bridge and join the other men. I didn`t need telling twice ! I left my clothes lying on the hot upper deck, hoping that no practical jokers were about who might try and hide them. I certainly did not want to finish the last couple of hours of my watch `starkers`! I plunged over the side. The sea was pleasantly warm .There was much joyous shouting and playful splashing. I was told by the Navigating Officer that the depth of the Pacific at this spot was 11,310 feet. If we drowned here at least we would make a proper job of it.

To compensate for the absence of fresh vegetables and fruit, lime juice was doled out twice a day. The crew looked forward to this. A long time at sea on any journey meant a strict control on the amount of fresh water available. Having a shower meant you took it in pumped sea water. Usually we would wash our clothes at the same time. We called it `dhobying`, from an Indian word (dhobi). We used a special soap for use with salt water. It did not lather very well but it sufficed. To rinse our clothes in the tropics, we would often tie a stout string to them and trail them in the foaming wake from the ship`s stern. It was easy to do this from a destroyer but I doubt if the KRs and AIs {King`s Rules and Admiralty Instructions} normally permitted this, especially from a battleship flying the C-in-C`s flag.

We arrived at Hong Kong on 15th September, in good time for the surrender ceremony the next day. How different this small colony was from the time when it was attacked by the Japanese, the day after Pearl Harbour. Then a Japanese division of some 40,000 troops overwhelmed a defending garrison of some 12,000 Commonwealth troops. There the Japanese committed one of their worst atrocities. They overran the British military hospital and bayoneted to death all the wounded in their beds and the nurses too, some of whom were raped before they died. Such barbarism is hard to comprehend.

The surrender ceremony on board HMS Glory, as with the one in Tokyo Bay, was brief. So actually our three ships had been present at two surrender ceremonies by Japan..

* * * * *

CHAPTER FIFTEEN

IN DEFAULT

With the war ending I couldn't help wondering whether without an enemy to look out for, life in the Navy was going to become dull and boring. I soon found out that it was not - far from it. Britain now had a large Navy, completely out of proportion to her peacetime needs. And so a reduction of the Senior Service started almost immediately. Conscripts and volunteers, who were only in the service for the duration of the war, were soon to set sail for home. As I had only been abroad in this theatre of war for one year, I doubted if I would be returned to the UK with my shipmates. I was right. It would be another year before I was to see my loved ones. The enormous scale of that war was such that it took two years to return all Allied troops (world-wide) to their homeland.

One of the first things the Royal Navy did after Japan finally surrendered was to make contact with the Chinese Navy. This involved a meeting between Admiral Fraser and a Chinese Admiral, at Canton, which is not very far from Hong Kong. Because of her draught, the flagship Duke of York was far too large to approach Canton, so Wager was allocated the task. On 21 September 1945, Admiral Fraser was piped on board and we set sail, flying his flag at the masthead and the White Ensign astern.

When once Wager was underway I was ordered to go aloft, to keep the Admiral's flag flying clear. There was very little wind at the time. I thought the order a bit strange, because I doubted whether any Chinese peasants looking up from their paddy fields would know what the flag was or the purpose of it. However who was I to question ? I made sure I kept the flag clear. As the war had only just ended, I couldn't help thinking that there might be one or two Japanese soldiers still out in that rough terrain who had not yet heard about the surrender. I felt very vulnerable up aloft, as I presented an ideal target to anyone who might feel inclined to take a pot-shot at me. I was a sitting duck.

Suddenly from the bridge below, the voice of Captain Watkin bellowed :
"Shailer, have you got the boards ?" I thought, `The boards, what is he talking about?`
"No sir," I shouted down.
"Come down at once you bloody fool!" he shouted. When I reached the bridge the Captain turned to me and said, "Go down to the wireless office and fetch the boards, report back to the bridge and then go back up the mast."
"Aye aye sir." I saluted and proceeded to the wireless office, but as I left the bridge the Captain turned to the OOW and said, "I want him put on First Lieutenant's report."

I reached the wireless office, told them about the trouble up top and confessed I did not know what the boards were. It was explained to me that the boards consist of two narrow rectangular signs. One is displayed in the wireless office and the other is handed to the OOW on the bridge. The signs are worded `SAFE  TO  TRANSMIT` and `DO  NOT  TRANSMIT. MAN ALOFT`. These are essential to prevent someone from being electrocuted, because of high voltages generated in the overhead cables during wireless transmissions. On this occasion I took the `SAFE TO TRANSMIT` board up to the bridge and the wireless office displayed in its place the other board -`DO NOT TRANSMIT. MAN ALOFT.` When I reached the bridge I gave the `SAFE TO TRANSMIT` board to the OOW and proceeded back up the mast.

The following day I reported to the Master-at-Arms. I stepped forward in front of the First Lieutenant and saluted. The Master-at-Arms ordered,
"Off cap." Once I had removed my cap smartly down to my side, the charge was read out. This officer, who was very popular with the ship`s company, asked me if I had anything to say in my favour.
"No sir," I replied.
"Very well, Shailer. Now I don`t mind you forgetting to fetch the boards, going up aloft and electrocuting yourself, but I do object to having to organise people to clear up the mess." How could I forget something I had not been taught ? They were in the wrong for forgetting to teach me, but I loved his sense of humour. Enough said.

My punishment - six days extra duties for two hours a day. This entailed any cleaning jobs they could find, but I tackled these mundane chores with a cheerful heart, as I found this was the best way to help pass the time. Also I felt mollified that out of the entire ship`s company, I had been given the best seat in the house, so-to-speak, to see the coastal topography of China from such a vantage point.

*　　*　　*　　*　　*

SHORE LEAVE IN HONG KONG

The Wager returned to Hong Kong from Canton the same day. Admiral Fraser was immediately piped ashore and returned to his flagship, the Duke of York.

From 22 September Wager soon busied herself with activities normally associated with a warship in peace time. One of her first tasks was to paint ship. This task had already been partially completed at sea, on the way from Japan. After so many long and arduous journeys, most ships of the Fleet were badly in need of repainting.

A flotilla regatta was organised, to take place in Hong Kong harbour, which had so recently been under the yoke of Japan. Wager was part of the 27th Destroyer Flotilla. Each destroyer entered a whaler for a race through the Fleet. I was detailed as bow oar. Every morning at 06.00 the crew climbed into the whaler and we were lowered over the side into the water. Each time we would row round the harbour, giving it our best effort. Practising continued for one month and towards the end of that time we stuck to the actual race course.

Finally the day of the race arrived. This time the whaler was lowered at a more godly hour. As we climbed into the whaler, members of the ship`s company shouted encouragement. It was with considerable pride that I was able to write home that same evening, informing my loved ones that we had won. Using that 16-foot oar had certainly put some extra muscle on my shoulders.

No sooner had we got over the excitement of the race, than one of the officers suggested to Captain Watkin that he thought it would be a good idea to hold a ship`s concert. Volunteers were called for to take part. Anyone who had a musical talent, such as singing as loudly as possible in the shower, or in my case playing the harmonica (though I hasten to add not in the shower) was roped in.(I still have the concert programme after sixty years). I notice I was also roped into a gang of sailors to sing sea shanties. I suspect some of their words were rude . . .

The programme was headed : -

H.M.S. WAGER

PRESENTS

AN ALL STAR NON STOP REVUE

`UP SPIRITS`

It was at about this time that Lt. R. Trowbridge (Jimmy-the-One) left Wager to move on to bigger things. I have already mentioned how popular he was throughout the ship. So much so, that on the evening of the day before he was due to depart, a few members of the wardroom and of the lower deck, forcibly carried him round the upper deck. This culminated in his being dropped over the side into the waters of Hong Kong harbour. He took it all in good part.

Some fifty years later I was to be put in touch with shipmate Ron Dunning, a gunner from Wager, who lives in Australia. After the war he emigrated and got a job as Superintendent, Government House, Western Australia. Imagine his surprise when Sir Richard Trowbridge arrived in 1980 as the new Governor, a position he held until 1983. He was the same Lieutenant who had been chucked overboard at Hong Kong. The amazing thing was that Sir Richard remembered Ron from his Wager days, after thirty five years. His first words on seeing Ron were, "What are you doing here ?"

Shore leave in Hong Kong was always enjoyable, mainly because it is such a colourful port. There were many small shops selling curios, carved camphor wood chests, intricately carved ivory objects relating to their religious beliefs and artefacts, some of which were quite valuable. There were tea houses, brothels, photographers and plenty of fresh fish stalls. Chinese tailors were of particular interest to the sailors, as they were so efficient. You could be measured for a suit or uniform at 14.00 hours and it would be run up and ready by the evening. Not only that, the garments were always a superb fit. Places of entertainment soon sprang up after the war. They displayed glowing Chinese lanterns and large gaudy placards, dancing girls in exotic costume accompanied by live, loud, whining music. Dragon decorations were everywhere and the Chinese let off fire crackers on the slightest pretext. A ferry trip across to Kowloon (New Territories) was worthwhile, as was a ride in a rickshaw.

Shore leave usually ended up with a good meal in the China Fleet Club. My favourite was a lobster tail salad. The first time I paid the club a visit with some of my shipmates, I ordered such a salad. On the plate were one or two red chillies. I had never before encountered these. I was soon to make an unforgettable mistake. I started to chew one and immediately experienced a searing choking sensation in my throat, watering eyes, a flushing of facial skin, a gasping of breath and a desperate need for heat quenching water. That was another lesson I learnt the hard way. My shipmates were in hysterics of course.

From almost the first day Wager arrived in Hong Kong, we were to receive a daily visit from a sampan, manned by two cheerful Chinese girls. They came from a local Catholic orphanage. They would call early in the morning to fetch our dirty washing and would return it in the evening, immaculately washed and ironed. They were not allowed to set foot on board, so the washing was placed in a canvas bag or bucket and lowered and retrieved by rope, along with their payment. Their rates were very cheap. Sometimes they would offer to sell us artefacts. Some of these were superb. I bought a couple of carved ivory figures to take back to England as presents.

Occasionally whilst we were ashore, our money would run out. Then we would stroll about the jetties, examining the junks which were tied up alongside in great numbers. I always admired those craft of ancient design. Whole families lived aboard them. With their sails set, they seemed to me a craft of great strength, grace and beauty.

Another thing we would do when money was scarce was to climb a small hill, Mt . Victoria, to catch a panoramic view of the colony. There were cultivated tiers on the slopes. We saw Chinese peasants (mostly women) tending their crops. There was no irrigation system. All water had to be carried to the crops. This was done by means of a yoke across the women`s shoulders, supporting two cleverly constructed buckets full of water. The weight must have been considerable. In addition we were shocked and disgusted to see human excrement floating in the buckets. After that experience, we regarded all vegetables in the China Fleet Club with some suspicion.

Before she left Hong Kong for good, Wager was sent out on several Anti Piracy Patrols (APP).

I may have created the impression that life in the Royal Navy since the end of the war was one long round of pleasure seeking, but that is not true. Yes we had our times of relaxation, but we still had a serious job to do - the jobs we were being paid for. Signal traffic in this Far East Fleet base was quite heavy, as there were still many warships anchored there. The Royal Navy was still on a wartime footing.

On a couple of occasions while Wager was in Hong Kong, there was the threat of typhoons. For such storms, we would weigh anchor and proceed out of harbour to ride out the storm at sea. This was preferable to remaining in harbour and risking the ship being torn from her moorings, or dragging the anchor, with the resulting damage that might occur. No sailor wants his ship to run aground.

*   *   *   *   *

ANTI-PIRACY PATROLS

Land-based Chinese pirates had become a serious post-war menace. The pirates would frequently obtain berths on coastal ships, mingling with legitimate Chinese passengers, until the vessel was near to their coastal hideouts. Then they would hold up the crew, rob the passengers, loot the ship of anything they considered of value and steer it towards their lair. When once the ship had been run aground, other gang members would approach in sampans or motorised junks to take off the loot. Any resistance by passengers or crew was met with death. As a precautionary measure, owners took to installing grills around the bridge, to prevent the pirates from capturing the ship. Loading gates were kept locked until a ship reached its destination.

On 30th October 1945, shortly after a typhoon had abated, Wager set out on anti-piracy patrol. We were to patrol the coastal waters off Hong Kong and the near Chinese mainland, but outside the three-mile limit. Hardly had we left harbour, when we received a signal that a Chinese steamer was in distress. We sailed at full steam to her last reported position. All we found was a scene of floating wreckage with no sign of life. It was assumed that all those aboard the steamer had drowned, but later we were happy to learn some sixty people had been picked up by two junks. It was hardly a cause for celebration, as the original number of passengers and crew had been nearly two hundred. We searched the coast but failed to spot any survivors.

Not long after we completed our search, we sighted a waterlogged junk. We hailed it but got no response. It was thought the recent storm had overwhelmed the vessel. For one or two days we sent a small armed party ashore to the New Territories, to try and gather information about piracy in the region. On the last day of our patrol our armed party entered the small village of Peng-Chau. Nothing was learned.

Wager returned to Hong Kong harbour on 3rd November and refuelled. It was at about this time that the destroyer left Hong Kong for the last time. She headed west into the Gulf of Tonkin. Near Hai Phong she `dropped the hook`. A small armed landing party made for the shore in the ship`s motor boat. I believe we were looking for stranded prisoners-of-war. None were discovered, but as the boat neared the shore it was fired upon by small-arms fire. Needless to say the party made a hasty retreat back to the ship, taking no retaliatory action. We were soon under weigh again and heading south for Australia.

The ship arrived in Sydney about 22nd November 1945. I knew the Navy was about to draft me to another ship. This was a time I dreaded, when I would have to say farewell to Wager (a `happy ship`) and to many good shipmates. We had gone through a lot together this past ten and a half months. Most of her crew were men who had joined only for the war. In a few weeks they would be back with their loved ones , because the ship would shortly set sail for Britain. I cheered myself up with the thought that when I did eventually get back to England, in a year`s time, I would be due for two months leave - 28 days `End of War` leave and 28 days `Foreign Service` leave. I was now in receipt of what was called `Japanese Campaign` money.

*   *   *   *   *

DESPERATE WOMEN

There was a shortage of men in Australia. The Aussies had fought bravely in several theatres of war. Many had been killed, wounded or made POWs. Many had fought in jungle terrain and as a result, some had succumbed to debilitating tropical diseases.

During one of my last days on board Wager we witnessed a disturbing incident. One of the fleet carriers, adapted for trooping and moored near Circular Quay, was very soon to cast off and depart for the UK. Her gangway was still down. Along the quay was a large group of Australian women, who had struck up friendships with our servicemen (mostly sailors) and in some instances had married them. Some women were sobbing. On the quay the gangway was guarded by two Royal Marines. Many sailors, before manning the side for the departure, were leaning over the side shouting their farewells. "See you in UK," or "Hope to see you again," or, in the case of those who had become engaged or married, "I`ll be back as soon as my papers come through." Quite a few British sailors who were not due to complete their service with the Royal Navy applied for a transfer to the Royal Australian Navy.

All of a sudden there was a shout amongst the women. They made a concerted rush for the gangway. Standing at the top of the gangway, the Officer-of-the-Day produced a loudhailer. A warning was shouted at the women to keep off the gangway. They hesitated and quietened down, but suddenly they responded to further shouts from amidst the crowd. Again they stormed the gangway. This time the marines were

unable to restrain them and the women started to rush up the gangway.
They were met by a powerful jet of seawater from a well trained hose. Some were knocked off their feet by the force of the water. It was a dangerous situation, but eventually and soaked to the skin, they retreated to the quay. The two marines ran up the gangway. It was quickly raised, the lines were cast off and the carrier went astern from the quay. She was assisted out into Sydney Harbour by a couple of tugs.

I watched all this with mixed emotions. I was disturbed at seeing the hose turned on weeping women.

*   *   *   *   *

CHAPTER SIXTEEN

THE CRUISER

For a short time I was back on the books of HMS Golden Hind, but instead of returning to Warwick Farm (the racecourse barracks), I was billeted aboard HMS Tyne, a depot ship moored in Sydney Harbour. Thankfully I did not stay on her for very long and on the 13th January 1946 I was drafted to HMS Bermuda, a fairly new Fiji-class cruiser. She had previously been escorting convoys to the North Africa landings. The next month I would be twenty one and was due to receive my first stripe and an increase of three pence per day in my pay.

*　　*　　*　　*　　*

OVER THE TOP

I settled into my mess on the Bermuda and soon had some new shipmates. In those days, pubs in Sydney opened for two hours in the evening from 5 pm to 7 pm and opened again at 8 pm. Thirsty Aussies would head for the bars as soon as they knocked off from work. They would down their schooners of beer and then wend their way home for a meal. Because of the bar hours, sailors tended to drink more rapidly during the evening session with sometimes disastrous consequences.

On this occasion three of us went on a run ashore in Sydney. One of the three had been a Bevan Boy. He had been conscripted into the coal mines during the war, rather than the services but eventually ended up in the Navy. When the bars closed in the evening, we decided to cross the harbour by ferry, from Circular Quay to Luna Park, North Sydney. Luna Park was actually a fairground complex, which included a large dance floor. Unfortunately when we arrived at the fairground, the gates were shut and would not open for another half hour. We decided to return to South Sydney by walking across Sydney Bridge.

As we set off the ex Bevan Boy shouted, "Not that way. We will go over the top!" We managed to squeeze through some barbed wire, which had been strategically laid at the foot of one of the massive bridge support columns. Inside there were considerable flights of steps. We climbed these and eventually found ourselves stepping out at the foot of the arch of the mighty bridge. To allow the bridge maintenance staff to climb the steep arc of the girders, metal steps had been installed over them. As we climbed these shallow steps the sunset was fast approaching. Eventually the steps ceased and we found ourselves walking on bare girders. We were impressed by the hugeness of the rivets - the size of dinner plates and the sheer width of the arch girders. As I have mentioned before, I suffer from vertigo (the Navy never found out). It is amazing what a few drinks will do. Strange as it may seem, I didn`t experience giddiness or fear but rather, a sense of heady excitement. Perhaps there is a lesson in there somewhere for vertigo sufferers.

We progressed up the arch until we reached a hut at the peak. There was a similar hut on the corresponding girders, on the other side of the bridge. Both huts were used as small stores, for paints etc. Each hut had doors at either end but these were locked. There was nothing for it but to climb out onto an adjacent platform, which swayed in the wind. It is fixed in my mind that when once we were out on the platform, we started to sing popular war-time songs to the citizens far below, although I doubt if anyone could hear us. Grippo suddenly decided he urgently needed to relieve himself. I couldn`t help wondering, on whose head it might be falling. He was certainly doing his best to upset the Sydney weather forecast. Now it was dark the lights of Sydney presented us with a spectacular panorama - a terrific contrast to all the war-time years of blackout we had had to endure. Eventually we decided to descend, scrambling off the platform to the other end of the hut. We had no difficulty in making our descent . After climbing through more barbed wire onto the road, on the South Sydney side, we returned to the ship.

We did not realise how grimy we were, until we stepped off the gangway into the light on the quarterdeck, when the bosun`s mate pointed it out. We told him what we had been doing. At first he wouldn`t believe us. The ex-miner said,
"The Aussies boast about their bridge, but it was designed and built by British engineers."

Word soon carried on the grapevine about what we had been up to. The following day (Sunday) some bright spark `obtained` a White Ensign and organised a small party of sailors to repeat our performance.
"We will show them whose bridge it really is," he said. And so three men went ashore in the evening, one carrying the ensign tucked in his jumper. On the way to the bridge they picked up some weighty stones, as they needed something to weigh down the flag.

At first light the following morning many of the ship`s company proceeded to the upper deck. With necks craned expectantly aloft, they eagerly looked for the ensign. What a disappointment ! The bridge was so large and the flag so small, it was unrecognisable as a White Ensign. It could easily have been mistaken for pigeon droppings.

I read somewhere in the 70`s that two Frenchmen had been arrested for climbing Sydney Bridge. They should have said in their defence that "It wasn`t us, it was them." They received a heavy fine.

Nowadays the general public has access to the top of the bridge. A walkway with safety rails has been installed. For a small charge people can walk over the complete arch of Sydney Bridge. It was very different for us, tackling it in the dark with no safety rails and the three of us slightly inebriated, trying to get past a locked painters` hut.

*   *   *   *   *

DRESSED OVERALL

HMS Bermuda sailed for Tasmania on 5th February 1946. It was my twenty first birthday. The ship was to be flagship to the annual Royal Hobart Regatta. This was the resumption of an event which had been put on hold ever since the start of WW11. The next day the cruiser anchored in the mouth of the Derwent river and was dressed overall for the occasion.(Page 117).

The local branch of the RSL (Returned Servicemen`s League) laid on a couple of

Page 117   HMS Bermuda dressed overall at the Royal Hobart Regatta, Tasmania.

coaches for the off-watch sailors, for a trip to the top of Mt. Wellington (over 4,000 feet to the summit). Everyone was rewarded with a magnificent bird`s-eye view of Hobart Harbour. This was followed by a visit to a local brewery. The free samples were very much appreciated. There were no complaints. The RSL is comparable to our Royal British Legion back home.

Our skipper was Captain C.D. Howard - Johnston , DSO, DSC, RN, the youngest cruiser skipper in the Royal Navy at that time. Shortly after completion of the Royal Regatta, the ship returned to Sydney.

On 24th February Bermuda departed for Hong Kong. This was not to be a straightforward journey. For the entire journey the ship had in tow a large floating battle-practice target, for use by the Far East Fleet based at Hong Kong (like the one used back at Scapa Flow). For this reason she navigated a more sheltered route, between various island passages. The crew nicknamed the target `Hezekiah`.

To add more interest, I have set out the ship`s progress as a log. *(An old atlas might be helpful).*

24.2.46   Set course for Darwin.
28.2   Arrived Darwin. Temperature 102F. Temperature on board 120F. Metal
           decks in direct sunlight almost unbearable to walk on, even with sandals.
1.3   Left Darwin. Steamed into the Arafura Sea.
2.3   Off Tenimber Islands.
3.3   In the Ceram Sea
4.3   Passing through the Molucca Passage. One famous island in this group
           during the war was Morotai, on which the Aussies played the biggest hand in
           the fighting.
           In the tropical belt. Conditions now very warm and clammy.
           The ship is now using up to sixty five tons of water per day.
           Pay increased by nine shillings per week whilst in the tropics (equivalent to
           one fifth of a working man`s weekly wage back in Britain).
5.3   Passing Celebes Islands.
6.3   In Basilan Straits (off North Borneo).
7.3   In the Sula Sea (off the Philippines).
           Discovered an empty outrigger canoe. The Captain had the `prize` winched
           aboard to take back to the UK, possibly for his children.
8.3   Off northern tip of Luzon.
9.3   Ran into the monsoon. Target `Hezekiah` bounced all over the place.
11.3.   Bermuda reached Hong Kong, with her charge still safely in tow.

*   *   *   *   *

A SPOT OF LEAVE

By this time the ship was in need of some dockyard attention. Some sailors, including myself were sent on four days` leave to Repulse Bay, on the other side of Hong Kong island. Whilst in dock the ship had her hull scraped and painted.

On the first day of my leave I walked to Stanley and back. I was talking to a commando outside the notorious Stanley prison when they brought in the Japanese ambassador. He had been wounded and arrived on a stretcher. He was listed as a war criminal.

All buildings in Hong Kong were in a poor state of repair. The only building put up during the Japanese occupation was the new Government House. The Japanese had also erected a war memorial on top of Mount Cameron. It was supposed to remind the Chinese of the might of the Japanese Emperor Hirohito and honoured their dead. One of the senior Japanese officers there is reputed to have stated that if the Allies retook Hong Kong, the Japanese had intended to carry out mass hari-kiri.

On the second day of my leave I walked to Aberdeen, a Chinese fishing village. It was a bustling place, with many junks and sampans tied up to the jetty. On the waterfront carpenters were busy building new boats. I was particularly fascinated by a Chinese toy shop which sold paper balloons, dragons, kites, snakes on sticks and of course Chinese crackers. There were many other novelties and everything appeared to be hand-crafted.

I spent the last two days of my leave in Repulse Bay, relaxing on the beach and swimming. To the right side of the bay was what appeared to be a castle, but was in fact a folly, which some wealthy person had had built in pre-war days. It was quite large and the walls on the seaward side descended right down to the water`s edge. The terrain behind the bay was very rugged and would have been a tough area to defend.

We returned to the ship on 12th April, whilst she was still in dock. It was then, while sleeping on the upper deck, I was stung inside the index finger of my left hand by a scorpion. How it got there is a mystery. My guess is that it came aboard hidden in some stores. Initially the pain was excruciating and my hand was quite swollen. After a couple of days it turned septic. I reported to the Sick Bay and it was examined by the doctor. He made an incision in my finger. Then to my surprise, he used a pair of tweezers and pulled out from the puss, a long wormlike core, more than an inch in length. I still have the scar.

*   *   *   *   *

A TOUR OF THE WAR-TORN FAR EAST

In early June, 1946, Bermuda steamed out of Hong Kong harbour at the start of a Far-East tour. It was a journey I shall never forget for several reasons. The ports of call, in sequence of our arrival, were :-

Shanghai, China (East China Sea).

Tsingtao, China (Yellow Sea).

Kure, Japan (East of Hiroshima), on the island of Honshu.

Hiroshima, Japan, on the island of Honshu.

Nagasaki, Japan, on the island of Kyushu.

Fukuoka, Japan, on the island of Kyushu.

Chemulpo, Korea (a small port on the West Korean coast).

Seoul, Korea, (Yellow Sea).

Return to Hong Kong.

The Far East Fleet was still being run very much on a war footing. We were warned to stay in groups when ashore especially when in Japan. We were allowed shore leave in Shanghai. It was an overcrowded busy city, trying to get back to some semblance of normality. There wasn`t much for us to do ashore. A few places had dancing girls in beautiful Chinese dresses, serving tea. Unlike in Australia, one got the feeling we were not welcome - a sort of underlying resentment. We suddenly became aware of small groups of nationalist soldiers, gathered at the end of every street and alley, as though expecting something to happen. A large number of Chinese people gathered in the main street, shouting and waving banners. We suddenly realised their anger was directed at us. There was nothing for it but to make for the ship. We ran like hell. The ship quickly cast off and we made for Tsingtao in China.

Before the war Tsingtao had been a German white settlement. When we arrived it was being used as a base by the Americans. Unfortunately I was unable to go ashore there. This was probably just as well because Bermuda had not been there many hours before the sound of heavy artillery fire was heard. The gunfire was coming from the direction of the rapidly advancing Chinese Communist Army and was thought to be only about eighteen miles away. As soon as all our men were safely back on board, the ship left and set course for Kure.

When the ship arrived at Kure I was on watch and was unable to take shore leave. It was the same when we proceeded `just down the road`, so to speak, to Hiroshima. Our call at the atom-bombed city was brief. When the sailors returned from shore leave, they were not the usual happy, raucous band one is accustomed to seeing. They seemed subdued, as the enormity of what they had seen sank in.

I did manage to get ashore at Nagasaki. I was surprised how many houses had been erected since the A-bomb of eight months before. But the number of new houses built was `peanuts` compared to the vast decimated expanse of the city that met our eyes. It was noticeable that brick or concrete buildings of Western architecture such as churches, although badly damaged, had stood up to the A-blast better than any other type of building. (Page 102) . All the same, they had been virtually destroyed.

A group of us walked a short distance across the almost dead city. We approached a modern flat-roofed, single-storey building. An American soldier stood guard by the front entrance. Leaning out from the flat roof were several beautiful, laughing Japanese women, who were making gestures to us to come up onto the roof. I was jokingly encouraged by my shipmates to climb up to them. I spotted a rainwater down pipe round the corner and started to climb. The women were shouting encouragement, as were my shipmates. The commotion alerted the sentry. He suddenly appeared round the corner. Pointing his rifle in my general direction, he shouted, "Come down." I very quickly descended the short drop. "Do you know why these girls are being kept in this place sailor ?"
"I have no idea," I replied.
"They have all got VD" he said. We were taken aback. He shared out a packet of `Lucky Strike` cigarettes with us and we quickly left. Ribald comments soon came, thick and fast, mostly directed at me, although it was they who had put me up to it.

As we returned to the ship we came across a small curio stall. I purchased an

120

opium pipe, which bore fine floral metalwork, although I hasten to add I had no intention of using it. I also purchased a silk facsimile of the Nippon Times, dated 2nd September 1945, which headlined the surrender of Japan. It hangs in my hall, framed behind non-reflecting glass.

On my way back to the ship I picked up several pieces of glass, which I kept. I took these to be fragments of window glass. They had been distorted by heat and were translucent - a sort of frosty appearance on their surface.

Note :- After leaving the Navy in 1955, I worked in a research laboratory. I lent the glass fragments to a Dr P.W.McMillan, a ceramics expert. He wrote me a short report, which I quote verbatim :-

To :- MR J. SHAILER   2 / 10 / 58

Thank you for the glass sample. I have broken a small piece off one corner. The glass has devitrified (crystallised) on the surface and from this and in view of the distortion, it seems likely that the temperature has been raised to at least 800 degrees centigrade. This would mean that the glass was fairly close to the centre of the explosion because the heat generated by the explosion is only a momentary flash, but the glass has been heated to red-heat throughout its thickness and it has cooled fairly slowly - perhaps it was buried beneath other hot rubble ? We cannot check if there is any residual radio-activity (this is very doubtful) because it would require a very sensitive Geiger counter.

Signed   P.W.McMillan

*   *   *   *   *

BACK TO AUSTRALIA

It was about mid-August when Bermuda left Hong Kong and steamed south for Sydney. She carried a crew of some seven hundred. Of these fifty sailors were married to, or intended to marry, Australian girls. Twenty five men, not from the crew, were also transferred to HMS Bermuda for demobilisation in Australia.

The ship also carried thirty Chinese, signed on at Hong Kong on short term agreements. They formed part of the crew and augmented the post-war demobilisation. They wore a regulation steward`s uniform. They served as stewards, batmen, laundrymen and one or two as cabin boys.

The ship progressed through the sweltering tropical belt and arrived at Sydney by late August. She spent a week in Sydney before commencing a short round of good-will visits to Melbourne and Adelaide.

Bermuda arrived at Melbourne on Thursday 5th September 1946.

*   *   *   *   *

A HUSBAND SEEKER

On 5th September 1946, the ship berthed at Melbourne for four days. During our short stay I managed to get ashore twice. Grippo and I went to discover the delights of Melbourne.

We entered a milk bar and two attractive young girls spoke to us. We paired up. We were relieved to find they were not prostitutes. They took us around the city to show us various features of interest. We ended up in a cinema (I can't remember what the film was). It was a pleasant run ashore. Before returning to the ship we made a date with the girls for our next shore leave.

Two days later we set off to keep the date, not knowing whether the girls would be there. When we got to the milk bar, sure enough they were waiting for us. After a spell in the milk bar, they suggested we take a ferry trip on the River Yarra. This was very enjoyable. During the trip my date became very talkative. Suddenly she said, "You can kiss me if you like." I duly obliged . It suddenly occurred to me that she might be very young, although when we first met she looked about eighteen.
"How old are you ?" I asked.
"I'm sixteen," she said and seeing me looking surprised she added,
"My auntie got married at sixteen. We marry young in Australia." Alarm bells started ringing in my head and although I continued to be pleasant to her, I was now very careful in what I said.

When it was time for us to return to the ship, the girls arranged to meet us at the same milk bar. It was a date I had no intention of keeping. The Bermuda was to sail for Sydney the next day, so that is my excuse.

On the 9th September 1946, the ship sailed for Adelaide. She arrived next day and tied up to No.1 berth Port Adelaide.

*   *   *   *   *

AN INVITATION TO TEA

It was the 10th September, during the Australian winter. Part of a signalman's duties whilst in port is to man the ship-to-shore telephone. I was on watch in the wireless office when the phone rang. A woman's voice said,
"I would like three sailors to come round for tea this evening." I thanked her and said that I would organise three sailors to be there. As soon as the lady rang off, I mentally put my name down on the list and then went down to the mess. I managed to persuade two more volunteers to join me.

The three of us went ashore. One, who was a sailor for the war only, was a barrister in `Civvy Street`. We labelled him `Prof`. He bought a bottle of whisky which he stuffed in his coat pocket.

We finally found the address. A pleasant middle-aged lady answered the door. "Come in," she said and ushered us into the hall. She pointed to where we were to hang our coats. We were shown into the drawing room where there was well polished furniture, including a piano.

Without further ado, she sat herself down at the piano and said,
"Now I know sailors like a good sing-song so gather round." By this time we were all feeling a trifle uncomfortable, as this wasn't the normal start of an invitation to tea. The time was already 4.30 p.m. After all who wants to sing when there is good food about ? But worse was to come. I saw her music book opened at the first tune - `Abide with me`. We sang that half-heartedly and then came `Onward Christian Soldiers` and so our evening continued thus, for about half an hour. To make matters worse `Prof

had an appalling voice, quite unmusical and `Grippo` and I were not singing with gusto either. Halfway through the singing the lady informed us that she was a deaconess. We had our suspicions already that she was something of the sort, but until then we were not sure. I would never ridicule anyone for their religious beliefs, including deaconesses, but I don`t think hymn singing in someone`s drawing room is a sailor`s idea of a run ashore. We do have a Church Parade on board every Sunday (Sunday Divisions) even at sea, unless the weather is too rough or in wartime, if the enemy is about.

When `Prof` found out the lady was a deaconess, he began to worry about the whisky bottle that was protruding from his overcoat pocket. He made an excuse to go to the toilet, but his real purpose was to transfer the bottle to the inside pocket of his overcoat.

Eventually it was time for something to eat. We mentally sighed with relief. Needless to say on the way back to the ship I received some very uncomplimentary remarks, although in the days to come we were to laugh about it. After all it was like a home from home, even to be standing in someone`s drawing room, compared with being crammed in our mess.

The ship left Adelaide for Sydney on the 14th September. On the 23rd she sailed for Hong Kong. The ship`s company was feeling a bit low. We had had some wonderful times in Australia and had met some very nice people. I was reflecting on this and felt very sad to be saying goodbye to Auntie Minnie, Helen and Lillian. I never saw them again.

HMS Bermuda stopped off at the Great Barrier Reef on 27th September. A boat was lowered to take a small party to land on Frederick`s Reef. There some seeds were sown on behalf of the Government of Australia. I only hope they germinated. We were never told what they were the seeds of, but over fifty five years later they may well have developed into magnificent tropical trees.

* * * * *

CHAPTER SEVENTEEN

THE HOMECOMING

HMS Bermuda finally sailed for the UK in October 1946, leaving Australia, Hong Kong and the Far East far behind. Although I had set out from England in 1944 and sailed to Australia via the Panama Canal, I was now returning to Portsmouth via the Suez Canal. What one might call a round-the-world voyage, during which there had been several lengthy `diversions`.

Britain was suffering one of the worst winters on record with icy unrelenting blizzards blowing in from the East. The snow was very deep. The sudden change from a tropical climate to one of Britain`s worst winters did not help me at all. The tropics had taken their toll and I was now in poor health. I had a fever. Ever since the scorpion sting and the infection in my hand, I had become more and more run down. I had a boil under each arm (very painful when trying to remove a sailor`s tight jumper) and a septic left forearm, which if squeezed near the elbow would exude puss from a sore near the wrist. The smell was awful.

As soon as I reached HMS Mercury, the communications barracks at Petersfield, I was put to bed in the Sick Bay and designated `unfit for sea`. They kept me there for about a month. I distinctly remember my doctor in his spare time, skiing up and down the slopes of adjacent fields; a very rare spectacle in the south of England. I nearly lost my arm, but with an intensive course of penicillin, a better diet and plenty of rest, my fever abated and I soon began to mend. The doctor said I was recovering from a tropical fever.

As soon as I was well enough, I was sent on Foreign Service leave and War leave. I reached my mother`s street. `I wonder if she will look any different ?` I thought. My mother no longer lived next door to Mrs Phillips, but just up the road in a first floor flat. I knocked on the door. Mother opened it and beamed. I finally stepped over the front doorstep of our new home. There were big hugs and kisses and even a few joyful tears. She didn`t look any different to me after all that time.

It was during the last two weeks of my leave that I called on Mrs Phillips, who, when I was a lad of fifteen, had been so kind to me during the Blitz. Her niece, who worked for London Transport, was staying with her. As soon as I was introduced to Glad I was smitten. She had a lovely calm face and the most beautiful brown eyes. I asked Glad`s aunt if I could take Glad out. She turned to Glad and said, "Would you like to go out with John ?" Glad nodded. I walked back up the hill to the flat, feeling as though I was walking on air.

The next day Glad and I went on our first date. We climbed to the top deck of a London bus. I turned to Glad and said," I don't like that coat you are wearing." She was quite shocked, but at least she knew she was going out with a bloke who called a spade a spade. We ended up in a cinema in Ealing and saw a James Mason film. In my opinion he was badly cast as a farm worker. His accent did not suit the character he was playing. It was such a boring film we left halfway through. Not a very good start, for me or for James Mason!

A week later I returned to HMS Mercury. I wrote to Glad and proposed to her. I know that I put in the letter, "I am giving you one week to decide." To be fair to her, I emphasised that I had another eight years to serve. Glad wrote back and accepted my proposal. She also put in her letter, "Eight years or twenty years, I will still wait for you." When I received her reply I was `over the moon`. We were married four months later, a marriage that was to last fifty one years. How blessed was I! I had quite a gallery of portrait photos of girls I had met on my travels. I tore them all up in front of Glad on my next leave (I never called her Gladys).

I was still unfit for sea, so the Navy decided to send me to London to work at the Admiralty.

*   *   *   *   *

CHAPTER EIGHTEEN

HMS PRESIDENT - WHITEHALL

On the 10th February 1947, I was drafted to the Admiralty in London, which was the hub of Royal Navy operations and of course communications. There I was trained as a radio-teleprinter operator. My shipmates were an assortment of communication ratings - telegraphists, Wrens and a few signalmen, all under the watchful eye of a duty officer. We worked in the wireless room in a building known as the `Citadel`. You can see it on your right, as you walk from Horseguards` Parade into The Mall. The room was below ground level. There were no windows. My specific task was to receive and transmit incoming and outgoing naval messages but primarily, ship-to-shore telegrams from naval and merchant ships at sea.

The set-up for passing telegrams from ships at sea back to the UK was not entirely straightforward. Wireless receiving stations were strategically positioned ashore in various parts of the globe. To describe the routing of signal traffic more easily I give here an example :-

A luxury liner making for Singapore is passing Ceylon, some five miles off shore. A passenger on board wishes to send a telegram to his mother-in-law in England, to tell her how much he misses her. He goes to the Purser`s office and writes out his message on a telegram form. The telegram is handed to the ship`s wireless operator, who transmits it locally by Morse key.

The message is received in Ceylon, by a telegraphist at the local shore wireless receiving station. He hands it on to the radio-teleprinter operator, who types it onto a reel of paper tape. This tape may already have several messages punched on it. At the best time of day in Ceylon for transmitting (i.e. the time of least atmospheric interference) the messages are automatically transmitted in plain language, by radio teleprinter using the punched tape. The message is received simultaneously on the Admiralty radio-teleprinter and is printed out on both the sending and receiving machines in plain language. At the Admiralty end, the telegram is passed on to the Post Office, via Portishead for distribution to the passenger`s mother-in-law.

Official signals received at the Admiralty which concerned naval matters, were folded and rolled up to fit into a lidded rubber cartridge. This was then fed into an inlet valve of a hissing pneumatic pipe distribution system. As soon as the suction grabbed it, you could hear the cartridge racing along the pipe to its destination. Before the war, Selfridges Store in London used a similar pneumatic distribution system for their sales. This all seems very antiquated stuff now, but I can assure you the radio teleprinter service worked very well, although it did have two major weaknesses.

The principle fault was the multiple handling of the same message, which increased the possibility of mistakes arising. Surprisingly there were very few, in comparison with the large volume of signal traffic that had to be dealt with on a daily basis. That tells you a lot about the operators. The other weakness was that the system was at the mercy of atmospheric conditions, such as sun spots etc, so messages had to be stored on tape, until transmitting conditions were at their best. This meant delay. Nowadays the Navy has the benefit of computers and communication satellites.

I can`t help thinking that those of my generation who survived the war, are so lucky to have seen the amazing progress of Man in technological advancement over the last eighty years. Each generation benefits from the progress made by all previous generations, in the search for knowledge and subsequent progress. I predict that in the next five hundred years the homo sapien species will have reached the zenith of its achievement. Then it will become like the dinosaurs !

*   *   *   *   *

THE TEA BREWER

At the Admiralty wireless office the night watch was from 22.00 hrs to 0800 hrs the next day. Every signalman had his name on a monthly roster for tea brewing. Telegraphists and Wrens were not included, because of the nature of their work. The duty tea brewer provided an urn of tea and progressed around the office, pouring out for those telegraphists with their headsets on, who were receiving messages. The Wrens however, were required to leave their teleprinters and form a small queue.

Several Wrens had special preferences when it came to their `cuppa` and would often turn on the charm, to ensure their tea was uniquely acceptable.
"Can I have a touch more sugar John ?"
"Do you think I could have a dash more milk ?"
"Could I have another half spoon of sugar ?" and so on. I knew exactly what they were doing. They were using the tea-brewing session as an excuse to get up out of their chairs <u>twice</u>. You try sitting for ten hours non-stop. I didn`t blame them. As if all this wasn`t soul destroying enough, there was one girl from the East End who would swear loudly if she thought her tea was too strong.

Needless to say it was with great relief that I relinquished my one month stint as duty tea-brewer.

*   *   *   *

BENT FORKS IN THE MALL

I was married in St. Peter`s Church, in the village of Hixon, Staffordshire, on the 17th May 1947. We honeymooned in Blackpool. To get there we had to change trains at Crewe. We were standing on the platform there when I happened to look down at my shoes. I was amused to see piles of confetti, which had been trapped in the top of my uniform, trickling out of my bell bottoms. I glanced along the platform and saw a soldier with his partner, also waiting for the train. The same thing with the confetti was happening to him, so we knew they had just got married that day too. We laughed about it and when the train arrived we all got into the same compartment. A ticket inspector opened our compartment door and asked us if we would like the blinds down. We thanked him but jovially declined.

Our boarding house was run by two elderly spinsters. Confetti was still escaping from my uniform and I apologised for the mess. "Don't worry about that, we are used to it," one lady said. She was very understanding.

The first night of our honeymoon was a disaster. Glad woke me up at about two in the morning to tell me in a frantic voice, "A thunderbolt has just gone through the room!" There was a terrific storm in progress, but until Glad woke me I didn't hear a thing.

The only other memory I have of the honeymoon was when we had a meal down town in a posh restaurant. A ten-piece Hungarian band started playing. We both thought it wonderful, although I felt out of place dressed in a sailor suit. The Navy

127

hadn't yet got round to allowing its sailors to wear civvies ashore.

I continued to live at my mother`s flat in Ealing, but now Glad also came to join us. We were very happy and I was grateful that I was working at the Admiralty. I had a regulation bicycle, loaned to me by the Navy. I also used sometimes to borrow my sister`s bike. I used to go on watch by riding the ten miles from the flat in North Ealing ,via Chiswick , Hammersmith , Knightsbridge, then up the Mall to Admiralty Arch. This meant of course that I had another ten mile journey back when I came off watch. These arrangements worked perfectly well, but in the winter I was obliged to wear a heavy uniform overcoat, which was not conducive to cycling great distances. If the weather was too bad I would catch a tube train from Ealing Broadway to Trafalgar Square, although it wasn`t very often that I did not cycle.

At the outbreak of the Second World War, there were some roads in London with a top layer of tarmac, laid over vast numbers of vertically placed, wooden, brick-shaped teak blocks. As the war progressed, many roads fell into a state of disrepair. The Mall, leading from Buckingham Palace up to Admiralty Arch was one such road. The tarmac had worn off in places, leaving the wooden blocks exposed. This was not too much of a problem if the road was dry, but if it had been raining for some time, then it was a very different ` kettle of fish`. The blocks would become extremely slippery and would swell, causing one or two to pop up above the normal road surface.

On one particular winter evening, I cycled my usual route from Ealing to the Admiralty. I was wearing my regulation overcoat and it was raining. The journey was uneventful until I was passing Buckingham Palace. I turned left into the Mall, by the Queen Victoria Monument and on that corner collided with a swollen wooden block. I was flung into the road and was narrowly missed by a taxi going in the same direction. The buttons were torn from my coat. Luckily I was only bruised. My luck ran out with the bike. The front forks were bent. Ruefully I lifted the bike onto my shoulder and limped up the Mall. I took it into the Admiralty workshop and explained what had happened and then walked round to the wireless office.

The following morning at 0800 hrs, I came off watch blinking at the daylight and went round to the workshop, but I wasn`t holding out much hope of using the bike. I was pleasantly surprised however, to find that they had worked wonders with it. The forks had been straightened and you would hardly guess it had been in an accident. And so I was able to cycle back to Ealing, sore but happy.

I have often wondered in my imaginings whether our monarch, if he had witnessed my mishap through a palace window, would have sent out a royal servant to me, carrying a brandy on a tray or better still, a rum. I doubt it somehow.

*　　*　　*　　*　　*

THE COLD WAR

I will never forget an incident that occurred in 1948, while I was on night watch at the Admiralty (22.00 hrs - 08.00 hrs). It happened during the early days of the Cold War between the Western Allies and the Soviet Block. Most of the signal traffic was dealt with by the early hours, then the wireless room fell quiet.

On this particular watch however, a Wren operator, who was manning an ordinary Post Office-type teleprinter (not radio), was teaching another Wren how to operate the machine. Her machine was connected directly to the War Office by ordinary land line. These machines are quite noisy, so the peace of the office was unavoidably disturbed at about 06.30 hrs, when her machine suddenly started to chatter with an incoming message. The Wren shouted excitedly and I ran over to see what the trouble was. "Look at this!" she exclaimed. I leaned over her shoulder. A message on the machine read, `TOP SECRET - AS FROM 11.30 hrs A STATE OF WAR EXISTS BETWEEN THE USA AND THE USSR`.

Having experienced six years of war already, my heart sank. I hastened to the Duty Officer.

"Sir there is a Top-Secret message on the War Office line, stating that a war has started between America and Russia."

"If it is in plain language (uncoded) then I don`t believe it," he said. All the same he ran round to the machine, read the message for himself and rushed back to his desk. He immediately started to make urgent phone calls to the most senior staff in the Admiralty.

While all this frantic activity was in progress, the same teleprinter started clattering again. I was very relieved to see the purport of this new message, which read - "It's alright mate. I am just practising for when it does happen." I was amazed at this crass stupidity but laughed with relief, as did everyone else in the know. I quickly informed the DO. However it was too late, as the damage had already been done. Admirals, Vice Admirals, in fact the whole upper echelon of the Navy had been aroused from their beds. The DO now had the unenviable task of ringing those same senior officers to advise them to disregard the message.

During this excitement a leading telegraphist, whose duty was to receive and transmit messages to Hong Kong by Morse-key, had transmitted a message prefixed with an operator's code (used between operators to clear up signal queries) which went - "XYZ, Have you heard about the war with Russia?" Upon receiving this alarming message, the telegraphist at Hong Kong must have jumped up with excitement and blabbed his exclusive information to all and sundry. It wasn`t long before an official signal was received from Hong Kong, wanting to know about the war that wasn`t.

As a consequence of this serious incident, the instigator, an Army corporal at the War Office, was soon court marshalled, as was the leading telegraphist. Two burley naval policemen appeared at the door of the wireless room and escorted the unfortunate man down to Portsmouth . But that wasn`t the end of it.

We were due to be relieved at 08.00 hrs, but at about 07.00 hrs a Vice Admiral suddenly swept into the office. He didn`t waste any time in making his presence felt. "I want the key to this door," he demanded. A Wren duly obliged. He locked the door and addressing himself to us all said,

"No one leaves here until I say so. If word of this gets out, my shares will plummet !" It was 10.00 hrs before the door was finally unlocked and we were allowed to go home to our beds.

*   *   *   *   *

OFF THE BEATEN TRACK

After coming off the night watch, I set out from the Admiralty for Euston Station, tired but happy. Glad was now expecting. She had returned to Hixon to have the baby and to be with her family. I had weekend leave and intended to spend it with her in Staffordshire.

When I reached the station I strode onto the usual platform and asked the porter, "Is this train OK for Stafford ?"

"Yus Mate," he replied. I boarded the train, found an empty seat, put my small case on the overhead rack, sat down and promptly fell asleep. I awoke when the train was passing through Rugby Station at high speed. I thought this odd because my usual weekend train normally stopped at Rugby before reaching Stafford.

"Excuse me," I said to the other passengers "Where is this train going ?"

"Euston to Liverpool, non-stop," came the reply. What I said about that porter back at Euston cannot be repeated and won`t be found in the Oxford Dictionary !

I thought the train might slow down as it passed through Stafford Station, or even stop at a signal. Then I intended to jump off with my small case. It wasn`t to be. The train tore through Stafford Station as though it knew what I was thinking. I returned to my seat and started chatting to the other passengers.

When the train drew into Lime Street Station, I alighted and ran to the ticket collector. I explained my problem. I was worried, as it was getting late and Glad would be wondering where I had got to. He told me to cross over to the down line. I ran round to the other platform. The ticket collector there laughed, when he heard what had happened. The smile soon disappeared from his face when I said, "I know your bloody sandwiches are no good but your damned porters are even worse ! Now can you tell me about trains for Stafford please."

"There are no more trains for Stafford," he said, with a smirk of satisfaction. Then all of a sudden he took a more sympathetic attitude. "The train now waiting at this platform will take you to Stalybridge. That`s the nearest you will get to Stafford tonight."

Eventually I arrived at Stalybridge. What a dismal station. Everywhere was in darkness. To make matters worse the station buffet was closed . I hadn`t had a bite to eat since the previous evening. I stood on the platform for two hours before I heard a train approaching. It was a mail train and thankfully it stopped. I persuaded the guard to allow me to board it and travel with him, as he did confirm the train would be stopping at Stafford.

When I finally reached Stafford at about 1am, tired, cold and very hungry, I was pleased to find a taxi waiting outside for a train that was due in from London. I was driven the seven miles to Hixon. The house was in darkness. I tapped on the door. A light came on and Glad shouted, "Is that you John?" When my wife opened the door I gave her such a hug. "I went to meet you at Stafford Station but gave up in the end," she said.

"Never mind," I said "I'm here now," and we both went to bed. I had reached the stage when now, I was even too tired to eat.

*   *   *   *   *

CHAPTER NINETEEN

AN EQUATORIAL POSTING

During my time at the Admiralty I had got myself a wife, recovered in health and learned new skills. It had been a good posting and I had the benefit of a normal married life. But as the end of my two year stint approached I began to feel despondent, for I realised it was very likely I would shortly be posted overseas again. Glad and I could be parted for a very long time. I was soon to become a father and Glad presented me with a lovely daughter, Janet on 13th March.

My new posting wasn't long in coming. I was finally drafted from the Admiralty (HMS President) on 22nd February 1949. I was now twenty four. I was only billeted at HMS Mercury for about three weeks, when I was sent on embarkation leave. During that time I visited the hospital to see Glad and our new daughter. Later in March I found myself boarding the TS Dunedin at Southampton. She sailed that same day for Ceylon (Sri Lanka). My posting was to Ceylon West Receiving Station (CWRS) which came under the main administrative base HMS Highflyer, Trincomalee. We were situated almost on the Equator, some eight miles inland from Colombo the capital. The camp was located on an old coconut plantation, in the small village of Welisara. Nothing of note happened on the outward journey. This was the second time I had passed through the Suez Canal, whilst in the Navy, but this time going south.

We berthed alongside the quay at Colombo. A RN lorry was waiting to transport us to the camp. I was soon on my way, to what was to be my new home for the next twenty six months. I gazed from the back of the lorry, intrigued by the new sounds and smells of this small capital city. I was not so impressed however, as we passed the Pettah fish market. It stank to high heaven ! I also found the sight of some of the locals chewing betel-nut and spitting the resultant blood-red saliva onto the ground a revolting habit.

I soon settled into my new environment. We lived in a bhanda, a glorified long shed with a white corrugated roof and large open windows. There were two rows of beds, each bed canopied by a substantial mosquito net. Both the washroom and the heads were in separate huts, which each bore roofs of coconut thatching. Outside the camp and hidden by undergrowth were a few bungalows. These were for married couples. The CO also lived in a bungalow with his wife and young son, but this was within the camp perimeter.

My job was again as a radio teleprinter operator. At the Admiralty I had been dealing exclusively with signal traffic for Ceylon. Now I had changed places and was at the `other end of the wire`, so to speak.

To get to the wireless room we had to descend a short hill. This led to a small raised path, which crossed a paddy-field and had a large monsoon ditch situated on the camp side. Once across the paddy-field there was a very sandy track, which led through thick bushes to the wireless room. At the side of the track we would come across the occasional termitarium - a substantial mound, in which each grain of sand had been stuck together individually by termites. It was said these mounds were as hard as concrete and would require dynamite to destroy them. Snakes were seen quite frequently along the track. The climate was very hot and oppressive. Because the wireless room was air-conditioned it was sometimes quite a relief to be on watch, to escape the tiring tropical heat.

An interesting feature of the camp was the different types of tropical environment to be found in any direction, beyond the camp perimeter. To the north was the dusty main road to Colombo. To the east was the main entrance and the camp road leading to the Colombo main road. To the west were a few paddy-fields and beyond these a river estuary. The wireless station and the `dust bowl` were situated to the north of the paddy-fields. To the south was a mixture of thick jungle, more paddy-fields and the occasional village. Estuarine crocodiles were known to live in the river.

Monsoon ditches abounded. These had been dug to channel flood water away from the camp buildings during the monsoon season. Our bhanda was virtually in no danger, as it stood on a hill. This did not mean however that it was immune to everything, as I remember a monsoon storm in 1949 when paddy-fields were washed out, violent winds tore the roofs off the flooded police bhandas and a spectacular electrical display played havoc with the camp electrics. I still have a vivid mental picture of a sixty foot palm tree being struck by lightning, which split the trunk open from top to bottom (Page 133).

My wife had had the chance of coming out to me in Ceylon but she could not come to terms with living in a foreign country. She had never been abroad. I think London was probably the farthest she had travelled. When she decided not to come, I was devastated. Many a marriage would have failed for that reason, but our love was deeper than that, so I came to accept the situation. I understood Glad much more when I eventually returned to England. At the time, our daughter Janet was only two years old. I had noticed the very young children of other wives, who had joined their husbands out there, were not comfortable in that tropical climate. They also seemed to pick up a variety of illnesses and the mothers were frequently taking their children on the camp lorry to attend the hospital in Colombo. So perhaps it was for the best that my young family stayed at home.

During the many happy years of marriage we enjoyed, when once I finally left the Navy in 1955, Glad often expressed her regret that she didn`t come out to me in Ceylon. I missed being a proper father too and when I got back to England my daughter of course did not know me.

*   *   *   *   *

THE NEAR MISS AND A MONITOR LIZARD

On one occasion I was trekking in the sandy, scrubby area between the `dust bowl` and the paddy-fields. As always I was looking for snakes. Soon I heard voices. Then suddenly there was a shot and a bullet whistled over my head.
"Don`t shoot," I shouted in alarm, jumping out from the thick vegetation. There stood a startled and very apologetic, red-faced Master-at-Arms, carrying a .303 rifle pointing skywards. He was accompanied by the C.O`s wife and young son.
"We didn`t realise you were there," he said. "I was shooting at a Kabaragoya," (the

132

Page 133.　Monsoon-damaged police bhanda at Ceylon West Wireless Station.

Singhalese name for a large monitor lizard). He was obviously as much shaken as I. We laughed with relief (especially me) that nothing far worse had happened. We made our way back across the paddy-field to the NAAFI, for a thirst-quencher. I don`t remember him standing me a pint for the trauma he had put me through.

Later I decided to go back to the same area. I had recently made a spear, so this time I took the spear with me in addition to my usual snake-stick, in case the monitor was still about. These lizards can grow very large. I have a photo of one which was some eight feet in length, but that is exceptional. They are carnivorous scavengers and if cornered, have a reputation for lashing out with their tales. Their bite is invariably infectious, because they feed off rotting flesh. They are well able to take on a cobra. They do not attack the snake directly but circle round it. Meanwhile, the cobra rears up with an extended hood, displaying the familiar spectacle pattern. The snake strikes at the monitor, time and again. Somehow the lizard is always just out of reach. Eventually the snake is exhausted and the giant lizard rushes in for the kill.

These lizards normally walk at a slow gait, rather as one would imagine a dinosaur to progress, but of course on a much smaller scale. However don`t be misled. When the need arises they can run at about 12mph, but because they are cold blooded creatures they are unable to sustain such fast movement for very long. As they walk they frequently flick out a long purple tongue.

I resumed my search for the monitor. There was no sign of it, so I decided to call it a day and made my way back. As I reached the paddy-field path, I suddenly spotted the large reptile in a monsoon ditch. This gave me an advantage, as being at a lower level the monitor could not lash out at me effectively with its tail. I quickly speared it in the neck and then struck it hard on the skull with the handle of my snake-stick. I struggled back to the bhanda carrying this large dead lizard. As I walked, its long purple tongue dangled from its mouth and swung from side to side. As soon as I came off duty the next day, I skinned the lizard (not a pleasant task) salted the inside of the skin and pegged it out in the sun. I took the skin over to the small tannery in Welisara village(Page 135).

A few weeks later I was making very handsome leather watch-straps for my mess mates. I have regretted killing that animal ever since. If I found myself in the same situation now, I would be thrilled just to have the opportunity to photograph it. I certainly would not kill it.

*   *   *   *   *

Page 135.   Death of a monitor lizard at Welisara.

FILLING THE GAP

I had only been at the camp about a month, when the frigate HMS Amethyst, called at Colombo on her way out to join the Far East Fleet. One of her signalmen was taken ill and was sent ashore to the local military hospital in Colombo. At the camp, I and another signalman were ordered to pack our kit and to stand-by. Whoever was off duty when the call came, would be sent to the Amethyst as a replacement. At the last moment however, the situation changed. Her signalman suddenly made a rapid recovery and was returned to his ship. The Amethyst cancelled her need for a replacement and we were both stood down.

Little did we realise how fortunate we were, because on April 20th 1949, HMS Amethyst proceeded up the Yangtze River to relieve a guard ship, HMS Consort, at Nanking. Preparations had been made to evacuate British and Commonwealth citizens who were caught up in the advance of Chinese Communist Forces. What is known as the `Yangtze Incident` is well documented, but in short, the Amethyst was fired upon by Communist shore batteries and received many hits. During the melee she ran aground and was stuck in the mud for six days. She was trapped. I can`t think of a worse situation for a ship to be in, other than to be on fire or sinking. She suffered many casualties - twenty five dead, including her skipper Lt Cdr Bernard Skinner, who died from his wounds the next day. The ship had received over fifty hits. HMS Consort and two other ships, HMS London and HMS Black Swan gave support, all suffering casualties. Total casualties for the whole incident were forty six dead and many wounded.

Months of negotiation passed before finally, on July 31st, the Amethyst, under the command of Lt Cdr Kerans, made her famous successful dash for the open sea under cover of darkness. She was again fired on, but confused the Communist gunners by putting out a smoke screen.

How fortunate was I . I had escaped by the skin of my teeth yet again ! I felt very humbled by the suffering endured by those brave sailors and couldn`t help wondering if the signalman who had been taken sick at Colombo had survived. When on watch he would have worked on the bridge - a very exposed position.

* * * * *

THE SWOLLEN FOOT

During my two year or more stay in Ceylon, I can recall only two occasions when I was medically unfit for duty. The first was when I contracted a virus, which caused me to suffer sickness and diarrhoea. It lasted several days and was extremely weakening. The second occasion was when I had severe athlete`s foot - a fungal infection between the toes. This condition became more complicated when one foot turned septic and swelled to an enormous size. I was in considerable pain. I was now unable to walk properly and reported to the sick bay.

It was not long before I found myself being transported by lorry to the military hospital in Colombo. I had been provided with a walking-stick, but this proved to be more of a hindrance than a help. When I finally reached the hospital, after a bumpy, sweaty and painful journey, I had to climb down from the lorry, gingerly dangling my rotten foot over the tailboard and at the same time carrying a small case

136

containing my pyjamas and toilet gear.

Hobbling into the hospital, I reported to the office of the ward Sister. She looked quite fearsome. Definitely not the sort to cross. She directed me to a bed at the near end of a vast ward. In a ward of some sixteen beds there was only one bed that was occupied. The occupant turned out to be a cheerful RAF bloke. He was endowed with a very infectious laugh. I hobbled over to my bed and was surprised to see three towels of various sizes laid out on the bed. Soaked in sweat and in pain, I asked "Is there anywhere I can get a bath or shower?" He directed me to a double door at the far end of the ward. "Why have I got three towels?" I asked.
"I don`t know," he replied and then laughing, "I suppose one is a bath towel, one a face towel and a special one for your rotten foot."

I grabbed the folded bath towel and hobbled down the highly polished floor of the ward and made my way to the showers. After much effort, I managed to undress and to remove my canvas shoe. When I had set out for the hospital I could not get my other shoe on, but optimistically I had packed it, just in case the swelling should go down.

I soaked under the shower for several minutes. What a relief ! What luxury ! Suddenly a female face peered round the door. I instinctively grabbed the folded towel to cover up my `personal belongings`.
"Have you nearly finished?" the young nurse asked smiling. "The Sister wants to see you."
"Yes I will just dry myself," I said red-faced. The nurse withdrew. I started to unfold the bath towel but there seemed to be yards of it. It turned out to be the counterpane belonging to my bed. I quickly dried myself on the counterpane, hoping no one would notice it was now damp. Then without getting dressed, I wrapped it round me and grabbing my clothes left the shower room.

I pushed through the swing doors. Oh blow ! The Sister was down the far end, talking to the `laughing man`. Luckily she had her back to me and didn`t even look round. I got down onto the floor behind the end bed unnoticed. Then I heard the sister leave the ward. I was about to try and stand up but suddenly heard her voice approaching again. She spoke to the `laughing man`.
"Is he not back yet?" she asked exasperatedly. She decided to look for me and headed for the shower room. She soon spotted me of course.
"What are you doing down there ?" she said with stern indignation. "Get up and why are you wearing that counterpane?" I stood up as best I could, feeling particularly small. During my explanation, I glanced at the `laughing man` and realised he was trying with great difficulty to stifle his mirth.

It may seem ridiculous that I had gone to all this trouble, instead of dumping the wet counterpane on the floor by my bed, but remember I didn`t want the Sister to see me in the counterpane or `starkers`, even though she was probably used to seeing various well endowed specimens of the British male, be they short, tall, fat, thin or hairy. Also in those days punishments were quite severe for the most trivial misdemeanours. As soon as the Sister had swept out of the ward, the `laughing man` and I rocked with laughter.

However it was the Sister who had the last laugh. I had to endure an intensive course of injections over the next three days. Because my skin had been thickened by the sun, she often found it difficult to get the needle to penetrate my skin and frequently bent it. As it was withdrawn, I swear it was given a slight tilt. I know after three days my arms were very sore. However I mustn`t complain. They made me better so I should be grateful. I was lucky compared to an RAF Warrant Officer who was brought in with peritonitis. Sadly he died during the last night of my stay there.

*   *   *   *   *

AN ENGLISH GARDEN

During my off duty hours I found time for several pastimes, apart from jungle trekking, tennis, football, athletics and of course, letter writing. In March 1950 I decided to start a major project, by laying out a large garden right outside the bhanda windows. It was to be English in its concept and would comprise several features. Namely : a crazy-paved area, a reasonable size cement pond, a rockery, flower borders and a large rustic trellis down two sides of the entire layout and finished off with a rustic arch. I extended the trellis as far as I could along the side of the bhanda, so that everyone would get a share of my English garden. The CO was very sympathetic to the idea. What little I knew about gardening I had picked up from my two grandfathers, one of whom had been awarded two RHS Banks medals.

I managed to obtain a few packets of English flower seeds from home. In my photo album there are snaps of the garden, taken at various stages of development. Surprisingly when I compared the snaps of a bare, newly sown garden, with the snaps taken of the same garden one month later, showing the garden full of flowers, you have got to admit that is a very rapid growth rate. Luckily I always wrote a brief description and date on the back of most of my snaps. These brief records have been very useful in the compilation of this book. After all this garden was laid out over fifty six years ago (Page 139).

One afternoon my mate `Symo` entered the bhanda and said,
"John I have just seen a piece of your trellis fall off," I went outside and found the offending piece of wood lying on the ground. As I went to pick it up, another piece fell off. I peered more closely at the trellis and then tugged at one or two pieces to see if they were secure. Next instant, the entire fifty foot length of trellis collapsed to the ground in small heaps of dust and bark. This was the handiwork of termites. They had consumed the entire insides of the whole structure. For the last few days my trellis must have been left standing on a `wing and a prayer`. That experience taught me another lesson. To only provide food for those termites that have lost their teeth. It was very disheartening. I had no intention of constructing another trellis. I couldn`t see the sense of it. It would only get eaten again.

Whilst walking in the jungle on one occasion, I suddenly noticed a plant with a tall stem which supported several flower pods. It was very similar to an amaryllis. I decided it was a type of lily and would look well in the garden. I went back to the camp for my trowel. As I entered the bhanda, most of the men were asleep under their

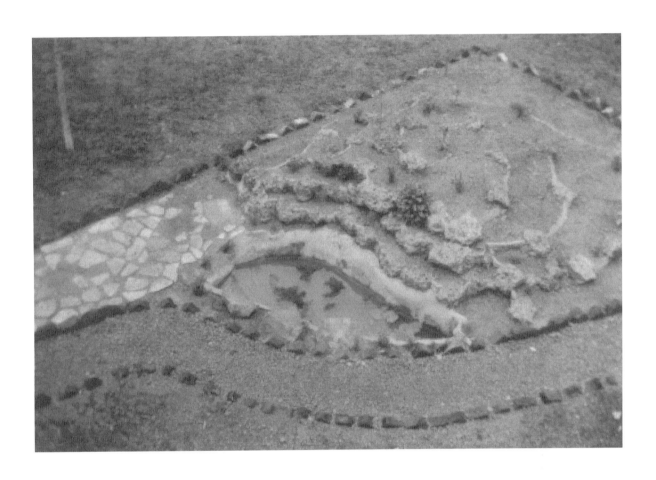

Page 139. Layout of the `English Garden` at Ceylon West Wireless Station.

mosquito nets. I thought, `They don`t know what they are missing`. I transplanted the lily into my garden. It didn`t even flag, which surprised me. Next day the pods burst open to reveal several large, lily-like, flawless white flowers. I photographed the plant for the album. It became quite a subject of conversation until a few days later when the flowers faded and died.

*   *   *   *   *

THE DUST BOWL

An area beyond the paddy-fields and to the left of the wireless room, was referred to by everyone as *The Dust Bowl*. It was about the size of a football pitch and although extremely sandy, was a popular venue for soccer matches. Every time the ball was kicked, clouds of choking sand and dust rose into the air, invariably finding a way into our eyes, noses and mouths. There was a convenient small bank on one side, which served as a grandstand. It was impossible to mark the pitch but there were goalposts, corner and centre-line posts.

Some men were accompanied by their wives, who would sit on the bank as spectators, to give their partners some moral support. As the climate was so hot and oppressive back in their bungalows, each wife was assisted with her housework by a native female servant, so consequently they had plenty of spare time on their hands. During a football match there were many roars of encouragement but few goals. In that climate and on a loose pitch, legs and body soon became tired, so normally a match was only played for half an hour each way at the most.

*   *   *   *   *

MOUNT LAVINIA

Every day a lorry was laid on to transport off-duty personnel (including wives) to a seaside hotel at Mount Lavinia, which is located on the west coast, south of Colombo. There was a small beach for swimming and surfing, where everyone could relax. Most of us chose to surf. Fibreglass had not been invented, so surfboards were usually made from elm.

Mount Lavinia seemed about the only place we could participate in an energetic pastime without breaking into a profuse sweat. The cooler hills, where most Europeans retreated to during the height of summer, were beyond our reach, distance-wise and cost-wise. I suppose it would be reasonable to describe the surf as `moderate`. Not as big as at Bondi Beach, Australia, but bigger than the surf at Newquay, Cornwall.

Apart from surfing, the only memory I have of Mount Lavinia, is of a female tourist who was caught in the surf by a big wave, which broke the neck halter of her costume. Of course the men lounging on the beach couldn`t let that pass without hooting and whistling (topless bathing had not yet caught up with us). Personally, I couldn`t quite see why they were making such a fuss. After all the embarrassed woman was quite flat chested.

*   *   *   *   *

SNAKES ALIVE !

I have always had an enquiring mind and so, by the time I reached Ceylon, I was quite knowledgeable about reptiles, particularly snakes. In the heat and often high humidity of an afternoon, while most of my mess mates were sleeping their lives away beneath their mosquito nets, I was in the jungle looking for snakes, lizards, exotic butterflies and interesting plants. I tried to avoid villages and their rabid Pi dogs and instead made for areas of intermediate jungle. There was a better chance of seeing and catching things there. I cannot say I was afraid of snakes but I did deal with them with cautious respect, particularly the venomous ones.

I paid a visit to Dehiwala Zoo and came to a large snake pit which housed two very large Indian pythons. Their keeper was a small Sinhalese man. We had a short discussion about snakes in general. I had my camera with me. He assured me the pythons had recently been fed. I had already read somewhere that pythons go into a state of torpidity after gorging on a pig, or whatever. I offered the keeper one rupee to allow me into the pit to take a few photos. He took my rupee eagerly and gave me access to the pit. I stood in front of these two huge snakes, eighteen and sixteen feet long respectively and took a few shots. The sun was behind me, which was a good thing, except that there wasn`t much room to manoeuvre. Because of this it was difficult to avoid getting my shadow in the picture. Whilst taking my snaps I kept more than a wary eye on the snakes. Any sign of prehensile tail movement and I would have been out of that pit like a flash.

Hungry pythons have a nasty habit of girdling you in a fond embrace. Their coils tighten with every exhalation of breath from your lungs, until it comes to your last breath. Then you breathe out but can no longer breathe in again. By the time the snake has unhinged its lower jaw and grasped your head, you will be dead anyway. Just as well really, as you would now be heading for a bath in acidic digestive juices. There is a plus side to all this. At least you would die with your boots on.

Back at camp, I managed to catch a rat snake, some three and a half feet long. These are non-venemous. I decided to keep it as a pet and named it Rupert. I made quite a good home for it from wooden gin boxes, scrounged from the bar, adding some wire netting to the lid to let in some light. Having gained experience in the handling of Rupert, I used to let it out for `walks`, or perhaps I should say `slithers`. I was never without my forked stick during my off-duty hours, so that it was easier to recapture the snake and return it to its box.

It was during one such `walk` that I discovered I could `charm` Rupert. By `charm` I mean I could render the snake completely motionless. It would stop dead with its head and front length of the body raised clear of the ground. No amount of deliberate noise, such as clapping, stamping on the ground, or even banging a metal dustbin lid had any effect on the snake. It stayed stock still throughout. How was this achieved ? Quite simply by stroking the stick several times from beneath its body, from the ground up to its mouth. It didn`t work if you stroked it the other way.

Word soon travelled round the camp that there was a `snake charmer` in their midst. It wasn`t long before the Master-at-Arms called at the bhanda to see me. He explained that the CO would like me to give him and his family a `snake charming` demonstration. At the prearranged time I drew Rupert from his box and placed him on the road. `I hope Rupert doesn`t let me down,` I thought. The CO with his young son stood at a respectful distance, while I went through my `snake charming` routine. "That is amazing ! Thank you John," said the CO. He and his son strolled back to their bungalow, discussing with some amusement what they had seen.

Whenever the native camp security guards sighted a snake, they would immediately contact me, except when I was on duty in the wireless room. I would grab my forked stick. Usually the snake would turn out to be harmless and most commonly a rat snake. There was one occasion however, in March 1951, when the snake discovered was a hump-nosed viper, a savage snake if disturbed. Although poisonous, it is not usually deadly to humans. I managed to put the snake into a shoe box and took it to Dehiwala Zoo. I was introduced to the Curator of Reptiles, a Sinhalese man. He gratefully took the snake and said,

"We will give you a certificate for this." Then he said, "Would you like to see the Reptile House and our laboratory?" I jumped at the chance.

We first walked round that part of the reptile house open to the Public. Amongst the exhibits was a king cobra in a very large glass case. This snake was at least twelve feet long. As we approached it reared up behind the very thick plate glass, displaying an enormous hood. The caption told of the snake having been caught by a German trapper. He was famous for his method of hunting. He would ride on the back of an elephant. A large lidded basket hung from the animal. He caught the king cobra by lowering a long pole with a wire noose on the end. This was manoeuvred over the head of the rearing snake. The noose was quickly tightened, the snake was hoisted up (with some difficulty I should imagine), forced into the basket and the lid safely secured. The zoo caption also explained that when this snake was being hoisted it managed to bite the elephant`s leg and the unfortunate animal had died within thirty five minutes.

We continued walking and came to a snake-pit in which there were at least fifteen Indian cobras. When I had first been introduced to the curator, I had become aware he had a thumb missing. While I gazed into this pit of death he suddenly explained.

"It was here where I lost my thumb. One cobra managed to bite me. I knew I had very little time, so I cut my thumb off." A cold feeling crept into the pit of my stomach as I tried to imagine what it would be like to carry out such a horrendous act. I have in fact found a book on the reptiles of Ceylon, in which it does recommend this action, but only if there is no medical aid to hand. It talks about `the removal of digits`.

We left the public area and the curator showed me into the laboratory. He handed me a very large book entitled `Snakes of the World`, by Ditma. He explained that the book illustrated and described all known snakes. I was very impressed by the book, but then he said,

"However we have a problem." He drew my attention to a small glass case which contained a small, beautifully marked snake. "This snake was brought in to us only yesterday and is definitely not referred to in Ditma`s book. Therefore, it is a species completely unknown to us." I felt very privileged to be one of the few people to have seen this snake. Incidentally the slightest movement on our part caused the snake to strike vigorously at the glass. He told me it was not poisonous. What puzzled me, because it was so aggressive, was why this new species had not been discovered sooner, because aggressive snakes soon make their presence known.

In the laboratory, besides their other duties, they `milked` snakes of their venom, by forcing the snake to bite on the rim of a glass, as part of the antivenin process. Antivenin is made by injecting small doses of snake venom into a horse. Later the size of the dose is gradually increased. This results in a substance developing in the horse`s blood which can destroy the venom. The serum is obtained by bleeding the horse. The blood serum free from corpuscles is sterilised, bottled and sealed for use. Antivenin can only destroy the venom of certain snakes. It is not possible to produce antivenom for all species of poisonous snake.

Treatment of snake-bite is best left to the experts, but if you are bitten out in the wild, urgent self-action is essential and unavoidable. Make a deep 1" to 2" long cut over the area of the bite. Suck the cut strongly and frequently, spitting out the blood. Beware of unsound teeth or mouth ulcers, otherwise you may poison yourself. A bite on a finger or toe means a quick amputation. Either you or a companion must do it. Better to lose a digit than to suffer a slow and painful death. The resulting wound should be cauterised.

One of the problems in Ceylon stems from their religious beliefs. Buddhists will not kill a snake and as a consequence the island is overpopulated with these reptiles. Superstition and fear also encourage their proliferation. One superstition tells that if one snake is killed, ten more will appear on the same spot. What rubbish !

My two years of experience with snakes taught me a lot about these fascinating creatures. For instance, most snakes prefer to slip away rather than attack. To improve the chances of seeing one in the jungle, a hunter must practise stealth with caution. I have seen a beautiful green tree-snake create an illusion. Its body appears to be moving in one direction, but as soon as the front portion becomes concealed by thick foliage, that part of its body then moves in the opposite direction. I moved to the spot where I expected it to reappear, but it never materialised.

The Russell`s Viper (tic polonga) is one of the most dangerous snakes and causes more casualties to the population of Ceylon than any other snake. It is extremely poisonous, very aggressive in attack and can jump its own length. It is at its most dangerous in the evening when, like many snakes, it tends to lie on roads and pathways, which retain the heat long after sunset. There are many instances of people being attacked by this viper. Sadly I have to tell of a sailor who came out from the UK as my relief. He joined the camp about a month before I left. It wasn`t until three months after I got back to England that I learned of his death. He had been bitten by a Russell`s Viper, which was lying on a pathway. He was rushed to the hospital at RAF Negombo (sixteen miles away) but died within two hours.

One day someone entered the bhanda to tell me Rupert was strangling himself. I ran out to his box and found he had somehow managed to work his head through the wire mesh, but could not withdraw it. The snake had obviously been struggling for some time, as there was an injury around the neck. Having extricated the reptile, I secured another piece of mesh over the old piece. This reduced the size of the mesh openings. Rupert`s wound soon healed but he was left with a light-coloured scar. A few weeks later, someone decided to let Rupert out of his box and I did not expect to see that snake again. Two weeks later however, one of the Sinhalese camp policemen came running to tell me he had seen a snake near the canteen. I ran to the spot and suddenly saw a rat snake slithering away. Incredibly I instantly recognised it as being Rupert, owing to the scar behind its head. I thought it deserved its freedom and allowed it to continue its progress towards the camp perimeter and thence into the jungle. Rat snakes are encouraged to live in the roofs of native houses where they help to keep down the vermin, so perhaps the jungle was not the best place for Rupert. I was sure he would find his way back to the camp, if he wanted to.

Shortly afterwards I was informed by the same policeman that there was an Indian cobra nearby. Grabbing my stick I ran outside. By this time, I had adopted the German hunter`s method of using a stick with a noose, but on a much smaller scale. There indeed was quite a large cobra. It was up against the wall of the bhanda. As I

143

approached, it reared up and expanded its hood. Any sudden movement on my part could cause the snake to strike. I continued my approach with the utmost caution and jangling nerves. I slowly raised the pole and lowered the noose over its head. It tried to bite the end of the stick. I immediately tightened the noose. I lifted the cobra off the ground. It was caught.

To finish it off I gave it a lethal injection, in preference to hitting it with the stick. In that way the skin remained undamaged. The body continued to writhe for some time although dead. When the snake was at last still, I broke off its fangs with a knife. Then I slit the skin from around the edge of both jaws and underneath down to the tail. Then using gloves at the head end as a precaution, I pulled the skin from the body. I flung the body over the perimeter fence into the jungle, knowing that there were plenty of scavengers that would devour it, including hordes of ants and the occasional monitor lizard. The skin was pinned flat on a wooden board, with the inner surface facing the sun, every vestige of flesh having been removed. A generous quantity of salt was rubbed into the skin. The skin lay curing in the sun until it was completely dry and almost as hard as the board on which it was pinned. After removing the surplus salt, I took the skin down to the local tannery in Welisara village.

One month later I collected the skin, which was now a patterned piece of thin leather. When I arrived back in England, I turned the skin inside out, taped the join, reversed the skin, inserted a specially shaped piece of fairly rigid stout wire and filled the snakeskin with sand. This rearing cobra with hood extended, stood on guard in the hall of our bungalow for several years. It gave some visitors quite a start, it looked so alive. Eventually my wife started to complain that she kept finding sand in the hall. Upon examination I found the tape I had used to seal the skin had deteriorated and the sand was indeed leaking out. I emptied out the sand and relegated the skin to a drawer.

I was on duty in the wireless room one day, so the security police contacted the Master-at-Arms instead, to inform him they had seen a cobra in a small hut. Arming himself with a stick, he entered the hut and found not one, but two cobras. He killed them both. Now facing a cobra in the open where there is space to manoeuvre is risky enough, but it is a very different circumstance from having to deal with two such snakes in a dim, confined space. When I heard what he had done, I considered his actions to be extremely courageous but reckless, but who am I to judge ?

Probably my luckiest experience was when I set out on a jungle trek. As I left the bhanda two of my colleagues asked if they could join me.
"Of course. Better than sweating under those mosquito nets," I said. One of the men was my relief, who was soon to die. For some time I had known of an old, fully-grown Indian cobra, which lived in impenetrable undergrowth at the rear of the canteen. I had been told of its existence by a camp policeman but had never seen it. The three of us walked past the canteen over sensitivity plants, which lay flat to the ground. Turning to look over our shoulder, we witnessed them folding up tiny rows of leaves wherever our feet had trodden, a curious sight. As we approached some tall dry grass I impressed upon the others, that should we make any kind of noise, we would be unlikely to see anything.

Hardly had I finished speaking when right in front of me, across this infrequently used track, I spotted just a dark, thick, three-inch length of large snake. Most of it was hidden in the long grass. It was motionless. I stopped dead in my tracks. My companions froze. Treading very light-footedly, I drew back and immediately brought

144

my stick down hard on its back with an enormous thump. There was an instant guttural sound, like someone bringing up phlegm, from which we all recoiled in alarm. The snake moved very slowly away towards the canteen. We still could not see it, but we watched its slow progress by means of the tops of the tall blades of dry grass bending and straightening to the shape of its body.

Unfortunately at the point where I had struck the snake, the ground was very sandy. This had dissipated the force of the blow, but because this very big old cobra moved so slowly, I felt sure I had badly injured it. I regretted I had not managed to kill it outright. It was far too risky trying to find it in the thick undergrowth behind the canteen, where it seemed to be heading. In any case we would have needed a machete to make any way through and would have increased the risk of being bitten. We returned to the bhanda and told our messmates of the incident. I can never forget that experience - the frightening guttural sound from the wounded snake and upon reflection, the fact that had I taken one more step I would have trodden on it. Almost certainly I would not now be here to write about it.

*   *   *   *   *

INSECTS AS SOUVENIRS

I had in my possession a bottle of formalin (a colourless solution of formaldehyde and water) which was used to preserve biological specimens. I used it in a small hypodermic needle to preserve butterflies and moths. Through the two years I was in Ceylon I managed to form quite a large collection, which upon my return to England I presented to the local school, St Peters at Hixon in Staffordshire.

When I sallied forth into the jungle I invariably took with me a large butterfly net, a killing jar, cotton wool a small bottle of ammonia and a pipette. The idea was to knock out any `prisoners` until I could get them back to camp to preserve them. If a captured specimen seemed particularly fine or rare, I would take it back to the bhanda straight away to reduce the risk of damaging it.

Then followed the tedious operation of preserving the insect. This involved pinning it to a smooth board. The pin was inserted through the thorax between the first and second pair of legs. I then injected the thorax and abdomen with a drop of formalin. This gave me about one minute to set the wings, legs and antenna to a lifelike position. After that the soft parts would set rigid and no amount of prising or teasing with a fine needle would have any effect, so I had to `get my skates on`. The aim when setting, was to try and make the posture of the dead insect appear the same as when it was alive.

The largest insect in the collection was an Atlas moth, one of the largest species of moth on the planet, with a wingspan of nine inches. I caught it in the canteen early one morning, after the Petty Officer chef had drawn my attention to it . Maybe he was worried about it getting into the salad, in case the men might think he had not washed the lettuce.

On observing my activities with insects, several of my messmates persuaded me to catch and preserve insects for them. Scorpions and colourful beetles were the most popular choice. To catch a scorpion I used a long piece of string, looped in the middle. As the insect was approached or teased, it would assume a threatening posture with the stinging tail raised forward over the thorax. I would lower the loop over the tail and quickly pull the two ends of the string apart. I could then lift it off the ground, keeping my arms well outstretched. Scorpions and beetles for that matter, are surprisingly strong and so I had to be very careful when securing dangerous insects prior to preserving them. I came across a huge Imperial scorpion in a monsoon ditch. It was a foot long and jet black. I caught it in the way I have already described. As I lifted it off the ground by the string it made a hissing noise. I don`t believe it could make a respiratory sound, so I can only assume this to be some sort of vibratory noise.

On one occasion I was sitting on the side of my bed, writing a letter home. Willy Wild, a Yorkshireman in the next bed, decided to clean his shoes. He pulled out a shoe-box from under his bed. At that moment I just happened to look up. Strange to tell I had not looked at his box, but some sixth sense caused me to shout out to him, "Don`t move !" I grabbed my stick and gently prodded at a yellow duster. It moved. I tipped the box over, expecting to see a small snake, but out ran a large, brown scorpion which I killed. Willy was very grateful and when the NAAFI opened, he ran down and fetched me a bottle of brown ale. He couldn`t understand how I knew the scorpion was in his shoe-box but then neither could I.

* * * * *

A NEW PITCH

In early 1951, one of the duties to fall upon my shoulders was to oversee two Sinhalese labourers, in clearing numerous bushes from a large area of scrub. This was the preliminary preparatory stage to setting out a new soccer pitch, not far from the NAAFI. As both their names were so long, difficult to pronounce or spell, let alone remember, they were given the nicknames Gabriel and Eusabie. As a team we worked well together.

A naval lorry was put at our disposal, in which they transported their tools and carted away debris from the site. At first the bushes were not easy to remove. After some digging however, a chain was attached to each bush in turn, which was forcibly torn from the ground by moving the lorry forward just a touch. Invariably under nearly every bush there were several brown scorpions, with pincers thrust forward and stinging tails arched menacingly. Some of the larger scorpions carried numerous young ones on their backs. Gabriel and Eusabie wore a type of loin cloth and cloths over their heads to keep off the sun, but no footwear. I was amazed they wore nothing on their feet with all those scorpions running about. For myself, I wore plimsolls, a white shirt and shorts.

As a fair-haired bloke with freckles, I had through patience and I hope with some common sense, managed to achieve a reasonable tan, except for my nose. That peeled, layer after layer, for my entire stay on the island. Whilst working on the new pitch there was no way for me to avoid the sun. I wore a hat of course, but a hat retains body heat so I always had a problem. To oversee the job properly, I needed to be in the vicinity of the work, so it was no good me trying to find shade or shelter under the numerous palm trees dotted about.

Soon it was time for me to leave Ceylon and return home to my loved ones. I was sorry to leave in one way, as it was such an interesting island. I didn`t manage to finish my part in laying out the new soccer pitch, but together with Gabriel`s and Eusabie`s considerable help, at least we had made a fair contribution towards the completion.

Ceylon is noted for its precious and semi-precious stones, especially sapphires. I struck up a friendship with a Sinhalese jeweller when I first arrived on the island. He used to use me as a go-between when selling to my messmates, as he spoke very little English. I did have some knowledge of gemstones, so that was a help. Just before I left, he mounted a wonderful amethyst in a signet ring my wife had given me. It was a real dazzler. Back home if I entered a jeweller`s they would invariably comment on it. One jeweller in fact wanted to buy it, but I refused. Unfortunately when we eventually moved into the first home of our own, I lost the stone in the garden while building a sandstone wall. It was foolish of me not to have removed the ring beforehand. I suggested to my family that if anyone felt like digging my garden over, they could come and look for it. There were no takers!

I arrived back in England on 17th May 1951, which coincidently was our wedding anniversary. A customs officer gazed quizzically at the gin box housing my insect collection.

"Bugs and beetles eh," he said, with an amused smile. "Now I'm very interested in insects." "What sort have you got in there?" I offered to show him but the lid was screwed down.

"Can you lend me a screwdriver?" I asked. He declined and waved me through. He saved a lot of fuss. All I wanted to do was get home to my wife as soon as possible. I had plenty of `rabbits`(presents) for her and the rest of the family. Homecoming is a particularly happy time for a serviceman, unless their wife has run off with someone else. Mine hadn't. After twenty six months away, I had plenty of leave to come and we made the most of it.

* * * * *

CHAPTER TWENTY

THE TEA URN

I arrived at about 14.00 hrs at the beginning of a three-month stay at my communications base, HMS Mercury. I tried to follow the normal procedure for getting myself messed by reporting to my Petty Officer. I was told he was in a field, engaged in running a children's party for children from a local orphanage. The sailors had rigged swings, a slide etc., and the party seemed to be, dare I say it, going with a swing. I approached my PO and told him who I was.

"I haven't time to talk to you now, but when the party has finished take the tea urn back to the NAAFI and then report to me." As an afterthought he said, "Make sure you take it round the back."

When the party was over and the excited children had departed, I lifted the large urn. It was fairly heavy. I emptied the rest of the tea on the grass and made my way to the rear of the NAAFI canteen . I was faced with three unmarked doors. I chose the nearest one and after putting the urn down, opened it. I received a nasty shock. There was a woman sitting on a toilet. She yelled and I shut the door quickly - very quickly !

Picking up the urn, I decided not to bother with the other doors and made my way round to the front entrance. I proceeded towards the counter, past the lads eating their sausage and chips or whatever. "Oh my God!" I had just spotted that same lady behind the counter. She was obviously telling the staff what had just happened. She suddenly saw me approaching. Immediately she pointed and shouted, so that everyone in the canteen could hear, "That's him, that's him." Everyone eating raised their heads in curiosity. I wished I was anywhere but there. It was the most embarrassing moment of my life.

I assume the three doors at the back of the canteen were for use by the staff. If they had been marked `TOILET`, that would have been OK from my point of view, but it would have encouraged all and sundry to use them.

*   *   *   *   *

A SHIP GOING NOWHERE

After being stuck in Mercury for three months, I was drafted to HMS Adamant on 10th August 1951. She was a depot and repair ship and was moored in Portsmouth inner harbour, as part of the Reserve Fleet (The `Mothball Fleet`).

I know that for the seven months I was on board her, I was not happy. In fact I was thoroughly bored. This ship wasn't going anywhere. I did manage to get home every fortnight though, which was a considerable consolation.

I do recall five days with Adamant when I did not feel as though I was stagnating. That was when I was included in a skeleton crew to take a destroyer up to the Tyne, for the breaker's yard. The vessel was towed all the way up the east coast of England by a single tug . There were seven other men in the crew. We were lucky as the North Sea was calm all the way. After we left the destroyer to her fate, we travelled back to Portsmouth by train.

Finally at the end of February 1952 , I was drafted to a seagoing ship - a frigate, which was to serve on the West Indies Station. She did however, stay in home waters for another seven months, so I was still able to go home on leave for some weekends.

*   *   *   *   *

CHAPTER TWENTY ONE

THE FRIGATE

I joined HMS Bigbury Bay, a 1,600 ton `Bay` Class AA frigate, on 28th February 1952. For the first four months she was located at Portland in Dorset. For some of the time spent there she was cradled in the small dry dock, having her bottom cleaned and other dockyard maintenance done to her. Once free of the dock, she either lay alongside the quay or was anchored in Portland Harbour. From time to time she exercised at sea. At weekends the majority of the ship`s company was on leave. Shore-leave invariably meant a bus into Weymouth.

On the 17th June Bigbury Bay headed up the east coast for Scotland, to take part in Operation `Castanets`, in the Firth of Forth. The ship carried out anti-submarine (A/S) sweeps. We passed close to the Royal Navy`s most modern and <u>very last</u> battleship, HMS Vanguard. She lay at anchor, rendered almost obsolete by the unstoppable advance in modern weaponry, particularly in aircraft capability. She had been completed too late to contribute to WW11. All the same she was a fine ship.

Most of us were able to take shore-leave in Edinburgh by catching a train from Rosyth. The city seemed little different from when I had set foot ashore there, as a boy signalman during the war, some ten years previously. The main differences were in the shops and streets, which were brightly lit and of course in the variety of food on offer.

At the beginning of July the ship left Portland and proceeded east to Portsmouth. From there she made for Brighton, Sussex, where we anchored off shore. It was a courtesy call.

After five days of overwhelming hospitality by the civic authorities and some of the local population, the captain (Commander A.W.F. Sutton , DSO and Bar), decided we should give back something in return. We were already `Open to Visitors` in the afternoons, with holiday-makers swarming all over the ship. After some discussion with local bigwigs, it was decided to lay on some entertainment, to be given by members of the ship`s company at the famous Dome Theatre.

All members of the crew who were singers, musicians or could tell jokes, suitable for a family audience I hasten to add, were `asked` to offer their talents. I put my name forward to play the harmonica. The authorities ashore decided to audition us. We were quite amused and pleased by this, as it meant we would miss our normal morning routine. We were taken ashore by motor boat and returned to the ship at lunch time.

The auditions went well. The next afternoon, those taking part were put ashore and made their way to a packed Dome. The audience indeed, consisted mostly of holiday-makers and were what might be described as `an appreciative family audience`. I wasn`t used to playing on a professional stage in front of a packed house and nerves gave me a dry mouth. As I moved the harmonica from side to side, it felt as though the corners of my mouth were trying to reach my ears. Apart from that, on the whole the entertainment went very well. We could tell by the favourable reaction of the audience.

Early next morning on the 6th July, we weighed anchor and proceeded to Dieppe in France. A coach had been organised to take us to Paris. Two telegraphists, Jimmy Green and Derek North, accompanied me to see the sights of that beautiful city. I managed to take some impressive snaps from the top of the Eiffel Tower.

When we arrived back at Dieppe in the evening, we paid a visit to a small club. There was a bar, round tables and softly-lit coloured lights hanging over a small dance floor. It had live French accordion music but unfortunately no female singer. We enjoyed the continental atmosphere, but the highlight of the evening came when we were introduced to a Frenchman who had been the leader of the Resistance in the Dieppe region during the war. He seemed a most unassuming man, spoke excellent English and insisted we have a table nearer to the musicians. He was very interested to hear of my time aboard the FFS Richelieu.

Bigbury Bay returned to Portsmouth to prepare for her long journey to foreign parts. In the meantime several of us took our shore-leave in Brighton. It was easily accessible by train. The ship was short of manpower at the time. To make up the deficit in the ship`s complement, the detention quarters ashore were `relieved` of several prisoners. They were a rough, tough bunch but funnily enough, the frigate turned out to be a very happy ship.

I said `au revoir` to Glad near the end of September. We were to be apart for well over a year. It was less than eighteen months since I had returned from Ceylon.

*   *   *   *   *

TO THE WEST INDIES AND FAR BEYOND

The Bigbury Bay set course for the Azores. The dramatic steep volcanic slopes of the Azores made quite an impression on me. They thrust up abruptly, for several thousand feet, from a boiling blue-green sea. Much of the vast slopes were cultivated terraces. We did not set foot ashore there. We finally set course for Bermuda and commenced our crossing of the Atlantic.

When once we passed over what is now known as the Atlantic Ridge, we headed into the Sargasso sea. What a difference. Stretching out before us was a vast expanse of floating weed, no waves and an eerie quietness. The surface was so still, except where the bow of the ship was cutting through the seaweed. It seemed endless.

The whole crossing from the UK to Hamilton, Bermuda, took about eight days. We arrived mid-October. The ship was not long in Hamilton before there was a hurricane warning. Bigbury Bay put to sea to ride out the storm. Later when things calmed down, we returned to Hamilton. As we passed Government House, we were surprised to see the roof had been torn off.

The ship left Bermuda, where one could observe beautiful angel fish swimming in the crystal clear water and headed for Jamaica. From there we worked our way down the east coast of Central America - Nicaragua, Costa Rica and Panama. The ship anchored off Nicaragua. Awnings were rigged over the quarterdeck and in the evening a cocktail party was held for the officers and their guests - mostly Embassy staff and their ladies and local Spanish-speaking bigwigs. Considerable diplomacy was involved in these social gatherings. Diplomacy however, was not on the mind of one particular Nicaraguan. Whilst the cocktail party was in full swing, he produced a revolver, excitedly shouted something and fired it above his head. He had to be escorted off the ship.

As we steamed down the coast of Costa Rica, a large shoal of sting rays was spotted. They are large fish in themselves, but to see them swimming by as a shoal in

151

the clear water reminded me of a flight of warplanes, or something out of science fiction. Anyway they made a wonderful sight.

Round about 22nd October we reached Panama. There were no plans for the ship to go through the canal. We were allowed ashore and I took the opportunity to go and view the working canal, which I had passed through on the troopship Athlone Castle, back in 1944. We were taken on an organised trip to a banana plantation, owned by the American Fruit Company. To transport the crops, lorries fitted with railway wheels were used along a narrow-gauge track. I caught a huge rhinoceros beetle, which ended up years later standing in my kitchen window. If I had been riding a motorbike I would not like to have collided with one. They are big.

We also saw a strange large brown spider. It wasn`t hairy, but had a smooth shiny exo-skeleton, rather like a crab. We had all heard of very poisonous spiders being found in crates of bananas, so I decided to leave well alone.

* * * * *

EXPLOSION AND VIOLENCE

We crossed the Bar at the Magdalena River entrance to Barranquilla in Colombia. Barranquilla is a small port, where the river flows north into the Caribbean Sea. The sea was quite angry over the Bar.

We were not prepared for what was about to happen. Firstly as the ship tied up to the quay, there was a very loud explosion upriver. A huge mushroom of smoke rose into the air, over what seemed to be a small island. Later we learned that a dynamite store had blown up, killing two workers. Secondly, it wasn`t long before a barge came downriver. It passed quite close to the ship. Two bodies could plainly be seen, lying on the hatch cover of the craft for all to see. No attempt had been made to cover up the corpses. Life is cheap there and the authorities` attitude to death seemed to lack the respect that we British would have shown.

Next day there was another shock. The dock workers downed tools. There was a lot of shouting. Shortly afterwards, two truckloads of helmeted troops appeared. They didn`t waste any time in getting amongst the workers. They assaulted them with their rifle butts. Men staggered from the dockyard with blood pouring down their faces. The place went quiet as the troops drove off. We could not believe the scale of the brutality.

* * * * *

A TOUR OF THE CARIBBEAN

By November 1952, our courtesy calls to the West Indies had begun. On 2nd November, Bigbury Bay called at St. Kitts. A coach trip was laid on for a visit to Brimstone Hill Fort. Way back in history, this fort had fallen to the French after many weeks of siege. We were told that the French were so impressed by the bravery of the English that they honoured all their prisoners and eventually freed them.

By the 4th November, the ship was moored at Bridgetown, Barbados. We were invited to use the facilities of the Marina Club on the waterfront. Apparently one of our shipmates, a man who was single, got friendly with two women, a mother and daughter. He was attracted to the daughter but she refused his advances. Eventually we were told that he ended up making passionate love to her mother. It wasn't long before he reported to the `Quack`(Medical Officer) and found out he had `caught the boat up`(caught a sexually transmitted disease).

On the 9th November, Sunday Divisions were held at Bridgetown, then we went on to Port of Spain, Trinidad. On 16th we visited the Doctor Jinnah Memorial Mosque.

On the 18th, the ship called at St. Georges, Grenada. The island had suffered extensive hurricane damage. There was hardly a building that had not been damaged. It was obvious that the population was extremely poor. Many were virtually destitute.

On the 21st the ship was approaching St.Vincent when we dropped a depth charge. The whaler was lowered over the side to gather in the `harvest` - dead fish, which soon ended up in the galley. On 23rd, we visited St. Mary`s Convent, Scarborough, St. Vincent. It is a very imposing building.

On 26th November, the ship was at St. Lucia in the Windward Islands, where we witnessed the schooner `Warspite` being rowed into Castries Harbour. Whilst on shore leave, some of us came across a church hall, where an afternoon dance was being held. We were invited to join in, which we did. There wasn't a white face to be seen. They played only calypso music and the dancing was easy, even for me. It was at least as easy as walking. Lift one foot up, hesitate, put it down. Lift the other foot up, hesitate, put it down. Those black people laughed at our antics. It was great fun. I found the West Indians very pleasant, as long as you showed them some respect. After all it was their country. They came across as cheerful and very laid back, which surprised me, considering how poor they were.

The ship returned to Port of Spain. There I went ashore with two shipmates. We had very little money and decided to walk out of the town. We reached the edge of jungle country, where we all climbed the side of a slippery waterfall. As we had approached the jungle, we had passed a bungalow. The owner was on her knees tending her small front garden. She was French but spoke very good English. She asked us where we were heading. We told her we were on a short walk and intended to see the jungle.
"When you return, you must call in for tea," she said. We gratefully accepted her offer.

We didn't go far into the jungle before we came to a clearing. I spotted a huge locust-like insect and picked it up. I had not realised it, but all the way down its back legs were sharp barbs. It kicked its legs to jump and the barbs punctured my skin. It drew blood and initially there was quite a sharp pain.

The French lady turned out to be the wife of a wartime Spitfire pilot. He was a West Indian, who had fought for us during WWII. He was not at home, which was a pity. We would have liked to have met him. Afterwards I did manage to get a bus and see Trinidad`s famous natural resource, the pitch lake.

The ship left Trinidad and sailed to Antigua. We arrived in St. John`s Harbour about the 30th November and on the 2nd December paid a visit to Nelson`s old dockyard. The original old black and white capstans were still on the quay. I was thrilled to be treading where our hero had once stepped ashore. It was of course a tourist attraction of considerable historical importance. Women vendors on the quay were selling their wares - necklaces of Crab Eye and Mimosa seed.

Bigbury Bay returned to St. Kitts on 10th December and dropped anchor close to a merchantman, the SS Biographer. We were to take part in a filming operation with RFA Broomdale (Royal Fleet Auxiliary). The film`s title was `Oiling at Sea`. Filming had already been delayed for five days, owing to Bigbury Bay fouling a propeller. Once filming was completed the ship sailed for Bermuda, to be there in time for Christmas, whilst Broomdale made for Port of Spain.

We tied up to the jetty at Hamilton, on 23rd December 1952. On Christmas Eve a group of us strolled up the main street and gazed wistfully into the windows of a few, brightly decorated shops. We came to a large store. A staff party was in full swing. They invited us to join them and we finished up by doing the Conga, snaking round the stacked tins of food and out into the main street. It was very enjoyable.

Everything in Bermuda was very expensive and I bought very little.

* * * * *

A RESCUE AND THE BLIMPS

The ship set course for Jamaica, but we were diverted. On 17th January 1953, Bigbury Bay went to the assistance of a Liberian ship, the SS Centurion. One of her crew had appendicitis and needed urgent hospital treatment. He was transferred to the frigate. We took him to the US Navy base at Guantanamo, Cuba.

The patient was transferred to a waiting USN cutter and we resumed our journey. As we left, we were interested to see two US Navy blimps flying over their base. They reminded me of our wartime barrage balloons, but these were narrower - more cigar-shaped. Quite an apt description I feel, considering they were flying over Cuba, where they make the best cigars in the world.

There were plenty of shops in Kingston, but my wages only went so far. I had to cut my cloth according to my purse string. I had already bought gifts and sent them back home for Christmas, so at this time I wasn`t buying anything.

* * * * *

CHAPTER TWENTY TWO

ARGY BARGY

From 2nd March 1953, increased Argentine activity in the Falkland Island Dependencies in the Antarctic caused furrows on the brow of the British Government. There was already a Royal Navy presence in the Falkland Islands and down in the Antarctic, particularly at Deception Island in the shape of a frigate, HMS Snipe.

Prior to the beginning of March, there had been some discussion leaning towards a withdrawal of our naval presence in the region. But now, as a result of the `back door` activities of the Argentinians, the political climate had changed . It was considered essential for the British naval presence to be maintained in the region .

At the instigation of Winston Churchill, HMS Bigbury Bay was ordered from the warm Caribbean and despatched to the cold Falkland Islands and the Antarctic region. The intention was to relieve Snipe from 12th March 1953. There was the possibility of British troops being sent secretly to the Falklands as well.

*   *   *   *   *

GOING SOUTH

It was February 1953. I was now twenty eight and experiencing my twelfth year of naval service.

We had a difficult departure from Port of Spain. The wind had got up. There was a lively gale blowing directly onto the ship`s port beam. Try as he might, Commander Sutton could not get the frigate to part from the quay. Every time the ship seemed to be putting space between herself and the quay, she was being blown back onto it. This continual battering could not be doing her any good, nor the quay for that matter . Large fenders were quickly draped over the starboard side to protect her hull. Eventually there was a brief lull in the wind. The captain sensed his opportunity. By clever revolutions on the propellers, a deft angling of the rudder and letting go the stern line at the precise moment, the ship came clear of the quay. We were underway at last. On 26th February the ship crossed the Equator and the usual `Crossing the Line` ceremony was held.

At the beginning of March we arrived at Recife in Brazil. The city is the state capital of Pernambuco. It struck me as a clean port, with neat bungalows down the side streets. There are several impressive buildings in the town centre, including banks, but it is not a very old city. The city was built at a confluence of rivers and has a number of bridges. It has thus been labelled, `The Venice of South America`.

Pushing on south, we had reached Rio de Janiero by the 9th March. As the ship approached the city, we could see from some 18 miles away the massive figure of Christ, poised atop the precipitous 2300 ft Corcovado mountain, beautifully floodlit. In the twilight, from that distance, it appeared as a giant cross in the sky.

As we entered Rio Harbour, we passed an old fort to starboard, against which were moored three Brazilian Navy vessels - a battleship and two destroyers. They did not look as though they often went to sea. The nearby domed peak of Sugarloaf Mountain with its soaring cable-car, made a great impression on us. Spectacular !

We spent most of our shore-leave on Copacabana Beach, a place for the young and the beautiful, although I hasten to add this description is not meant to apply to our `salty` matelots. Maybe perhaps `the young`, but certainly not `the beautiful`.

*   *   *   *   *

A BRIEF CALL

From Rio, Bigbury Bay set course for Montevideo, where we tied up at the quay between a couple of merchantmen. Montevideo is the capital city of Uruguay, a small country, as South American countries go, with a population of only 3.2 million then. There were some beautiful main buildings in the city, giving the whole place an old fashioned atmosphere. It was like being transported back in time.

I went ashore with a couple of shipmates. We discovered a small club bar, not far from the waterfront. It had a small dance floor. I played the harmonica there until late. Joe took his accordion with him and entertained the locals with a few tunes too. We played as many tunes as we knew with a South American rhythm. It was very late when we all spilled out into the street.

We found a small place where they served coffee. It was very strong. Joe stood his accordion on the floor. There was only one other customer in the place, a grubby looking man. He left shortly after we had been served. Joe suddenly realised his accordion had gone. We ran out into the street and spotted the man running away with Joe`s instrument. We chased after him. No one can run very fast carrying an accordion. We soon caught up with him. The man said something in Spanish, looked very apologetic and meekly handed the instrument over. We let him go, as we did not want any fuss with the local police.

By this time the reader might have gained the impression that a sailor`s life is one long round of pleasure. Nothing could be further from the truth. All the time sailors are on board ship they have a responsible job to do. Ports of call entail refuelling, re-victualling, mess cleaning, communications, watch-keeping, minor repairs, maintenance of equipment (including weaponry), spares, showering, laundering, keeping kit up to scratch, physical exercising, naval exercising, officer contact with port authorities and so on. Except when sailors are off duty, they are always occupied. It`s good for both mind and body. This philosophy keeps a ship up to scratch - a `fighting ship`.

*   *   *   *   *

THE FALKLANDS AND THE ANTARCTIC

HMS Bigbury Bay now set course for the Falkland Islands. The islands are 7,000 miles from England as the crow flies. They are divided into two main groups, West Falkland and East Falkland, separated by the Falkland Sound. There are 202 islands in total, which lie approximately 300 miles east of the Straits of Magellan and cover a total area of 4,618 square miles. The population density then was about one person per two square miles. On 12th March 1953 the ship anchored at Goose Bay. The local islanders went out and shot over forty wild Upland Geese and presented them to the ship`s company. From then on we were eating goose until it came out of our ears !

The ship left Goose Bay and made for Stanley, which is located on the east of East Falkland. Cape Pembroke Lighthouse came into view as we approached Port William, which is the outer harbour before entering the inner harbour of Port Stanley. We anchored on a calm day and the ship was refuelled. Shore-leave was granted and `Liberty Men` was piped. After inspection, the men were taken ashore in the motor boat.

Wooden houses lined the waterfront road. There were no trees to be seen, although there were plenty of hardy gorse bushes. I could see it was a very windswept place. I have read there are a few trees in some sheltered spots of West Falkland. These were planted and consisted of Patagonian Poplars, Scotch Fir and Cupressus Macrocarpa.

Actually the position of Stanley on the Globe is on the same latitude south of the Equator as Glasgow is north, but there is one big difference. There is no warm Gulf Stream to protect the islands from the ravages of the cold currents and the cold winds, that in winter seem to blow frequently from the west. Normally there is a gale on one day out of every five.

There was virtually only a choice of two things to do ashore : visit a tavern or go on a walk, to see the wild life. The pubs in Stanley are all small, sparsely furnished, cosy but drab. There were five pubs during my time there : The Globe, The Rose, The Ship, The Stanley Arms and The Victory Bar. I did not frequent all of them, I hasten to add. I favoured The Ship, where the famous actress Ellen Terry was born.

The islanders were friendly. Many were English or of English descent, but there was also a large proportion of inhabitants of Scottish descent. There was also some Scandinavian strain, from the days of sail and early whaling. The islanders were pleased to hear stories from back home.

An interesting feature of the pubs were notices pinned on the walls near the entrances. The notices bore a mug shot and barred a certain individual from entering that particular establishment for a period of usually one year. A notice would state what misbehaviour the miscreant had been convicted of by the local magistrate, such as drunkenness, brawling or foul language.

The peaty land was divided by barbed wire fencing, in some instances topping dry stone walls. It was obviously sheep country. Tufts of wool were caught up on the wire. Many wires had sheepskins draped over them, drying in the wind in preparation for tanning. Most of the sheep were Romneys and Corriedales and cross breeds of the two.

The islands` mean annual temperature is 43 degrees Fahrenheit and a minimum of 20 degrees F. The Graham Land Peninsula on the Antarctic Continent and some 800 miles from the Falklands, points icy fingers north. Occasionally icebergs drift up from the Antarctic and beach on the Falklands. They can be huge and take a considerable time to melt. The giant flat-topped ones are glacial in origin.

It wasn`t long before Bigbury Bay was ordered to Deception Island in the Antarctic, a distance of approximately 750 miles and almost three days sailing. After the first day we entered Drake`s Passage and encountered the `Roaring Forties` and thirty foot waves. These conditions continued for about two days and then calmed down. Deception Island, considered part of the South Shetland Islands, is aptly named. As the ship approached, there appeared to be no safe anchorage. It was only as we got very close that a narrow channel between two large ridges suddenly came into view. This is known as Neptune`s Bellows - the only entrance to a large sea-filled volcanic crater or caldera, the rim of which forms the island and is evidence of its torrid geological history. It is divided into two territories, British and Argentinian. It can boast a good small natural harbour - `Whaler`s Bay`, suitable for vessels of fairly shallow draught, such as a frigate.

Whaling ships used to anchor in the bay, but in the 1920s there was a severe earthquake. Huge tectonic forces lifted the floor of the bay, which made it much shallower. The massive earthquake wrecked a large whaling station, standing on the shore of the bay.

Every day whilst at anchor, a rating would be sent ashore as `ice lookout`. His job was to walk along the narrow beach from the jetty, past the old whaling station and the old whale bones still scattered about, to get to higher ground. Amazingly, there was still a faint smell of whale oil on the beach and the upturned hull of an old whaling boat, which would have been propelled by oars.

The ice lookout would ascend to the high ground until he reached a gap in the basin ridge, `Neptune`s Window`. From there he could look across the Bransfield Strait, towards Graham Land. The lookout was looking for a continuous white line on the horizon. If he saw it, he had to signify to the ship that the pack ice was advancing. When once sighted, it would only be a matter of time before it iced up `Neptune`s Bellows, our only access to the open sea and if that happened we would be trapped in the bay for most of the winter. This had happened on a previous occasion to one of our frigates. When it was my turn to be ice lookout, I used to enjoy the task. I wanted to be the one to cause frenzied activity (as long as I wasn`t left behind) by disclosing the news that the ice had started to move. The pack ice however, would probably not start moving until mid April, but we could not take any chances.

On one of the lookout turns I ventured along the ridge, so that I could look down on the Neptune`s Bellows channel. To my surprise I came across a grave. It had no gravestone but a large glass dome, under which were some flowers. The flowers were completely dried out and bleached. They had probably been there for many years, perhaps going back to Scott`s or Shackleton`s time.

A British Antarctic Survey base camp was situated by Whaler`s Bay (Page 159) and protected by a small detachment of Royal Marines. Outside the base hut were a couple of upturned sledges and a team of yelping husky dogs, sitting on the snow-covered ground. I found a sea leopard seal, some twelve feet long, which had been shot and dragged up the beach. Seal carcases were needed to provide food for the dogs. I cut one of the creature`s fangs from the jaw as a souvenir. It took me ages to remove it. Years later I gave it to my younger grandson, Damian.

The Argentines had a base camp at the far end of the sound. One day one of their armed trawlers put in an appearance and anchored in Whaler`s Bay, but made no attempt to communicate with us. A few days later, the Falkland Islands Dependencies` Survey ship, `John Biscoe`, entered Whaler`s Bay and tied up alongside us. She was a welcome sight in that godforsaken place. We last saw her in Port Stanley (Page 161).

I can remember that at the end of March Bigbury Bay carried out a landing exercise. We had to don battle kit, including ammunition belt, gaiters and pistol. We were lowered in the whaler (others in the motor boat) and taken close in shore. This was not opposite the beach but further in the sound, in the direction of the Argentinian base camp but not too close. We were faced with a ten foot crumbling bank of black volcanic ash. The temperature was minus fifteen degrees Centigrade !

We dropped over the side into the sea. My God, what a shock ! Brass monkeys would certainly not like to be here. Straight away all feeling seemed to have gone from my legs. Sparks, next to me, had a heavy wireless set on his back. When he dropped out of the whaler, he fell partially forward into the water and grabbed the gunwale of the boat to steady himself. He was soaked to the skin (no wet suits then). The ash bank crumbled away at every step. It was exhausting work trying to reach the top. By the time we managed it, poor Sparks was on the verge of hypothermia. Once clear of the ash, we had to run about a quarter of a mile across snow-covered ground to the base camp jetty. We stood there shivering, until the ship`s motor boat came

Page 159.   The British Antarctic Survey base camp at Deception Island.

round to fetch us. It reminded me of my training in the Isle of Man, but there, even though it was cold, it was nowhere near so cold as this.

I remember on one occasion that we were landed as a sealing party on the opposite ridge of Neptune's Bellows. There were five of us : Lt. Cdr. Rodger (Jimmy the One), Mr Field (Guns), Midshipman Cremer (Midy), George Collings and myself. We were all armed. The idea was to shoot a seal to provide food for the huskies. I was somewhat puzzled. We were over 1000 feet up. I didn't know seals climbed mountains. We didn't shoot any seals, but we did meet up with a group of small Chinstrap penguins. I must say we were all dressed in strange garb. I know I resembled Davy Crockett. (Page 162) .The penguins regarded us as a curiosity, which we were.

I can only remember on one occasion at Deception Island when naval discipline broke down. An Able Seaman (I can't remember his name) temporarily 'flipped his lid'.
He switched on the Tannoy, which the Bosun normally used to broadcast pipes and messages.
"Hands to stand easy," the AB shouted, followed by, "Up Spirits. How's that bastard?" The captain was on the bridge, as we had just passed through Neptune's Bellows, on our way out on ice patrol.
"Who the devil is that?" the skipper said. "I want that man's name." In the meantime, the errant AB had grabbed a butcher's cleaver, normally used on deck by the cook to chop meat for the galley. The AB chased a Petty Officer round the ship with it. The PO must have been terrified. The AB was arrested, but I heard nothing of what happened to him. It was all kept hush hush.

It was now the 5th April 1953. HMS Bigbury Bay headed out into the Bransfield Strait, in the Bellingshausen Sea. There was quite a lot of brash ice on the surface, together with the occasional 'bergy' bits. We soon started to see big icebergs. There were many. Some were coloured pink or brown or blue, presumably because they were carrying mineral impurities encapsulated in the ice, from that part of the terrain where they had broken off. Some icebergs appeared to have partially melted and had adopted fascinating tall shapes, like ghostly church spires.

We did pass a distant massive tabular iceberg, several miles long. This type of iceberg is large enough and flat enough to land aircraft on. A few have been reported in excess of sixty miles long. They are certainly the world's largest, the like of which would not be seen in the Arctic.

The ship steamed south towards Graham Land. It was not long before we sighted the edge of the main ice pack, which girdles Antarctica. Bigbury Bay altered course through 180 degrees and headed back. The weather deteriorated rapidly and very soon we were in the thick of a driving blizzard. By the time we entered Neptune's Bellows, Deception Island had become cloaked in fresh snow. We piled on more layers of clothing, which was fine but I never seemed to be able to get my feet warm .

*   *   *   *   *

Page 161. The Falkland Islands Dependencies vessel, John Biscoe.

Page 162.   The author with Chinstrap penguins (I`m the tall one !).

FALKLAND ISLANDS PATROLS

The ship left Deception Island for good on a clear day in mid-April. We could see for miles and noticed the snowy peak of a large mountain, which the Navigating Officer told me was over one hundred miles away. When the weather is calm and clear, the Antarctic is breathtakingly beautiful.

It was around the 23rd April, while based at Stanley, that Bigbury Bay got down in earnest to the business of patrolling the Falkland Islands. There were several reasons for carrying out these patrols. Principally it was to deter any positive aggressive action by Argentina, as it had been laying claim to the Falklands for many years and from 2nd March 1953, had increased its activities. Another reason for maintaining the patrols was to make our presence known to the small island communities and isolated farms. It was hoped that this would give them some reassurance that the Royal Navy was in the region to give them some protection and that the British Government was continuing to show support for a Commonwealth community living so far from the mother country.

Argentine fishing boats often arrived off the West Falkland shores during the hours of darkness, with the intention of poaching the beautiful brown fur seals for their pelts. These would command high prices back on the South American mainland. With there being so many islands, to cover the entire coastal distance by one patrolling frigate was an impossibility, but I felt sure her very presence must have been an embarrassment to the Argentinians, particularly with her radar facility.

The patrolling of the Falklands gave me the opportunity to learn more about this far-flung colony and especially the wild life. Over 120 species of wild birds have been recorded. Seal are common, as are penguin. There are several different species of the latter : gentoo, rockhopper, king, magellanic and jackass. Their eggs are edible and are normally made into omelettes or are hard boiled. Of the seals, the Sea Leopard lives on birds (including penguin), smaller seals and squid. Sea Lions are found at certain spots along the coast (a bull can weigh as much as 1500 lbs). Sea Elephants however, can weigh as much as two tons. Fur seals are found in five locations around the islands.

The country rock of West Falkland and north-east of East Falkland is Devonian (410 to 355 million years old), whereas the country rock of the south of East Falkland is Permian (290 to 250 million years old). Geological surveys have not made any discoveries of significant commercial potential.

The field of botany has revealed about 180 species of wild plants in the islands. I particularly liked the tussock grass, which grows to a height of six feet or more.

Stanley has the Anglican Cathedral of Christ Church near the waterfront and so can claim city status. The cathedral can accommodate some 400 worshippers. Close to the lectern hangs the ensign, flown by HMS Achilles during the Battle of the River Plate with the German battle cruiser Graf Spee. All the principal roads lie in an east - west direction. Close to the town limits are vast peat bogs, from which the peat is cut and stacked into ricks for use as fuel. There is no coal available. The town has a Town Hall and a fine Gymnasium. The Falkland Islands Dependencies are the direct responsibility of the Governor, to the Foreign Office in the UK. They do not come under the control of the Falkland Islands Legislative Council.

Moored in Port Stanley was a rugged `Norseman` seaplane, used for the distribution of mail etc, and the essential flights to transport the sick between isolated farms and the hospital. The town cemetery is of poignant interest. It faces across the waters of the inner harbour. At the lower end of the cemetery lie the victims of a victorious battle - the Battle of the Falklands (1914). At the top end are the graves of three sailors of the Battle of the River Plate (1940).

*　　*　　*　　*　　*

THE WOOD CARVER

I happened to pass by an officer's cabin at the same time as the `Chippie` (shipwright) was dismantling a damaged chest-of-drawers. I noticed the wooden top panel was of mahogany.
"What are you going to do with that ?" I asked.
"It will be scrapped. Why, do you want it ?" he questioned.
"I thought I might try my hand at wood carving," I said.
"It will save me scrapping it," he said with a smile and thrust it into my hands. I carried it down to the mess.

I had no proper carving tools, but I had one or two cutting blades, the sort that can be interchanged using a master handle. I soon discovered I had a bent for wood carving. I set to work, fashioning the mahogany into a plaque of theme and beauty, comprising a boy`s head surrounded by real and imaginary plants (Page 165). The craft creates innumerable wood chippings and so I always ensured I made a very thorough job of tidying up after my efforts. It can also be a noisy craft when using a mallet, so I refrained from carving if anyone was asleep.

I called the finished plaque `Nature Boy`. Some thirty years later, I was asked to produce a reproduction in fibreglass. That is now displayed on the outside of an environmental centre in Staffordshire. The centre educates children in biology and botany, which is why the theme of the plaque was considered appropriate.

It wasn`t long before word got around as to what I had created. The next thing I knew, an officer appeared in the mess, accompanied by a stranger dressed in civvies. They made a beeline for me.
"This is Captain White," the officer said . "He is Captain of the Falkland Islands Company vessel, the SS Fitzroy (853 gross tonnage), which plies from Montevideo each month. Will you show him your carving please." I removed the plaque from my locker. Captain White seemed pleased when he saw it.
"My ship has no ship's crest. Do you think you could design and carve me one?" he asked. It was an unusual challenge. I agreed to set my hand to the task.

I worked at the crest in my spare time. I carved a Lloyd`s Crown at the top and encompassed the crest with a carved twisted rope. It was completed in two weeks and passed on to the officer. I didn`t think anything more of it. I had not carved it for payment, but just as something to occupy my mind. It was a challenge.

*　　*　　*　　*　　*

Page 165.   The `Nature Boy` plaque.

THE CORONATION

The Coronation of Queen Elizabeth II took place on 2nd June 1953. HMS Bigbury Bay was still patrolling the Falklands, but lay at anchor most nights in Port Stanley. In the last week of May, a temporary signal station was established in an empty house on Ross Road, the waterfront road. The intention was to communicate matters mainly concerned with Bigbury Bay's contribution to the local Coronation ceremony and the evening celebrations. For example, some sailors had drawn spectacular decorative panels for hanging in the Town Hall. I spent one night in the empty house and was taken back to the ship at 08.00 hrs the following morning. It was quite eerie in the house, with a strong wind muffling strange unidentifiable creaks in the woodwork. Two of us were seated in a long, enclosed veranda, with an Aldis lamp, signal log and most important of all, a heater.

The day before Coronation Day I was put ashore and told to report to the Governor's secretary, to collect the Royal Standard for the ceremony the following day. Everyone was in buoyant mood, as Mount Everest had just been conquered on the 29th of May, but that wasn't the only reason. No. On the morrow we were likely to 'splice the mainbrace' {an extra tot of rum) to toast Her Majesty.

I reported to Government House. On my way I passed an impressive monument of whale jawbones, which had been erected to commemorate the first one hundred years of whaling around the Falklands. I had already been given the secretary's name. I entered the office.
"Miss Onions?" I enquired, pronouncing her name like the common tear-jerking vegetable.
"Miss OH-NY-ONS," she retorted indignantly. I was handed a large Royal Standard. It was now my responsibility to take charge of this most venerated flag.

On Coronation Day a Guard of Honour was sent ashore to Government House. I was put ashore with the Royal Standard and at the Coronation ceremony, raised it in front of Government House. It was a very proud moment for me. The standard flew until sunset. We now had a Queen. Long may she reign ! (Now while I write this, she has just celebrated her eightieth birthday).

Special Coronation postage stamps were on sale throughout the Commonwealth. The ships company of Bigbury Bay all endeavoured to buy some from Stanley Post Office. We hoped they would increase in value, coming from such an isolated part of the world. There were two different stamps of the same denomination, a Falkland Islands one penny red and a Falkland Islands Dependencies one penny mauve. I posted some home, so that they would bear the Stanley post mark.

In the evening there was a celebratory dance in the Town Hall. Much of the dancing that evening was Scottish Country Dancing. I particularly enjoyed the Circassian Circle. The music was provided by skilful island fiddlers and an accordionist. I thought the decorative panels drawn by members of the ship's company were excellent (Page 167).

*   *   *   *   *

Page 167.   Decorative panels drawn by crew members of HMS Bigbury Bay.

THE SS GREAT BRITAIN

One of the patrols undertaken by Bigbury Bay involved taking a few sheep to an island of the Jason Islands group. The sheep farmer came with us. He was our guest and was allowed on the bridge. I heard him telling an officer that if the few sheep were landed on one of the islands now, in a year`s time the few would have become a flock. Whilst in that area we spotted a large rookery of crested penguins on one island and on another island a fair number of fur seals.

As the ship entered Port William, the outer harbour, on the way back to Stanley, we diverted into Sparrow Cove. There lying beached, was Isambard Kingdom Brunel`s SS Great Britain, the first large hulled, clinker-built, propeller-driven ship in the world. She had been beached and abandoned there for the past sixteen years. Prior to that the Falkland Islands Company had used her, firstly as a wool store and later as a coal store. It is believed she fuelled Admiral Sturdee`s Royal Naval squadron in 1914, which was involved in the Battle of the Falklands. In the early 1930s, she was offered to the Royal Navy for use as a target ship. Fortunately the Navy turned down the offer.

It is hard now to believe that this fine ship, once the pride of our nation and unique in the maritime history of the world, should have been left to rot in this way. We had no inkling then that in May 1970, she would be secured on a giant submersible pontoon and towed 7,000 miles directly to Bristol, to be returned to her former glory, but this time as a unique maritime museum in the Great Western Dock.

Rotting hulks are a common sight in the coves and inlets of the Falklands ; shadows from the glorious days of sail and after. I use the word `glorious` because none can fail to appreciate the magnificence of such ships under full sail. Their appearance however belies the extreme hardship endured by their crews, especially in the Southern Ocean and around the Horn.

*   *   *   *   *

FAREWELL TO PENGUINS AND SEALS

In June 1953, the frigate Bigbury Bay was still making her presence known around the Falklands. By that time the ship had its own band, if you could describe it as such. It was made up of an unusual assortment of instruments : two piano accordions, two harmonicas, a homemade double bass, drums and maracas. If playing ashore, one of the accordion players (Joe Stubbert) would also play the piano if there was one available. We called ourselves the `Calypso Killers`.

A ship`s company dance was held in Stanley Town Hall on 7th July, at which the `Calypso Killers` band gave a good account of themselves. This was something of a farewell dance, because the ship sailed from Port Stanley for the last time during the last week of July, setting course for Montevideo.

A surprise awaited me there. Captain White contacted the ship and invited me to dine with him on board his vessel. This was very unusual treatment for a lower deck rating. It was of course to repay me for my work in carving his ship`s crest.

When I met the captain I was introduced to another guest, a South American businessman. Apparently he was reproducing the crest, to retail in Montevideo. The meal was enjoyable, but that was not the end of the matter. When I finally got back to

England in November 53, there was a parcel waiting for me. It contained two interesting books, `Birds of the Falkland Islands` and `The Falkland Islands`, with a card inside the cover which read `Best Wishes from Capt. F.W. White, The Falkland Islands Co. Ltd `. It was a nice gesture.

In Montevideo, the British Society and the British Legion (now the Royal British Legion) hired the Lafone Hall for two evening dances for the 30th and 31st July. I played on the first night, with Joe on the piano. The following night, the `Calypso Killers` played for the entire dance. .It all went very well. We even got a mention in the local paper.

On 1st August, Bigbury Bay played Montevideo Cricket Club at hockey, of which I was a team member. The result : MCC 4, BB 1. It was nice to quaff a brown ale at their bar. Their club had such a homely atmosphere.

*   *   *   *   *

ONE DOWN AT RIO

We set course for Rio on 2nd August. The ship was tied up alongside there for several days.

The expression `run ashore` (meaning shore-leave), has different meanings for different men, depending on their tastes and whether they are married or single. Most married men from our ship seemed to stay faithful to their spouses. Some drowned their loneliness in drink. A few associated with prostitutes who frequented the clubs and bars of Rio. Single men are easy prey to the riff-raff who frequent any port, but having said that, not many went whoring around. Some just drank and drank and became so drunk they were an embarrassment to everyone.
There is great comradeship however, between members of a ship`s crew. Men will rally round to protect their colleagues from the sharks of any port and the majority will stay out of trouble.

Two things stand out in my recollection of Rio. When walking down a side street with my `oppos` we found much of the street was given over to squalid, open-fronted rooms which were heavily barred and in which women lounged in flimsy and revealing garments. Pimps abounded and several tried to persuade us that heaven was behind those iron bars. We knew differently ! We had already heard about such places and had been warned of the dangers. Vice, disease and violence were rife. The knowledge that most of these women had ended up as prisoners of the `white slave` traffic was certainly most shocking.

The other experience came about when the ship was due to leave Rio for Recife. One sailor (a signalman) had not returned to the ship. Captain Sutton ordered a search to be made of all the likely haunts - bars, clubs, brothels and finally, the City Morgue. The man wasn`t found. What amazed us most was the fact that there were ten bodies in the morgue which had been brought in that day. The attendant informed us that in the city of Rio de Janeiro, this was the average daily intake of the dead. Some had been murdered. This depressing fact opened our eyes to an even darker side of city life, in South America.

After some delay, we cast off and headed out to sea for Recife. Meanwhile the errant sailor, having missed his ship, reported to the British Consul.

Arrangements were made to fly him on to Recife. When he eventually came on board he was charged with desertion and was incarcerated in the chain locker, situated in the ship`s bow, for fourteen days.

*   *   *   *   *

CHAPTER TWENTY THREE

TROOPS AND THE DIVERSION

On the 16th August 1953 we were heading for Recife. We stopped briefly to refuel and the next day made for Trinidad. We were destined for Tobago, but while tied up at Port of Spain, a crisis arose in British Guiana (now Guyana) in early October. A certain Dr. Cheddi Bharrat Jagan, a Communist agitator, was inciting strikes and violence in Georgetown, the capital. As the mayhem stepped up and threatened to get out of control, Bigbury Bay was ordered to embark a detachment of soldiers of the Welch Regiment. We made two trips, taking a total of 350 soldiers. They slept on the mess decks and anywhere else they could find space to lie.

Conditions below decks in that climate became very oppressive, especially for the soldiers who felt seasick. At least we had a hammock to sleep in and were used to the rolling and heaving of the ship.

We steamed up the River Demerara and disembarked our soldiers. The civil unrest was resolved when the rioters discovered they were facing a strong force of soldiers, backed up by armed sailors if needed. The mob greeted the soldiers with sullen stares, but did nothing and soon melted away.

We were not allowed shore leave in Georgetown. It was too risky with the present simmering unrest. We were however invited by the Canadian Bauxite Company to send a limited number of men ashore for a jungle trip. I was one of the lucky ones to be chosen. This was a rare opportunity to see for ourselves the open country, well away from Georgetown.

We met very early next morning. Each of the party was armed with a .303 Lee Enfield rifle and two rounds of ammo. We climbed into the truck. The vehicle followed tracks (you couldn`t call them roads). The jungle was in patches, like green islands in a swathe of tall savannah grass. Splashing through a stream, the lorry drove through an overhanging canopy of jungle. We were amazed at the flashes of electric blue from the wings of clouds of metallic-blue butterflies. The flashes occurred when a butterfly happened to cross a beam of sunlight, shining down through gaps in the forest canopy.

Along the bank of a stream we saw some ten feet of a huge snake disappearing into the water. We were informed it was an anaconda. Later in the day, just before setting back, we were walking on an open track with only thin vegetation on either side. Our guide stopped and motioned us to stand still. We could now *hear* and *feel* the activity of the jungle, like I was used to in Ceylon. It wasn`t long before we saw a large animal walking away from us. One of the party knelt and removing his safety catch, fired a shot. He missed. The animal streaked off. There was no time for anyone else to fire, but at least some of us had had a fleeting glimpse of a jaguar. I was surprised that we even saw it. Meanwhile, some men who were not able to go on safari, were able to play football in Mackenzie.
(Note: Dr. Cheddi Jagan became President of Guyana, from 1992 to 1997)

*   *   *   *   *

HOMEWARD BOUND

Two days later the ship left British Guiana, refuelling at Port of Spain, Trinidad and made a short stop at Tobago (the Robinson Crusoe island), where we were able to go ashore. The ship then sailed the 1,200 miles to Bermuda. A quick shore-leave, a last look in the shops and another look at angel fish in the clear waters of Hamilton harbour, more refuelling, then we set course for Portsmouth, England. It was the 6th November 1953. We were going home !

Because of the trouble stirred up by Cheddi Jagan, our homecoming had been delayed by two months. The trouble also caused us to miss the opportunity to visit Galveston and Houston, USA, which had previously been on our itinerary for courtesy calls. The ship`s company was not very pleased and nor were our families. The exception I suppose, was for those who had been on the short safari. I know I would not have missed it for the world, but I was also very disappointed at the delay to our homecoming .

HMS Bigbury Bay docked at Portsmouth on 14th November, after being away from our loved ones for nearly twenty one months. I consoled myself with the thought that this was to be my last overseas service. We had taken eight days to cross the Atlantic, with a following wind. I was left with some interesting memories of my experiences which, on my salary, I could never have gained in Civvy Street .

Note: On 14th May 1959, HMS Bigbury Bay was sold to Portugal, where she was renamed Pacheco Pereira. At least two Bay Class AA frigates continued to fly the flag in the South Atlantic, after Bigbury Bay came home. Like most ships, she had an ignominious end. She was sold off on 6th July 1970, and then scrapped.

*　　*　　*　　*　　*

OUT LIKE A LAMB

My last year and two months` service in the Royal Navy was, in the main, a disappointment. I was once more transferred to the `mothball fleet`. This fleet comprised surplus warships no longer required for active service and there were plenty of those after WWII. The Navy was now oversubscribed with warships. They hardly knew what to do with them. Some were eventually sold to friendly foreign powers, but the majority ended up in the breaker`s yard. Much of the defensive capability of these ships had been rendered obsolete by the modern developments in military aircraft, weaponry and radar.

The cocooned ships idled away in secondary harbours, awaiting decisions on their future, sometimes for years. Many of them had distinguished battle honours. I was messed on board HMS Mauritius and then HMS Liverpool, both cruisers but not of the same class.

Time was fast approaching when I would find myself in Civvy Street. I decided I needed to do some studying. I took a horticulture course, through the auspices of the Navy. I also took a correspondence course in Public Health and Hygiene, with a view to becoming a School Attendance Officer. I obtain my certificate in hygiene at Aston University. My correspondence college tried to persuade me to continue my studies, with the aim of becoming a sanitary inspector. This was not where my interests really lay, so I turned down that opportunity.

Whilst on shore-leave, I took driving lessons in Portsmouth and managed to pass my driving test after nine lessons. No, I didn`t run over any old ladies, but I did go through one red light and negotiate a roundabout doing 35 mph.

*　　*　　*　　*　　*

CHAPTER TWENTY FOUR

BACK ON TERRA FIRMA, FOR GOOD

On 7th January 1955, I was transferred to HMS Mercury for the very last time. After a boring month, the next day would be my thirtieth birthday. I would qualify for a £100 long-service gratuity. To qualify for a pension, I would have to serve for a further ten years. Although the Navy encouraged me to sign on again, I turned them down. My reasoning was that if I left the Navy now at thirty, I would probably have a better chance of getting on in Civvy Street, than if I waited until I was forty. I didn't want to end up as a hotel commissionaire. Not that I have anything against hotel commissionaires, but I thought I could make something better of myself. Time was to prove me right. But there was another reason. My dear wife Glad had stuck by me for eight long years and now I wanted, above all else, to be with her and my daughter Janet.

Shortly before I completed my naval service, Glad and I were allocated the keys to a Council house in Hixon, Staffordshire. Unbeknown to me, Glad had borrowed the money to furnish the house with basic furniture and had paid off the entire loan, by the time I walked through those barrack gates for the very last time. I was so proud of her.

I was placed on the RN Emergency Reserve for seven years, but I thought it unlikely I would be called to the Colours, unless the next war was world-wide again, which I thought doubtful. The world in the main was still recovering from WWII.

I remember a Labour MP giving a talk in Hixon Memorial Hall on `The Atom Bomb and War`. He stated emphatically that, because of the atomic bomb, there would be no more war, meaning that none would fight in the field, owing to the threat of a retaliatory A-Bomb. How wrong he was ! Since WWII there has always been armed conflict in the world, of one sort or another. The Korean War for instance, was not all that long in breaking out after WWII. In that vicious conflict there was considerable hand-to-hand fighting.

*   *   *   *   *

JOINING THE RAT RACE

I entered the rat race of Civvy Street at the age of thirty with some trepidation. I had only known life as a student and as a sailor. I thought the knowledge gained from my studies, including the three years at Acton Technical College, would stand me in good stead. The practical skills of having been a Navy signalman however, would be of little use. Who needs flag signals and flashing Morse code in a manufacturing or office environment? Perhaps I would be useful to the Coast Guard Service, but I could not have lived further from the sea. In any case, modern technology, in the form of the silicon chip and satellite communication, would soon be overtaking many of the 19th and early 20th Century communication skills, although I did not know of them at the time.

I managed to get a job as a pen-pusher in the working environment of an electrical engineering research laboratory. My job entailed writing and issuing work orders to the shop floor, some technical drawing and recording accurate details of the conducted research experiments. It was quite a stressful job.

The laboratories had been set up in ex - RAF WWII huts and in their large motor transport building. All the buildings had been part of an operational OTU bomber base, which during the war had supported thirty Wellington bombers. Some aircraft of the American Air Force were also involved in operational flights from this aerodrome. When one of the American aircraft was in trouble when returning from a raid, it managed to fly back to Hixon airfield, but made a pancake landing on a nearby railway embankment. When the RAF rescue team frantically raced to reached the plane, they found the American crew inside playing cards !

The laboratory management structure was to say the least chaotic. At the top was a Director of Research, who gave his instructions to a Works Manager, who in turn gave instructions to just about anybody, including his immediate assistant.

A working day on the shop floor saw the preparation and assembly of vacuum envelopes, for switchgear rectifier valves. The work mainly involved the furnace firing of steel pressings and ceramic insulators, which when fused together formed vacuum envelopes.

The trouble was that the Director would interfere directly with the progress of work on the shop floor, without necessarily delegating the changes through the Works Manager. He would change technical work sequences and materials at the drop of a hat. Because of this, technical orders placed on the shop floor were rendered obsolete. Bearing in mind that the technical sequences and the materials used were all part of research experiments, for which I had written the orders, it was vital to amend the orders to record what had actually been done.

Things got so bad that I dreaded going to work. As soon as I entered the laboratory gates and heard that the Director had called in during the night, I knew I was in for a hard time. I had to go to the men on the shop floor to find out what had been changed. I then amended the orders, accordingly. At the peak of the programme, it was not unusual for me to be writing sixty orders a day and working sixty hours a week.

The Director had an extremely intimidating manner and I saw grown men actually hiding when they saw him approaching. In the laboratory there was an area of neatly cut grass surrounded by Nissen huts. Each morning he had a habit of selecting a `victim` and walking that unfortunate employee back and forth across the lawn. At the same time he would wildly wave his arms about. He knew perfectly well that he was being observed by his employees, working in the huts nearby. They would remark to each other,
"He has got So-and-So today."

The Director collared me one day and while he was talking to me I was obliged to follow him out of my office. We ended up walking the lawn. I can`t remember exactly what the conversation was about, but I do remember him turning to me and saying, "Some of you men talk to me as though I am the chairman of a communist committee." Of course when I returned to my office my colleagues wanted to know what he had been raving about.
"I haven`t a clue," I said.

Out of my office window I observed the gardener planting bulbs in one of the long flower borders. The Director approached and apparently said,
"I don`t want tulips, I want daffodils." The unfortunate worker was obliged to lift the tulip bulbs, which took some finding and replace them with daffodil bulbs. I thought the Director`s behaviour was unreasonable to say the least.

I always remember an amusing incident, when the Works Manager's assistant,

174

who was responsible for site security, suddenly put in an appearance at around 10 p.m. As soon as he had breezed through the gates, the security man rang the workshop to warn them he was on the prowl. Eventually the phone was answered.
"Watch out, Smith is on his way in," he said. The voice at the other end of the line said," This is Smith speaking." Nuf said.

I had worked there for some two years when they started to build a new laboratory site on the eastern outskirts of Stafford. A police car was cruising past the new site at 1am, when they noticed a torch waving about in a footing trench. Upon investigation, they discovered the Director with a torch in his hand. When challenged he is reputed to have said, "I am the Director of Research and this is my new building." Apparently he was examining the footings. The police asked for some means of identification, but he had none. "I can get some identification from my office," he said. His office was about a quarter of a mile away. He went to get into his car but the police would not allow this, so he had to walk. He was eccentric to say the least, but then aren`t we all to some extent ? I know I am.

After my eight years working for the laboratories, they were closed down. I , like many others, was made redundant. Apart from bereavement, this is about the worst feeling imaginable. One`s feelings are of rejection, of uselessness and as though one is completely worthless - cast on the scrap heap.

Thankfully, I soon obtained a job in the company main works at Stafford, making bakelised tubes. These are electrical insulators. The work entailed operating a machine that rolled and glued brown paper. After two weeks I was `promoted` to making cork gaskets for large transformers. I worked with an old chap who had been doing the job for so many years he was part of the furniture, so-to-speak. He always wore his cap.

After about a fortnight, the Personnel Officer came to see me and offered me a job on the staff, working in an accounts office. I accepted my new post and was eventually promoted to supervisor. The work was subsequently computerised. I did not enjoy computer work. It seemed to take away the interesting aspects of the job. I felt as though I was just an extension of a machine, which in effect I was. I finished up keeping the Switchgear Company order book.

The factory had set up their own computer department. I was working in the office one day when the phone rang. It was the head of that department.
"Can you spare a couple of minutes and come over please John?" I left the office and walked over to the computer office.

In that department, they used NCR machines to record and tot up invoices etc . All the machines were operated by women. My sister had started a business in London which used NCR machines. Eventually, together with her business partner, they devised a course on cassette tape, to teach people how to operate one of these machines. The head of the computer department said, "Just listen to this John." He inserted a cassette into the player and handed me a set of earphones. I was amazed. I could hear my sister's voice giving instructions. "Thanks very much for letting me hear that, " I said gratefully. I had not heard the tape before. Now that has all been overtaken by video recorders and DVDs, etc.

I was a member of the factory safety committee. Once a month the committee would go `walk-about`, looking out for safety hazards. I only discovered one and that involved a sand pit. Men filled wheelbarrows with sand and always shovelled it from the bottom of the pit. Eventually the damp sand formed a cave, with several tons suspended in a precarious overhang. I could see there was a danger of the sand collapsing, with the likelihood that someone would be buried without anyone knowing about it until it was too late. I remember that the Safety Officer had a grisly museum - a collection of bits and pieces (some human) from horrendous accidents that had occurred on site. The specimen that stands out in my mind was a long tress of woman's hair. She had apparently been operating a drilling machine and had neglected to tuck her long hair inside her cap. As a result, she ended up being scalped.

*   *   *   *   *

THE SLIP-UP

In 1957 my wife presented me with another lovely daughter, Gillian. Both my daughters were born by Cesarean Section. That same year my grandfather, at the age of ninety, travelled from London to pay us a visit. He arrived on the Friday, but on the Saturday my wife had to go to work in Stafford Market. There were potatoes in the garden which needed lifting, so in the afternoon I decided to fork them up. Before I went into the garden, I asked Grandad if he would like to have a bath. He nodded. I went upstairs and ran the water for him. I couldn't find any bath salts, but I found a packet of Daz washing-powder. I sprinkled a small amount in the water.

I shouted downstairs that his bath was ready. Grandad slowly climbed the stairs. "I will leave you to it Grandad," I said adding, "I am just going into the garden to lift some potatoes."

I had been digging in the garden for about ten minutes, when I suddenly remembered Grandad. I thought that I had better go and see how he was getting on. I shouted up the stairs,
"Are you alright Grandad ?"
"No I'm not," he said in an aggrieved tone of voice. I bounded up the stairs with my wellingtons on.
"What is the matter? " I asked anxiously.
"I can't get out of this damned bath !" he exclaimed.
"Shall I come in ?" I asked.
"Yes come in , come in," he said testily.

I entered the bathroom and, grabbing a large bath towel, wrapped it around his shoulders. He was sitting in the bath but there was no water in it. He had apparently pulled the plug and every time he had tried to stand up, his feet had shot from under him.

I felt guilty over his distress, realising it was my fault. It was the Daz ! That was why he couldn't keep to his feet. When Glad arrived home I told her what had happened. "I suppose you wanted him to be `whiter than white`," she quipped.

*   *   *   *   *

THE BUNGALOW

In the autumn of 1958 a board went up in a Hixon village field. It advertised the proposed building of four detached bungalows on that spot. The site fronted a winding country lane - Stowe Lane, along which it is thought Mary Queen of Scots was taken in 1586 from the manor house at Chartley Castle, just a mile away, to Tixall Gatehouse, some two miles away. My wife and I discussed the possibilities and decided this opportunity was meant for us. We had just enough money to put down the deposit. Now we were happy, but broke.

In the following Spring, the footings were excavated and the bricklaying began. We were extremely fortunate. From the time the first brick was laid to the time the roof was completed, there was no rain - not a drop. That has got to be very unusual in this country. Every lunch-time I would visit the site to see how the work was progressing. We eventually moved in, in the August.

The front and back gardens were large and beyond the back garden was a field, which gave us the peaceful scene of a few grazing horses and cows. The animals were owned by a smallholder, Percy. He knew all his animals by name. He was quite a character.

Percy had a couple of small stables and a cow shed on his smallholding, which was about fifty yards away. He lived in a tiny cottage, situated by the stable yard. One day he saw all his cows were lying down except one. He leaned over the gate and shouted, "Lie down, Daisy." The cow didn't budge. Percy walked over to the back of the animal and somehow managed to ease the back legs from under it and down it went. "Do as you're told, Daisy," he said.

I can remember at Christmas, he gave a present to the young daughter of the family living in the bungalow next door to his cottage. The girl's mother had just made some jam. She approached Percy and said,
"It is very kind of you to buy my daughter a present. Would you like some jam ?"
"Jam, missus !" Percy said. "No thank you. I've got jam in my pantry my mother made forty years ago."

One day, Percy was found collapsed in the yard. He was taken to hospital. He would insist on wearing his cap in bed. Word has it that after he had been there several days, he asked the Sister,
"When can I go home ?"
"When you are better Percy," she replied.
"There is nothing wrong with me that a bit of Germolene won't cure," he said.

Sadly, Percy died some months later. After he died, his tiny cottage was demolished and his animals sold. His field was sold and became a housing estate. A large house now stands where his cottage used to be. All trace of him and his endeavours have been wiped off the face of the earth. It is as though he never was, but I fondly remember him.

The first week in our new bungalow did not pass without incident. The fences had not yet been erected. Our bedroom faced onto a field, backed by the large Manor Farm house opposite. A long drive led from our lane, through a yard to the farmhouse. A large iron gate at the entrance to the farm drive was usually left open. By the yard stood a large barn, in which cattle were kept overnight.

We had been in the bungalow for a few days. On this particular night, at about 1am, my wife woke me.
"What's the matter?" I asked .
"There is someone prowling about," she said worriedly. I slid out of bed and peered through the curtains but failed to see anything in the darkness. I climbed back into bed and lay listening. Suddenly I heard several heavy thumps. I jumped out of bed, put on a dressing gown, went into the kitchen and grabbed a long poker. Unlocking the back door, I stepped out into the dark night.

My next door neighbour Joe's light came on. He appeared, dressed in his night clothes and armed with a broom.

"We've some blessed cows in the garden," he said.

"So that's what woke us," I laughed. The `intruders` were black and white heifers. Joe said, "I don't know who these cows belong to. The Bankhouse has a few black and white heifers and so does Manor Farm opposite."

"So does old Percy on the corner. He has a few," I said.

"I am going to knock Percy up and ask him if he has any missing," Joe said and he walked off down the road.

Meanwhile three cows were still in our gardens, munching whatever they could find. A few minutes later Joe returned.

"They are not Percy's," he said. After a short discussion, we decided to drive the animals into the road. We had to be careful, as there was a ten-foot drop from the end of our front gardens. We managed to get them off our land safely, but what were we going to do with them ? They could not be left on the road in the dark, as they presented a serious traffic hazard. We decided to get them to go into the farm drive. We shut the big iron gate behind them. "The farm will sort things out in the morning," Joe said. We both retired to our beds. I told my wife what we had done and climbed back into bed.

At about 5.30 am, a farm-hand (we called him `the cowboy`) came roaring down the lane on his motorbike. This was the normal start to his day, or so he thought. He attempted to turn into the farm drive as usual, but the gate was shut. Showers of stones shot up as he braked violently. He finished up with the bike laying on its side. Luckily, he was unhurt.

But that was only the beginning of his troubles. He let the large herd of cows out of the cowshed onto the yard, not realising there were already three loose heifers about. They soon mingled with the main herd. It was not long before it was realised there were some `foreigners` in their midst - possibly spotted by their coloured ear-tags.

By this time the farmer had joined in. The two men had a job to segregate the three wayward cows, but looking through our curtains it was very amusing to watch. It never did come to light as to whose cows they were. They certainly gave us a sleepless night and an entertaining early morning.

*   *   *   *   *

A REORGANISATION

It was a bright sunny day in 1959 and not the sort of day to be at work. In the Laboratories, it was suggested by the Works Manager that I should reorganise the stores. Jobs were being held up because certain materials could not be found. As this work was in addition to my normal work I went home in the evening as usual, but returned to the site at 19.00 hrs.

I was busy applying new shelf codes to the stores` racking, when who should walk in but the Director, accompanied by the Head of Administration.

"What are you doing here ?" asked the Director.

"I am reorganising the stores Mr Bunting," I said.

"Who told you to do that?" he shouted excitedly.

"The Works Manager, Mr Bunting," I replied.

"I don`t want the stores reorganising," he bellowed, thumping a fist into the palm of his hand. I could feel the hairs starting to stand up on the back of my neck. `Keep calm,` I thought, `Keep calm.`

"Mr Bunting," I said firmly, "In the Navy we always obeyed the last order given." He turned to the Head of Admin` and said,

"This man is trying to run the place like a ruddy ship!" I couldn`t resist it. Trying not to sound too sarcastic, I said

"The Navy did have some very well run ships Mr Bunting. The Admin` Head winked at me knowingly. I just said, "Goodnight gentlemen" and walked out into the darkness and headed for home. At work the next day, not another word was said about it. Not even by the Works Manager. No apology, no discussion. What a set-up.

*   *   *   *   *

METEOROLOGICAL SABOTAGE

The Laboratory ex-RAF motor transport building was the pride and joy of the Director of Research, Mr Bunting. He had the wide gaps between the roof brick support columns blanked off with large prefabricated wooden panels. This converted the gaping MT building into a useful, closed-in, spacious machine-shop. It incorporated a caged storeroom. I thought it was a good idea.

Unfortunately and I think it was in 1960, a severe gale blew up. Powerful gusts struck the village. One such gust hit the MT building. A sudden change in pressure, sucked out the prefabricated panels and rendered them unusable. As a result, the worst possible chaos was inflicted on the workshop and stores.

All the paperwork - invoices, orders, drawings etc, exited the building and were last seen whirling through the air over Hixon. Mr Bunting frantically sent out a party of men to search the village for them, but very few were retrieved.

*   *   *   *   *

CAUSING AN OBSTRUCTION

Although I had passed my driving test whilst still in the Navy, it was eight years before I drove regularly. I knew very little about cars, except the operating principles of the internal combustion engine. So it did not come as a complete surprise when my first purchase in 1963, a pre-war Ford Ten, managed to travel the six miles from Stafford, before collapsing in the drive. The suspension had gone. That taught me a lesson.

My next three cars were a 850cc Morris Minor, a 1000cc Morris Minor and then a Mini Traveller. That last one was a fantastic little car and would fetch a handsome price today. All the cars were second-hand.

After driving the Mini for two years, I could at last afford a brand new car. I believed in supporting the British car industry, so I bought an Austin 1100cc sports saloon. It looked very smart, with spoke wheels and chromed bumpers. Unfortunately for me, all that glittered was not gold.

My normal routine on a Friday was to meet my wife returning from work, drive her into Stafford, park the car and then we would shop together. On this particular Friday I picked her up in the new Austin, but things did not go according to plan.

I drove into the heart of Stafford. On the way to the car park I had to stop at some traffic lights. There was just one car in front. When the lights changed, I tried to put the car into gear. The gear stick stirred about like a pudding spoon.

"What`s the matter?" Glad asked.

"This," I said, lifting the gear lever and waving it about. Luckily the car had stuck in first gear and so I was able to drive it slowly to the car park.

"What are you going to do John?" Glad asked, consternation showing on her face.

"I am going to drive it back to Hixon Garage where I bought it," I replied.

We completed our shopping and returned to the car. I drove it the seven miles, stuck in first gear, but the journey home was unusual for another reason. To leave town, we always followed the same route. I was driving down a narrow street, Mill Street, in Stafford. Because of parked vehicles, there was not enough room for both lanes of traffic to pass and today of all days, a fire-engine raced towards us with lights flashing and siren blaring. My heart sank.

I stopped the car but was unable to reverse. The fire-engine screeched to a halt. There was not enough room for it to pass. My wife was getting quite agitated. "Don`t worry Glad I`ll sort things out," I said, although mentally I was wondering what to do. Two irate firemen jumped down, one waving an axe, the other waving his arms and gesticulating that he wanted me to get out of the way. As they walked angrily up to the car, I wound down the window.

"Get out of the way," one of them shouted in my right ear. "Can`t you see we are trying to get to a fire?" This was more of a statement than a question.

"I`m sorry but I haven`t any gears so I can`t move," I said, apologetically.

"Then how did you get here?" one said disbelievingly. I waved the wayward gear stick at him.

"Blimey he`s right!" he said and added, "Let`s give him a shove," and with my foot depressing the clutch, they managed to move our car out of the way.

We slowly continued our journey, during which time I prayed that another situation would not arise where I needed to reverse. I said to my wife,

"Out of all the times we`ve been down that road Glad, this would happen when a fire-engine is trying to get to a fire."

Three months later the paint was peeling from around the side lights of the Austin.

"That`s the last time I buy a British car," I said. Since then I have always patronised Renaults. Spares are expensive, but their cars are comfortable and economical and after driving them for years, I have never been stranded.

When it came to changing our car, my wife was very superstitious. As I left the house she remarked, "Don't buy a green one and the registration number must not add up to thirteen."

*   *   *   *   *

A LOAD OF BULL

In 1965, being a keen gardener, there were not many days when I was not working outside, trying to improve the landscape. The bungalow being a detached property, had a small alleyway between our garage and the neighbour`s garage. This led from the front drive to the back garden.

I was forking over a raised rose bed in the back garden, when I heard a commotion coming from the drive. Several children were exercising their lungs with excited shouts. I strode over to the garage and peered round the corner down the alley, to see what mischief they were up to. I was in for a shock. I came face to face with an enormous bull ! I raised the fork level with the bull`s nose and lunged towards it, not to harm it, but to prevent it from getting into the back garden and more importantly, to protect myself.

The bull tried to turn round in the alleyway but there wasn`t enough room. Its large haunches boomed against the walls of both garages. I had visions of them collapsing at any moment . With the children still shouting behind the animal, it wasn`t at all keen to back off. "Children run down the drive," I shouted urgently. This they did. Again I lunged with the fork and the animal then backed off, extricating itself from the narrow space. It swung round and lumbered back to the road, much to my relief. The children had scattered.

It turned out that the animal was being transported by trailer. As a Land Rover was towing the trailer up a nearby hill, the trailer door had dropped down and the bull had tumbled out into the road. I got the impression that the children knew whose bull it was. Anyway I did not see anything more of the bull, nor of the children, so I assumed it had been caught.

In the same year, two other things come to mind which I consider are worth a mention. We used to visit my mother in Folkestone for a holiday. I always carried a camera but typical of fate, on this occasion I forgot it. We entered an arcade which boasted the usual petty gambling games. I suddenly spotted three nuns playing on a `one-armed bandit`. We were amazed. I have regretted not having had my camera with me on that occasion ever since.

The second event worth mentioning for that year, is the fact that I received a summons from the Chief Constable of Nottingham for a parking offence. I had never been to Nottingham in my life. Luckily, or unluckily depending on how you look at it, that year the village policeman, the village garage owner and myself caught chicken pox, all at the age of forty. It is not an illness that I would recommend to any adult. It was very unpleasant. Intolerable itching, especially on the head, blistery spots and worst of all, blisters in the mouth and throat. I was off work for nearly a month, but the day I went back was the day I was reputed to be in Nottingham. I saw the doctor that morning. He declared me fit and I went straight back to work. Using my clock card, I clocked in at precisely the time I was alleged to have committed the parking offence.

I wrote to the Chief Constable explaining the facts and received a reply saying there had obviously been a mistake. I did not receive an apology however.

* * * * *

CHAPTER TWENTY FIVE

THE POWER OF A TORNADO

If I remember rightly, it was in September 1967, at about 7.45am. I was having a shave in the bathroom and my wife was in the kitchen, preparing breakfast. The weather was a mixture of sunshine and showers. The sky rapidly darkened. Without any warning a terrific wind suddenly sprang up. My wife cried out. I ran into the kitchen, with shaving soap still on my face.

"The wind !" she cried in a terrified voice. I could see it was bad. The rain was being atomised. It hurtled past the window horizontally as a fine mist, at very high speed. The bungalow seemed to shake. The noise was terrific.

"It`s only a wind," I said, trying to sound unconcerned, but I was very worried. I resumed my shave.

Just then my wife cried out again.

"It`s gone, it`s gone !" she yelled. I rushed back into the kitchen.

"What`s gone?" I asked. Glad pointed.

"Joe`s pergola."

Joe, our neighbour, had built a strong pergola to support several climbing roses. The structure consisted of high brick support columns, with substantial overhead timber cross-beams. The latter were bolted to the tops of the columns. My wife was looking directly at the structure when the wind took the first two columns. She described how they first went in the middle and then the entire open structure collapsed. Thirty seconds after that incident, the wind had died almost completely.

We had experienced a tornado and were very lucky that the roof was still intact. It fetched oak trees down on the Chartley Estate, just a mile away. Earlier Chris, one of our future son-in-laws, had looked out of the window towards Hixon, from his father`s pub, the Fox Inn in the next village Great Haywood. He described seeing a dark, cone-shaped, moving column, which descended from the sky as it approached Hixon.

I examined my back garden and discovered a narrow strip, no more than ten feet wide, where the `twister` had tracked across the ground. Every plant had been decimated, just as though someone had taken a scythe to them. It was interesting to note, plants further up the garden had not been touched. On my way to work, I had to steer round a hawthorn bush, which had previously been growing on top of a roadside bank at the edge of a field. It had been torn out of the ground.

Alf Ides, the landlord of the Bankhouse pub, had walked down to the field to fetch his cows, when the tornado struck.

"The cows stampeded," he said. "Tiles were flying from the roofs of the Council houses lower down in the village and were landing in the field, like a shower of meteorites. I didn`t know whether to lie down, or run for my life."

CHAPTER TWENTY SIX

THE HIXON RAIL DISASTER

On Saturday January 6th 1968, I was busily engaged in loading the car boot with perennial plants and a couple of small shrubs. These had been promised to my friends the Lloyds, of Stafford. The last plant was just being loaded when George, my neighbour, approached. We were passing the time of day, when suddenly there was the most strange loud noise coming from the direction of the new continental railway crossing. I can only describe it as a sort of roaring noise, a bit like a jet fighter or a skip-full of metal parts being tipped out.

Across the road was a large milking shed, which obscured our view.
"What was that?" George said.
"It seemed to come from the crossing," I replied. Even as I spoke, a huge mushroom of dust rose in the air from beyond the shed. "I`m just going into Stafford, so I will see what has happened," I said.

I drove through the village towards the crossing. The railway crossing cut across a mile-long straight road leading out of Hixon towards Stafford. I was shocked to see many people walking up the road, some with bloodied faces. There had been a terrible train crash.

As I neared the crossing, I could see that the last two coaches of a Manchester to Euston Inter-City express were still on the track, the tail-end one straddling the road. It turned out later that there were about two hundred passengers on board. The train consisted of an electric diesel locomotive, pulling some nine to ten carriages.

At the same time as the train approached, a 140-feet long, sixty-ton, multi-wheeled low-transporter lorry, with a pusher and a puller and manned by a crew of five, was half way across the crossing, progressing at 2mph. To make matters worse, the lorry was carrying a 120-ton transformer from Newport to Hixon. There was a police escort.

At such crossings there is a telephone, which is connected to the nearest manned signal-box. It enables people who are driving large or slow transport over the crossing to inform the signal-box of this fact. The signalman of course, would then set the signals down the line to stop all trains until the obstruction had cleared the crossing. Whether this was done for this transporter lorry, I cannot say, but as the load had a police escort, I find it hard to imagine that this was not done.

The train hurtled round a curved track and the driver would only have seen the obstruction when it was too late to brake in time. The train struck the transporter lorry at 75 to 80mph, cutting it in two. The huge transformer was lifted into the air and deposited, coincidentally, on the exact spot beside the track where a crossing keeper`s house had recently been demolished. Installing the new continental crossing had made the keeper redundant. The locomotive and several carriages veered off the track to the right and into a field. Four of the carriages, which came to rest at crazy angles, formed an enclosed diamond-shaped barrier in the field. Three carriages were very badly shattered.

I parked my car at the side of the road and ran round the tail-end of the carriage that was still on the crossing. I ran into the field to see what I could do to help. I must have been one of the first villagers on the scene, because no ambulances or any of the other emergency services had arrived by that time. I was shocked at the horrendous scene of destruction and carnage before me. I made my way inside the diamond of shattered carriages. Hardly any grass was visible. It was almost completely covered by debris. I came across a semi-conscious woman, lying on her back. She had the whole of one shin cleaved of flesh, from knee to ankle. She was moaning, "My husband, my husband."

I went to search for something I could use as a stretcher. I clambered between two carriages resting precariously and was shocked to discover a protruding white hand belonging to some poor victim lying crushed beneath. It was obvious they were dead. Perhaps it was the woman`s husband.

Just as a man was approaching, I found a proper stretcher. We managed to get the women onto it. Next we needed to move her out of the area of shattered carriages. We saw an upright carriage, with a gaping, torn doorway in its side (Page 185). The man climbed through the gap and said, "We could get her through here." He jumped down and helped me to lift the stretcher, until one end rested on the carriage floor. We slid it into the carriage with some difficulty. Then, we both climbed into the carriage. We could not get her through the doorway on the far side. It had been narrowed by the force of the impact. Surprisingly, the windows on that side were still unbroken. I looked around for something heavy. There were a lot more people arriving by now and I could hear the sound of rescue helicopters. Just then a railwayman arrived. I shouted down to him, "Can you chuck me up that piece of metal?" He heaved it up into the carriage. It turned out to be a piece of shattered bogey and was very heavy.

I shouted to stand clear and swung the lump of metal at a window. It bounced off. I tried again. This time the window shattered. The man assisting me jumped down and helped to manhandle the stretcher through the window. Others, now standing below, joined in. The woman was carried alongside the torn-up track and pushed under the last coach, to a waiting ambulance on the other side. I have often wondered how that unfortunate woman got on.

It was very noticeable that amongst the helpers were one or two youths who were regarded as the trouble-makers of the village. Now look at them, mucking in with the rest. The trouble with some youths would soon disappear, if they were given something worthwhile to become involved in, but it is up to their parents to guide them in the right direction. The goodness in all of us always becomes apparent at such times.

I went back into the field and offered my help to the Police Superintendent directing rescue operations, but he declined. It was quite a coincidence that only a week before, the County had set up a helicopter emergency service. It must have been a terrible shock for the policemen escorting the wide load, when the crash occurred. Many of the more seriously injured were ferried by helicopter to Stafford Hospital.

As I was returning to my car, I noticed a man standing quietly at the roadside. Two little girls were clutching his hands, pale faced and looking distressed. He turned out to be a Mr Harold Tunnicliffe of Atherton, Manchester, their grandfather. He was taking his granddaughters back to their mother in South Harrow. The girls

Page 185. An aerial view of the Hixon Train Crash, showing the carriage window-exit used for a stretcher victim. The point of impact on the huge transformer and the severed road transporter can be clearly seen. *(photo by permission of Mirrorpix)*

were each clutching a doll they had had for Christmas. I said to Mr Tunnicliffe
"I live in the village. You can come with me for a coffee and then I will take you to
Stafford Station and put you on a train for Euston." He expressed his gratitude.

As I was about to get in the car, I saw a schoolgirl passenger standing on her own.
She was carrying a bag and a hockey stick.
"You can come with us. We are going to get a train for Euston from Stafford," I said.
At first she walked towards us, but then suddenly let out terrible, hysterical screams. I
asked a women standing by her garden gate to take the child under her care. It was
very distressing.

I introduced the man and his two granddaughters to my wife and after coffee we
set off. Because of the train crash, I had to take a diversionary route, but managed to
reach the station. I explained their circumstance to the ticket collector. We were in
luck.
"That train standing at Platform No.1 will be leaving any minute for Euston," he said.
Things could not have been better. As they boarded I waved them goodbye. I read in a
newspaper the next day that they were the first passengers from the disaster to reach
Euston, where the little girls were swept into the arms of their anxiously waiting
mother.

Sadly twelve people died in the crash, including the driver. Thirty were seriously
injured and many more had minor injuries.

The following day, Sunday, the village was swamped by `gawpers` and `ghouls`.
People were even picnicking on the grass verges and this was in early January. My
wife and I could not believe it. I remember on the Monday, seeing many railway men
in driving snow, trying to cope with the wrecked carriages and the enormous volume
of debris scattered about in what, three days before, had been a peaceful rural setting.

The crossing warning time from the time the flashing lights and warning bells
starting, to the barriers actually beginning to come down was only eight seconds.
There was a further eight seconds allowed for the barriers to come down completely.
Then there was another eight seconds before the train would reach the crossing;
twenty four seconds for the whole operation. As a result of the Inquiry into this
horrendous accident the total crossing operation time was increased to twenty seven
seconds. That doesn't seem much of a time difference, but when you consider that
these trains are traveling at 75-80mph at that crossing, the difference of four seconds
equates to a considerable track-travel distance. From then on this new crossing
operating time was applied to all such crossings throughout the country.

*   *   *   *   *

CHAPTER TWENTY SEVEN

BLOOD ON THE CARPET

I believe it was still in 1968 that I had an `argument` with a circular saw. It was on a Sunday. I was using the saw to shorten some lengths of wood. The work was progressing smoothly for a while, but then disaster struck. Suddenly one end of a long piece of wood caught on something in the garage. It caused my thumb to swing into the rotating blade. There was an almighty bang and I knew I had done some nasty damage.

I stopped the machine, clamped my hand over the injured thumb and ran into the house.

"Can you get me a towel quick Glad," I said urgently.

"What have you done?" she asked, anxiously. She was turning very pale. Blood was dripping on the kitchen floor from my elbow.

"Please don`t faint on me Glad," I said. She ran and found a clean towel.

When I first did the damage I didn`t feel a thing, but now I was in agony. I wrapped the towel round my hand and jumped into the car. The doctors, a husband and wife team, lived in the next village Great Haywood, about three miles away. I drove the car more or less with one hand and an elbow. Blood was dripping everywhere, on the floor, the seat and onto my lap.

The wife of the practice opened the door.

"What have you done John?" she asked. She led me to the surgery and started to unwrap the towel. She had nearly removed it but some of the blood had congealed and dried. The towel was stuck on an exposed nerve. She bathed it with cold water and the towel came free, much to my relief.

Just then, her doctor husband entered.

"What`s John been up to?" he asked his wife. She told him.

"Have you stitched it ?" he asked.

"No, there is nothing left to stitch," she replied. The saw had exposed the end of the bone. "All I can do is bandage it and give you some antibiotic powder," she said.

The next day I set off for work, in much pain. I had had little sleep. At lunchtime I made my way to the dining hall and sat opposite a young man from the office, Arnold. He asked me what I had done to my hand and I explained. While I was eating blood suddenly started to ooze from the bandage. Almost at once Arnold keeled over face down onto his meal.

It is strange how some people cannot stand the sight of blood. My wife couldn`t. She was even unable to watch medical operations being performed on the `tele`.

*   *   *   *   *

CHAPTER TWENTY EIGHT

THE CANNON-BALL

In 1972, my wife and I were sitting in the drawing room of a very old cottage. It is situated in the village of Salt (Staffordshire) which is nearly three miles from Hixon. The cottage belonged to a work colleague of ours, Arthur. He was badly disabled owing to suffering from a deformed spine, which forced him to walk bent at a severe angle.

My attention was drawn to a small stand on the mantelpiece. I puzzled over its purpose.
"What is the stand for Arthur?" I asked.
"Oh, that," he said. "Well I was digging the garden and found a cannon-ball, so for a long time I displayed it on the mantelpiece. "This immediately aroused my interest, because I knew that on the higher ground overlooking the village, a bloody battle had taken place in 1643, between Oliver Cromwell`s Roundheads and the Royalist Cavaliers - the Battle of Hopton Heath. During the battle, 4-inch cannon were used, so I thought it very likely Arthur`s cannon-ball could be a relic from that battle.
"Where is it now Arthur?" I asked.
"Oh, my mother got fed up with it when she was dusting, so I chucked it on the rubbish heap." I was very surprised at this and said,
"I would have thought the Staffordshire Sealed Knot Society {a group of dedicated people who re-enact skirmishes of the Civil War) would be very pleased to have it, if you don`t want it Arthur."
"Well, he said, if you like, you can dig it up."
I promptly grabbed a spade and eagerly sallied forth into the garden.
"Where abouts was your rubbish heap?" I asked.
"I`ve had several but I think it was there," Arthur replied, pointing.

Full of enthusiasm, I started to dig. All sorts of rubbish appeared, but no cannon-ball. I continued digging and eventually struck something hard. It was not the cannon-ball, but the brick floor of an old pig sty.

I had uncovered a piece of history, but not what I was looking for.
"I am surprised you haven`t found it, said Arthur, but I`ve been thinking about it and I remember, I also had a rubbish heap over there," indicating another spot. After much strenuous and patient digging, no cannon-ball was found in that area either.

Eventually, after digging up most of Arthur`s garden, there was only one area I hadn`t touched, against a wall where an old English climbing rose was growing.
"What about there Arthur?" I asked, pointing.
"Well yes, I did have a rubbish heap there at one time, but I couldn`t possibly let you dig there because I really prize that rose," he said.

So after all my efforts, no cannon-ball was found, but at least Arthur had most of his garden dug over and, I might add, to quite a depth. Poor Arthur has since passed on, but I like to think the cannon-ball is still beneath his beautiful climbing rose and that perhaps, he is looking down on his garden with a broad smile of satisfaction.

*   *   *   *   *

A CHANGE FOR THE BETTER

In 1974, at the age of forty nine and after nineteen years with the same firm, I didn`t seem to be making any further progress. Admittedly while I worked there I had been promoted to supervisor, but after that nothing changed. For nearly the whole of the previous year I had patiently scanned the employment ads` in the local newspapers. One day my eyes were tracking down the columns when I suddenly spotted an advert for a supervisor`s job at a local power station.
"I could do that," I said to myself.

My qualifications and experience seemed to meet their requirements, so I applied for the job. I was short-listed. Only one other applicant was interviewed at the final interview. He was a much younger man than I. He smoked a pipe and looked intelligent and full of confidence. I felt flat. He was summoned into the room first. When he came out his expression told me nothing. He walked past me, looking straight ahead and without speaking. After all I was the opposition.

Now it was my turn. I took a seat in front of three `inquisitors`. If the interview had been held many years earlier, I would have broken out in an uncomfortable sweat. Since then life has taught me to avoid ducking and diving and to try and stay calm. It is better to meet things head on. With an outward display of confidence I said, "Good morning gentlemen," to which all three responded in kind. Now the ice had been broken, I immediately genuinely felt a touch more confident.

After several questions, all shrewd, some out of inquisitive interest and some very testing to see how I would respond, I was asked to express my opinion on the duties of a supervisor.
"In my opinion gentlemen, a supervisor should not just sit on his backside giving out orders, but rather should get involved in the work of the department to such an extent that he can perform every task of those personnel he purports to supervise. Only then will he be in a position to control the running of the department, to compensate for sickness and absenteeism, by applying energies directly to those aims which would otherwise suffer." Writing this now, it sounds terribly pompous.

Eyebrows raised ! The `inquisitors` gazed knowingly at one another and then one said, as though talking to an old friend,
"I see you have put down `woodcarving` as one of your hobbies. Tell me how you go about this." It turned out that he made violins in his spare time. When once I learned of this, he had my instant respect. From that moment I was almost certain I had got the job. A letter dropped on our doormat a few days later which confirmed this. My wife and I went out to celebrate. I only regretted I had not made such a move years before, but that is all `water under the bridge` now.

*   *   *   *   *

MAN IN A HOLE

In 1972 my sister bought an interesting old house at the back of Hastings, on the heights, going towards Battle. There was a flagpole in the garden. She could look down into the valley, where there was another house with a flagpole. By doing some research in the local library, it came to light that in the 17th Century the house had belonged to a judge. As well as dispensing justice he had also had a darker side - smuggling !

My sister`s partner Dennis deduced that the flagpoles had been used for signalling, probably to give warning of approaching Excise men. Within their boundary hedge they discovered the remnants of a Roman wall. I was quite excited about this. The place seemed to be steeped in history.

Quite near to the wall was a strange, brick-lined, circular pit, about nine feet deep. The diameter was too large for it to be a well. We pondered on its purpose. It was a complete enigma. At the bottom was a layer of soil. I had suggested it might have been used for storing blocks of ice, but then again, I might have been barking up the wrong tree.

In the end, curiosity got the better of me. I had to try to get to the bottom of it, literally. I offered to clean out the pit. Dennis fetched some steps. I took a spade down with me. I asked Dennis to pull up the ladder, as I didn`t want it to get in the way. Pat, Dennis and my wife Glad left me to it and returned to the house, where apparently my sister produced a bottle of wine and some glasses.

Meanwhile I started digging, throwing the soil over the rim. I noticed the bricks were very old. I also noticed something else. I suddenly became aware of some very strange shiny spiders, slowly appearing from cavities between the old brickwork. There were more than a dozen of them. Whether the warmth of my body was encouraging them to break cover I cannot say, but I certainly did not appreciate their company. I had never encountered this species of spider before. They were milk-chocolate brown in colour, had a smooth exoskeleton (like a crab) and were so slow in their movements that it was like watching a slow-motion film. I am an arachnophobe. I cannot bear to look at large spiders, especially if they are moving rapidly and not necessarily in my direction. To me they look evil and I dread August and September, when the large house spiders invade my house. Because of their slow movements, I had little fear of the spiders in the pit.

Eventually I managed to remove all the soil. The bottom was bowl-shaped and in good order. I decided it must have had some sort of storage purpose. Now that I had completed the task I was ready to get out. Unfortunately for me, Dennis had not left the steps near enough to the edge for me to jump up and grab them. I was trapped ! I shouted, but nobody came. As the women`s voices were getting louder by the minute, I imagined that the wine bottle was now empty by about two thirds. What with their raucous laughter and also the background music to contend with, I found it impossible to make my voice heard. The wine was working wonders, though not for me. I continued to holler, without success, but suddenly they realised I was missing and remembered where I was. They all rushed out to the pit to rescue me. By that time, the wine bottle was empty.

*   *   *   *   *

SLOW IN THE FAST LANE

Our holidays were often spent with my mother, on the south coast, where she lived. When starting a holiday, I usually drove to Stafford late at night to get onto the M6 on the other side of town. Setting off on this particular holiday, we followed our usual route through Stafford. This time we came up behind a car being driven by an elderly man, who seemed to find it an exertion to travel at more than 25 mph. Owing to oncoming traffic, I was unable to overtake and so we patiently dawdled through the town behind him.

Eventually the car in front reached the feeder road to Junction 13 of the M6. We were amused to see the car proceed up the feeder road, *still* doing 25 mph. I found it impossible to pass him, as he was half in and half out of his lane. I also was forced to feed onto the motorway at 25 mph. I did not like to do this. As every driver knows, when you feed onto a motorway you should be doing a good speed, so as to match the speed of the motorway traffic.

As I slowly drove up the feeder lane, I was suddenly aware of two dim headlights behind me. After slowing for a lorry on the motorway, I drove onto it. Half a mile on a police Range Rover overtook me and signalled me to stop on the hard shoulder. I slowed down from 70 mph and stopped behind the police vehicle.

A stroppy police sergeant approached the car and tapped on the window. I wound it down.
"Can I help you officer?" I said.
"Yes. I am a bit concerned about your driving sir," he said.
"What is wrong with my driving Sergeant?" I asked.
"When feeding onto a motorway your speed should match the speed of the motorway traffic." Of course as I said before, I was aware of this.
"There was this old bloke in front of me doing about 25 mph," I explained. "Also, there was a lorry -."
"There was no lorry behind you," he interrupted.
"No I mean there was a lorry..." I had intended to say, "coming down the motorway," but I received a sharp nudge from my wife and bit on my words. Diplomatically I said, "Thank you for your advice Sergeant." He walked back to his vehicle. We did think it unusual that he was on his own. I can only assume he'd had a bad day .

I turned to my wife in disgust and said, "What the hell am I supposed to do? You are always telling me to slow down and now the police are telling me to speed up?" After I had calmed down, we both looked at each other and burst out laughing.

*   *   *   *   *

THE DO-IT-YOURSELFER

During the 70s, my father rented a three-storey house in Bath. The basement was converted into a hairdressing salon, which was my step-mother Eileen`s trade. Occasionally we travelled down the A38, turning off for Stroud and Bath. The M5 didn`t exist then, so the journey from Stafford took at least six hours.

One weekend we were introduced to one of Eileen`s sisters and her husband, John. He was a retired Irishman, quite a jovial man. We were sitting in my father`s lounge, when I suggested that I would make them a `cuppa`. I went into the kitchen, to boil the kettle, but I noticed a strong smell of gas. I informed my father and he and John both went downstairs to the basement to turn off the gas. At first they could not find the valve key. Eventually they found the key and used it. They also rang the Gas Board, while we opened all the windows.

Meanwhile I had started to take up the kitchen floorboards, because I suspected the leak was somewhere under the floor. I shouted down to my father,
"Release the valve, Dad." He turned the supply on, temporarily, but I could not find a leak in the floor space. "Turn it off again," I shouted. I began to nail the floorboards back in place, just as John entered the kitchen.
"Here, let me do that," he said in his jovial way. I passed him the hammer and nails.

"Doesn`t he think I`m capable ?" I thought. "Be careful where you knock those nails in John. There are lead pipes under there," I said.

John happily hammered away and soon the boards were back in place. Just then the gasman arrived. He examined the cooker and detected a leak, which he repaired before going on his way. As he left, he said, "Don`t light anything until the gas has had time to disperse." We went to the family next door and told them what had happened. They said they could smell gas too.

I returned to the kitchen. The smell of gas seemed to be worse than ever. Suddenly I realised there was a hissing sound coming from under the floorboards. Not only had John driven a nail into a lead gas-pipe, but he had also driven a nail into a water pipe. Up came the floorboards again. I asked John to warn the neighbours again. I bunged the gas leak with some soap, but it was useless trying to do that to the water pipe. John returned, huffing and puffing. He reached into his pocket for a packet of fags. I stopped him lighting up just in time. Was he completely mad ?

Both the gas and the water were now turned off. The gas was bound to have seeped under the floorboards of the next door property too. It was a dangerous situation. The same gas fitter and then a plumber turned up. After about an hour things were back to normal. It was not exactly the best way to spend a Sunday afternoon.

*   *   *   *   *

CHAPTER TWENTY NINE

THE SAILING CLUB

After starting work at Rugeley Power Station in 1974, I soon found out what an excellent social club it had. There were several sports facilities, including a nine-hole golf course. On a small pond by the Social Club building, radio-controlled model yachts were raced to RYA rules (Royal Yachting Association). There were actually two power stations on the site : `A` and `B`. When I first arrived there, a 16-acre lake, situated near the entrance to the `A` Station and known as the Borrow Pit lake, was an ideal water sports facility, but was only used by fishermen.

The Borrow Pit was originally a gravel pit and was the aggregate source for building the larger and more modern `B` Station. It had slowly filled from the local natural water table and from surface water which seeped from Cannock Chase, to form a lake some 49 feet deep.

With the cooperation of the CEGB and the Station Manager, a few members of the Social Club (including myself) inaugurated a sailing club. And so in 1976, the Rugeley Electricity Sailing Club was born. I took on the task of Secretary and during the next twelve years I saw the club grow from a few members and no facilities, to a successful club with nearly seventy members and seventeen sailing dinghies. Sailing is a true `family sport`, as you can all be in the same boat, literally.

Eventually, a sailing room for changing and stowing our gear, a slipway and a jetty were added. Obviously these facilities could not be acquired all at once. When once we had a rescue boat, which was paid for by the main Social Club, no sailing was allowed to take place unless the manned rescue boat was standing by. The Sailing Club was now properly up and running.

A great deal of pleasure was experienced on that stretch of water, but there was also a more serious side to the sailing activities. A senior sailing instructor of the RYA, Don Harding, together with his wife Shirley, used to organise weekend sailing courses for non-sailing employees of the Central Electricity Generating Board. The safety aspect of these courses was always of paramount importance and each course was supported by several sailing instructors.

My wife decided to buy me a sailing dinghy. I managed to acquire an old Merlin Rocket, a clinker-built, wooden, racing dinghy - Sail No.1166. A Merlin Rocket was considered amongst the sailing fraternity to be somewhat `hairy`. It deserved such a reputation. During the first year of the club, I unintentionally capsized her several times and was labelled `the fishermen`s friend`. When once I got the hang of the technical niceties of sailing however, I was able to take her out to plane the water in a Force 7. After that I was invited to instruct on the weekend sailing courses. On a few occasions my wife presented the prizes and trophies to race winners.

Because the courses became so successful, some extra dinghies had to be brought on site. The instructors preferred to teach in their own boats. They towed them from all parts of the Midlands. The jetty was not big enough to accommodate all of these, so I obtained permission to put down a pebble beach.

I always remember an incident when two very attractive blond identical twins, Jane and Janet, asked me if they could try out my dinghy on their own. They had very little knowledge of how to handle a boat. As there was only a light breeze I agreed. `This will be fun,` I thought. It was !

They managed to do just about everything wrong and the result was a boat that was going round and round in small circles and getting nowhere. Members who witnessed this from the shore were in stitches. Jane and Janet still keep in touch. Their Dad, John, is one of my best friends. Jane used to crew regularly for me. John used to bring his daughter to the lake to sail . He enjoyed sitting in his car and watching our sailing skills. I think he found it relaxing.

*   *   *   *   *

THREE IN A BOAT

In 1976, before the Sailing Club had even acquired a changing room, I invited nephew Anthony Barlow and a friend of the family, Laura Gray, to an afternoon of sailing. Anthony is a big bloke and was at one time, until he suffered a dislocated shoulder, captain of the Stafford Rugby Team. Both he and Laura crewed the Merlin and I took the helm. Laura let it be known that she had no previous sailing experience.

We rigged the boat and floated her. I invited the crew to board. I told them to each hold a jib-sheet. I hoisted and secured the mainsail. I explained what they were required to do. Then I pulled in the main sheet and the sails filled. We were underway.

It was a bright afternoon with a fresh breeze blowing from the south ; ideal conditions for sailing. The crew was expected to balance the boat. That is, as the boat was heeled over by the wind, they countered this by leaning their backs over the side to the wind. So, if a boat went about (changed direction through the wind) the wind would now blow on the opposite side. If the crew did not move their weight quickly enough to the other side of the boat, they would cause the heeling angle to increase and the boat would become unbalanced and was likely to capsize.

We had been sailing up and down the lake on a broad reach for about an hour and a half, when suddenly, as we went about, the crew did not balance the boat properly and we capsized. We were all flung into the water. The Merlin completely turned turtle, with her mast now pointing straight down towards the bed of the lake. Although now upside down, she stayed afloat, because of buoyancy bags strapped within her hull.

In this situation, it is the job of the helm to right the boat. He does this by checking the rudder is secure. Next, he extends the centreboard(keel), grabs a sheet (a rope attached to a sail) and applies his weight to the centreboard with his feet, arching his back at the same time. The dinghy should slowly rise to firstly lie on its side. He can now free any secured sheets and allow the crew to lie horizontally within the boat, so that they can be scooped up when the boat starts to assume a vertical stance. The boat`s bow should be pointing into the wind. Now the helmsman can continue to apply his weight to right the boat. The mast should continue to rise until secondly the dinghy has completely righted itself. At the same time (hopefully) the crew should now have been scooped up inside the boat.

Now the boat is upright but full of water, some frantic bailing is required. If the helm can sail the boat, he opens the self-bailers. The forward movement will cause the self-bailers to suck out the water, but the boat has to have sufficient way before the self-bailers can become effective. When once the water has gone, the self-bailers must be closed otherwise, should the boat lose speed, water will start to ingress again. The entire procedure for righting a sailing dinghy varies, according to the class of dinghy and the conditions prevailing at the time, but basically the method is the same.

When we capsized, I suddenly realised I could not see Laura.

"Is Laura on your side Anthony?" I shouted, anxiously.

"Can't see her," he replied.

"She must be under the boat," I said. Although the Merlin was completely upside down, because of her buoyancy there is a sufficient airspace within the hull to enable a person to keep their head above water. Laura's head should be in that airspace, unless she was rendered unconscious as the result of a blow to the head.

Frantically, I attempted to right the boat by applying my weight to the centreboard. As the dinghy came up onto its side, with the mast now lying horizontal, Laura swam out. "Wasn't that fun?" she said calmly, just as though it was an everyday occurrence for her. I was amazed. I had imagined she would be quite terrified beneath the upturned hull, especially as she had never sailed before. It was a pleasant surprise to see her courageous reaction to the situation and she certainly gained our respect. While a crew member is under the hull, they can easily duck-dive beneath the gunwale and come up outside the hull, but perhaps Laura did not realise this. Not many modern dinghies turn turtle. Most lie on their side, but my boat had a mind of its own. Sometimes it did and sometimes it didn't.

Laura did not get off scot-free. As we capsized, she had sustained a nasty blow to her knee. By the time she arrived home her knee was so badly swollen she could not bend it sufficiently to climb her front doorstep. Her husband Tom had to assist her. Hard knocks are common . They come with the sport but are not often badly felt, because one's skin is cool and usually wet.

Indirectly it was as a result of that capsize that a changing room was allocated to the club. Obviously all three of us were soaked and had to change into dry clothes. Laura changed in my car, while Anthony and I turned our backs to her and stood `guard`, like true gentlemen. This was an unsatisfactory arrangement that could only be considered as temporary, until we had the proper facilities.

$$* \quad * \quad * \quad * \quad *$$

IN THE DRINK

It was, I think, during the summer of 1984 that I was asked if I was agreeable to having an experienced yachtsman from Bermuda as my crew. It was explained to me that this sailor had a full-time job teaching wealthy Americans to sail their yachts. I had no objection to this. In fact I thought I might pick up a few useful tips for the time when I might become a millionaire! I automatically assumed this man would make an excellent crew.

On the appointed day I had to rig the boat entirely by myself as my crew had not arrived. Having launched the Merlin and secured it to the jetty, I was standing up in the boat making final adjustments to the mainsail. Suddenly the Bosun appeared on the jetty, accompanied by a stranger.

"Here is your crew John."

"Welcome aboard," I said, "but first you'll be needing to wear this" and I passed my crew a buoyancy aid. He quickly put it on.

"Right jump in," I shouted. He did. If at all possible you should always step into a boat, but he took me too literally and jumped. He misjudged it and his feet landed squarely on the gunwale, while I was still standing. The boat tipped violently and he fell into the water. At the same time I was upended and fell into the water the other side.

Several club members, who were at the jetty rigging their boats, thought it hilarious and ran along the jetty to make sarcastic comments and give unhelpful advice. Although wet and cold, I saw the funny side of it, but my crew did not.

He scrambled out onto the jetty. When I asked him if he was going to get back into the boat he declined and walked off, leaving a wet trail behind him. He was never seen again.

Now this was a pity as it meant I had no crew. I decided to miss the first race and to get into some dry clothes. I was ready for the second race and sailed the Merlin single-handed, which was not what I was used to, but I enjoyed this new experience. I came last in the race but that was not important .

*   *   *   *   *

THREE KIDS IN A BOAT

In 1985 the club Commodore made arrangements for a party of very young children from Saxon Hill Special School, Lichfield, to be bussed to the Club lake. Some of the children were in wheelchairs. They were each allocated to a dinghy. The sailing club members were already rigging their boats when the bus arrived. I was allocated two small girls and a small boy.
"I am going to launch the boat now, so I will see you over there," I said to the three children, pointing to the jetty. I floated the dinghy off its trolley and pulled it round to the jetty, where the children met me.
"Now I must put a life-jacket on each of you," I said. While rigging the boat, I decided to reef the mainsail. This in effect reduces the sail area and the energy of the wind and so lessens the chance of a capsize. I assisted the children into the dinghy.

The girls were each told to hold a jib sheet (a rope controlling a small sail). I explained that they were only to pull it in or let it out, when I said so. This arrangement worked well. The boy sat to one side of the boat. He seemed nervous and subdued.
"You can help me later on," I said to him gently.

We headed for the centre of the lake. The girls were obviously enjoying the sensation of sailing, but the little boy looked unhappy. Soon there was another boat up ahead and I had to `go about`.
"Let your rope go slack," I said to the one girl. "Pull your rope in when I shout," I said to the other girl. "Ready about. Lee ho," I shouted and eased the tiller forward. As the boat tilted and went on the other tack, there were shrieks of excitement from the girls.

I had quickly moved to the other side to balance the boat. At the same time, a tremulous small voice said,
"Do you want me to get out now?" The little boy had mistaken `Ready about` for `Ready get out`!
"No lad," I said laughing "You would get very wet."

At that point the lake was over 40 feet deep. I swapped the boy over with one of the girls. It was very noticeable, when once he had something to do, how his confidence increased by leaps and bounds.

That was one of my most satisfactory sailing afternoons. Just to see those

196

unfortunate children really enjoying themselves made all the sailing club members`
efforts worthwhile.

*   *   *   *   *

DOOMED

On 19th August 1984, whilst sailing out on the lake, I can recall hearing the
sound of a propeller-driven aircraft coming from a southerly direction. I looked up
and saw an old twin-engine Vickers Varsity T1 (G-BDFT), accompanied by a small
Cessna. They were on their way to an air show. One of the Varsity engines started to
cough. As I watched, it retraced its flight path and headed back the way it had come.
The Cessna followed. I assumed the Varsity was returning to base to sort out the
trouble. Apparently the Cessna was filming.

About five minutes later however, the two aircraft appeared again. I was
puzzled. As I watched, one engine of the Varsity spluttered and then cut out. Shortly
afterwards the other engine cut out. The plane started to descend fairly steeply,
towards Uttoxeter. I was hoping and praying it would spot the old Hixon airfield,
which was only about seven miles away, whereas Uttoxeter was about ten.
Unfortunately it continued in the approximate direction of Uttoxeter. It was now
descending rapidly and silently. Sadly, I heard later, the pilot had made a brave
attempt to crash-land at Marchington Gliding Club but had hit some power cables,
resulting in the loss of eleven lives. I understand there were three survivors.

I have never been able to fathom out why the stricken plane did not make for
Hixon. The Varsity was carrying a party of vintage aircraft enthusiasts.

*   *   *   *   *

CHAPTER THIRTY

THE COLLISION

In 1979 my wife still worked in Stafford and I in Rugeley. On a day in November she had no transport, so I rose early and set out to drive her to work. It was still dark. Approaching a steep hill known as Weston Bank, we overtook a car being driven by her nephew Anthony. I flashed my headlights and drove on towards Stafford.

We had completed about half the journey when we came to a left-hand bend, just before the County Showground. I was behind another car. I was suddenly aware of a dark shape just above my line of sight, coming from the right. It seemed to be several feet from the ground and was immediately in front of the car. There was an almighty bang! Shape, bang! It was as quick as that. There was no time to brake.

A fully grown stag had decided to make a spectacular leap in the dark, just as we rounded the bend. It was still in midair when we struck it. The forelegs whipped round the side and dented a wheel arch. An antler broke off and went spinning away in the glow of the headlights. The animal dropped to the ground, close to a hedge.

I drove the car (a Renault 14TL) off the road onto the grass verge and got out. My wife was in a slight state of shock, so I waited by the roadside for Anthony to approach. He soon came round the bend and I waved him down. I explained the situation and asked him to take his auntie on to her place of work, which he did. I was relieved to see my distressed wife leaving the scene.

I walked over to the stag, assuming it to be dead or badly injured. It did not move as I approached. Its eyes glistened. There was no outward sign of injury and I could see it was still breathing. Perhaps it was concussed or injured internally. I decided to phone the police. I walked to the showground entrance, where two attendants were putting on their white coats in preparation for the day`s events.
"Can I use your phone please?" I`ve had an accident."
"Help yourself," one said. I told the police what had happened.
"This is a reportable accident sir, so please stay where you are and we will be along shortly." I walked the short distance back to my car.

This was the first time I was able to see the damage properly, as it was just beginning to get light. My heart sank. There was a dent in the bonnet, a leaking radiator, broken headlights, a bent bonnet lid and finally, as I previously mentioned, a dented wheel arch. I could not believe that just one animal could have wreaked such damage.

While I was standing by the roadside, a large white van drew up.
"What`s happened?" asked the driver. I told him about the collision.
"Where is the deer?" he asked. Suddenly I felt uneasy about this bloke.
"I`ve no idea," I replied.
"I have a good knife. We could look for it and I`ll cut it up," he said.
"I don`t want that," I exclaimed angrily. He scowled.
"Oh well, if you want to be like that," he shouted and drove off towards Stafford.

It was some twenty minutes from the time of my phone call before the police arrived in their white van - a sergeant and a constable. The sergeant walked towards my car, then stepping back, shook his head from side to side. Looking at his colleague with a wry smile he said,
"Dear, dear, dear!" Needless to say, I did not share his humour at the time, but I smile ruefully about it now.

"Where is the animal?" the sergeant asked.

"It is lying under that hedge," I said pointing. We walked towards the hedge. Amazingly the animal had gone.

"I'm sorry Sergeant. It <u>was</u> here," I said, apologetically. "It certainly did not pass by me while I was waiting for you to arrive."

"Don't worry sir. We will follow this hedge in the other direction."

We followed the bend in the road, keeping close to the hedge. Round the bend we suddenly came across a lorry with its wheels in a ditch. The driver was just climbing out of his cab.

"What happened to you?" the sergeant enquired.

"I was coming along the road when a bloody deer ran in front of me and I swerved," the driver said. `That deer is not only tough. It has a charmed life,` I thought.

The sergeant turned to me and said, "I think you should go back and wait by your car sir, while I take down the details of this incident." I made my way back towards the car. It was lighter now and as I walked by the hedge I glanced into the field and suddenly realised a vague animal-shape was in the middle standing stock-still.

"There is the deer," I shouted excitedly, pointing at the offending animal.

The constable drove up in the van. The sergeant got in and they drove into the field. I wasn't sure what they were hoping to accomplish but I wanted to be in on the action. I ran back round the bend and into the field. The constable wound down the window.

"Where are you going sir?" he shouted.

"I'm going to give you a hand," I replied.

"These animals can be dangerous and it is better that you go back."

"Thank you Constable," I said, "but if it is dangerous for me, it must be dangerous for you and three pairs of hands are better than two." Personally I didn't think they had a hope in hell of catching the animal. Events proved me right. As the van approached, the animal bounded across the field, leaped over the perimeter hedge, crossed a rough track, jumped over another hedge and disappeared into a dark wood. `That's the end of that,` I thought and walked back to the road.

When I reached my car, the police van drew up. I walked over and gave them the details of my collision.

"I have been in the Force twenty two years, mostly in this area and I have never heard of a deer on this road before," said the sergeant.

Later I learned that the police had contacted the Bostock family's head gamekeeper (they owned the wood).

"If the stag has managed to get into that wood, it is so dense I doubt whether I would be able to find it, even with a pack of hounds," he is reported to have said.

Some three miles away is the edge of the famous Staffordshire beauty spot, Cannock Chase, which is home to many deer. As my mishap occurred during the rut, it is reasonable to assume the stag had wandered from the Chase, seeking a mate. It had certainly wandered off the straight and narrow, as far as I was concerned. It cost me over £400 to have the car repaired.

*　　*　　*　　*　　*

CHAOS ON THE M1

In late 1979, I was driving my younger daughter, Gillian and babe-in-arms granddaughter Stacey, down the M1 motorway. We were to leave the motorway at Junction 13 and head for Bishop`s Stortford and Colchester.

Weather conditions were not good. It was very cold and the occasional snow flurry blowing across the motorway did not help. We had reached a point about half a mile from the junction, when we suddenly became aware of abandoned vehicles at the side of the hard shoulder. They were at all angles and some were up the embankment. There had obviously been a huge pile-up.

There were two cars travelling immediately in front of me, in the middle lane. The two drivers must have been gawping at the wrecks, because their steering was erratic. They approached a coach which had just slewed across two lanes and stopped. The car in front of me suddenly ran into the back of the car in front of it. They both stopped, which forced me to stop. Unbelievably, the driver immediately in front of me and his female passenger both stepped out onto the fast lane and harangued the driver in front of them. I could see in my rear-view mirror, a lot of traffic bearing down on us. Alarmed I said,

"I don`t like this Gill. I`ve got to get us out of here." Putting my left indicator on and getting a flash from an oncoming van, I drove across the inner lane onto the hard shoulder. I continued on the hard shoulder until I reached the junction turn-off. It got us out of trouble anyway.

We both sighed with relief and could not believe people would stand on the motorway, while traffic was still approaching at speed. It was almost certain that under those circumstances that if I had not taken the action I did, we would have had a vehicle crashing into the back of us.

*   *   *   *   *

GREENHORNS ALOFT

Our first flight in a passenger plane took place when my wife and I set off for a holiday in Gibraltar. We were to stay with our daughter Gillian, her soldier husband, Paul, and our two grandchildren . We were both a little apprehensive but when once the plane (a Boeing 347) was airborne we felt exhilarated. My pleasure at the sheer power of the high-angle take-off soon diminished however, when my wife looked out of the window and saw a wing and one of the under slung engines.

"There is water running off the wing," Glad said. I could see several oval inspection plates bolted onto the top surface of the wing. Liquid was flowing from beneath one of these. I had read enough about jet aircraft to know that aviation fuel is stored in the wings.

"I won`t be a minute," I said to her, unfastening my seat-belt.

Beckoning to the stewardess to follow me, I walked to the back of the aircraft. I explained to her what we had seen and that I had called her to the back of the aircraft in case I should be overheard and cause alarm to the other passengers.

"I will inform the Captain," she said.

Shortly after I had returned to my seat, the co-pilot appeared from the cabin and approached us.

"Are you the gentleman who pointed out a defect?" he asked.

"Yes," I said, "but embarrassingly, it has now stopped."

"Well thank you for reporting it," he said. "A seal needs replacing, but there is no need to worry as we will get it seen to in Gibraltar." "We won`t run out of fuel," he added with a smile. I suddenly thought how nice it would be for Glad to see the pilot`s cabin and this was a good opportunity.

"Would it be possible for my wife to see your cabin?" I asked.

"Certainly sir," he said. "I will send for you both in about thirty minutes."

Later and true to his word, we were invited by the stewardess to proceed to the cabin. The cabin door was shut behind us and we were introduced to the Captain. I was immediately struck by the vast array of instruments and the wide angle of vision. The pilot pointed out an instrument housed in the armrest of the seat between himself and the co-pilot. As we watched, the instrument flicked over and the word *BILBAO* appeared.

"We are directly over Bilbao now," the captain said. We were both very impressed. We returned to our seats feeling like VIPs. It was an experience we would fondly remember and it was a nice way to start our holiday. There is a lesson in all this. If you want the privilege of seeing the pilot`s cabin, then discover a defect and report it.

When we had first found our seats, a woman sitting in the seat immediately behind us must have overheard our conversation. She leaned forward and said, "Excuse me. Is this your first flight?" We nodded. "There is no need to be worried. I have done this journey lots of times." We both thanked her for her kindness, but neither of us was in a nervous state. The lady turned out to be an officer`s wife.

We learned that aircraft landing at Gibraltar are subject to the whims of the Spanish authorities. There are two flight approaches to landing on `Gib`, a gentle one and a `hairy` one. If the Spanish air traffic controllers are in a politically bad mood, they can force incoming British aircraft to make the more difficult approach. This entails a steep decent and sharp banking, to the discomfort of the passengers. Our flight took one such approach. As our plane undertook these uncomfortable manoeuvres, the lady behind let out a loud moan. It was she who turned out to be a bag of nerves, not us. I was amused but made no comment. I didn`t want to `put my foot in it`.

The Gibraltar airport was at that time, controlled by the RAF. The runway had been extended out over the sea. Embarking and disembarking passengers had to cross the runway, so access to the airport, the runway and to the town was strictly controlled, as was access to the Spanish frontier.

The holiday over, our return flight was not without incident either. The aircraft had two stewardesses. They dispensed cans of beer and soft drinks from their trolley. Later they came round with trays to collect the empty cans. The stewardess working on our side of the aisle tripped as she reached us and empty cans shot over me. She apologised profusely.

A short while later the same stewardess took her tray up the aisle, to gather in the `stragglers`. Upon her return, blow me if she didn`t go and trip up by me again, causing one or two more empty cans to strike me. She looked very embarrassed and exclaimed, in an exasperated tone of voice,

"Every time I get to you I drop everything !"

"Chance would be a fine thing," I said, grinning sarcastically. My wife knocked my knee hard, as much as to signify, "Don`t be rude!"

Turning a bright shade of red, the embarrassed woman picked up the empty cans

201

and disappeared up the aisle. We did not see her again. As we disembarked, I did give an apology to her colleague and asked her to pass it on.

*　　*　　*　　*　　*

THE JOKER

Every year, for ten consecutive years, my wife and I took a holiday in Jersey in the Channel Islands. We always stayed at Le Chalet Hotel, which overlooked Corbiere Lighthouse. We became good friends with the manager, Peter. He was a likeable Austrian who spoke excellent English. He and I were always leg-pulling.

I remember one particular year (1982) when I wrote to enquire about a room for Glad and myself. We soon received a reply. It read, `We can accommodate your wife but you will have to sleep in the boiler-house.` This gave us a great deal of amusement at the time.

When, a few months later, we arrived at the hotel for the holiday we had booked, there was an official-looking notice on the reception counter which read, `THIS HOTEL WILL BE CLOSED FOR TWO WEEKS FROM TOMORROW`. Suddenly because he couldn`t contain himself any longer, Peter appeared from behind the counter where (unbeknown to us) he had been crouching. He was very amusing. We still send one another a card at Christmas, even after all these years.

Unbeknown to Peter, his notice was a portent of things to come. In early 1998, we were on a short visit to Jersey with friends. We were staying for the four days in St. Helier. We took a coach trip and stopped at Corbiere, near where Le Chalet was sited. It cannot be seen from the road. We crossed the road with a friend, Ciss, to show her what Le Chalet was like. We were always singing its praises.

We walked round a blind bend onto the hotel car park and were shocked to find it was closed and all the furniture was stacked up inside. As we started to walk back disappointed, a man came out and said, "Can I help you?" We explained our reason for being there. "I don`t even know whether we shall be opening this year," he said sadly.

It was only recently in March 2006 that I heard that the hotel where we had spent so many happy holidays had been completely demolished. I know Glad, if she were still alive, would have been devastated.

*　　*　　*　　*　　*

THE MYSTERY BOLLARD

I believe it was in 1982 that a severe storm brought down hundreds of trees on Cannock Chase. Rugeley Power Station suffered some minor damage. The strongest gust recorded on the station measured 96 mph.

I had the interesting task of accompanying two representatives of the insurers around the `A` and `B` Power Stations, a middle-aged man and a young woman of about twenty five. We were looking for any storm damage. Station personnel would phone me to report any damage they found in their area of work. I listed all the damage as the reports came in. When I met the insurers I gave them a copy of my list. It was nice for me to work outside for a change. We set out to locate the damage. I was feeling a bit apprehensive, as I guessed I would have to do some climbing. I was worried about my vertigo.

We found out several large 8-feet by 3-feet, three eighths inch-thick, reinforced glass sheets had been sucked out of the roof of the turbine generator hall. I was obliged to follow the insurers up to the top of the coal plant. The young woman led the way. She had the agility of a cat - obviously used to her work and hard to keep up with. I could understand why she wore slacks. It was a dirty job. I did start to get vertigo as we descended, but I managed to control it.

A contractor Portakabin had been blown two hundred yards across an area between two cooling towers, then across a road and a car park and had ended up smashed to matchwood against the iron railings of a transformer compound. Various other listed damage was inspected and then I returned to my office. The insurers returned to a room which had been put at their disposal.

As soon as I sat down in my office at `B` Station, I received a phone call telling me that a bollard had been blown over at the `A` Station gatehouse. I phoned the insurers and arranged to meet them at the gatehouse, which was on the far side of the site.

When I arrived they were waiting for me. There were several traffic bollards there but they were all standing like sentinels. I went to the gatehouse and spoke to the duty security man.
"There is a bollard reported as being damaged but we cannot find it. Can you look in your log please?" I said. He scanned the entries for the previous night.
"Oh yes," he said, "There is an entry. It was one of those outside." I walked back to the insurers and leaning on a bollard and looking in their direction I said,
"I wonder which one it is?" I soon found out ! The bollard suddenly tipped over, leaving me sitting in the road. The insurance people rocked with laughter and I joined in. "That`s what I call being let-down," I quipped.

Everyone has amusing tales to tell about funny incidents at their place of work. One that sticks in my mind is when one of the contractor workers came into the office and asked me if he could use my phone.
"Go ahead," I said. He dialled.
"Is that you, Bill? he asked. "Do you think you could send me up some glue? I`m stuck without it".

*　　*　　*　　*　　*

BENEATH OUR FEET

It was in 1984 that I made a discovery which was to enrich my life. I was standing on the beach at the lake side, talking to the bosun of the sailing club. I glanced down and spotted among the beach pebbles a most unusual looking medium-sized stone. I picked it up and turned it over. It was only half a pebble, which was just as well, otherwise I would never have realised what a beautiful display was hidden within it. But it was the flat face that was so spectacular. It was like a piece of jewellery. I knew nothing about geology, but because it had a rough shape in the centre I assumed it was a fossil. I was wrong. My inquiring mind was working overtime. I decided to send the pebble to the British Museum for analysis.

The explanation I received back was to me an eye-opener. It made me realise that our world is an even more wonderful place, so magnificent but so fragile and ever-changing. It also brought home to me how little I knew about our planet. I became hooked on geology and took to studying the subject as a hobby. I joined the Geologists` Association and also the North Staffordshire GA.

As my family and friends learned of my new interest, they started to bring me back rocks and fossils from their holidays. It was thoughtful of them. Some turned out to be of very little use, but several were worth keeping and studying. I soon realised I needed to keep them in some semblance of order. I started a collection and in the numerical sequence, No.1 was allocated to the magnificent geode I had found by the lake. (Page 206).

In 1985 I was browsing through my newspaper when I was surprised to read about an elderly Japanese soldier on a remote Pacific island, who had just given himself up from WWII after all those years . He had still thought he was bearing arms in the cause of his Emperor. That is the only memory I have of that year.

It was in 1986 that my eldest grandson Jamie made us extremely proud. He passed out as a Grenadier Guard, at Pirbright. My family attended the ceremony. I remember, as we entered the barracks, passing a group of Paras`. They were looking quite depressed.
"Cheer up lads," I said, "it may never happen." A disgruntled voice immediately retorted from the back,
"It already has!"

Later on (in 1989) I decided to attend adult education courses in Geology, at Keele University. I learned about the Continental Plates of the Earth being slowly propelled by giant convex currents beneath the crust. The movement of such massive plates is an unstoppable force that brings about collisions, earthquakes and erupting volcanoes. In 2004 I gained an Open Studies Certificate in the subject. My thesis was on the craters of Mars.

Our continents still exist because continental crust is less dense than ocean crust and so the former overrides the latter, but there are exceptions.

The science of Geology started over two hundred and fifty years ago, but it was the exploration for gas and oil in the 1960s which brought to light how our Earth really functions. The rocks of our planet alter, in what is known as `*The Rock Cycle*`. I learned that oceans are widening or narrowing. Ocean crust is constantly being generated at ocean ridges and eventually, over vast time, is returned at ocean trenches to be consumed in the molten outer core beneath the Earth`s crust.

The phenomenon that really amazed me, is the fact that every so-many thousand years, the polarity of our planet has reversed. This is guaranteed to cause confusion to navigators ! How do we know that this phenomenon occurs? The evidence is `frozen` in the rocks. In the material that goes to make up a rock, magnetic particles are aligned with the Earth`s magnetic field of the time and are set in that direction as the rock solidifies - (*Palaeo magnetism*). By taking core samples from all over the world and comparing their magnetic direction, a picture emerges of how our magnetic poles were positioned in the past. If you see any rock faces where several neat core holes have been left, you will know geologists have been at work there.

I have now accumulated a vast number of geological specimens. As specimens they are ideal for use in discussions. I cannot see the point of shutting them away in a cupboard, where no one else has the advantage of seeing them, so I like to get them out for visitors to see. `To give them an airing` so to speak.

A married couple who lived next door but one to us (Jackie and Mike) decided to move into a small cottage near Inverness in Scotland. Mike in his university days had studied geology and had engaged in many field excursions. He had found some good

quality fossil specimens on those trips. He came to see me and said,
"We are moving to Inverness." He continued, "I know you collect things geological John and we won`t have room for my specimens. Would you like to have them?" I jumped at the offer.

Two days later I heard a rumble. No, it wasn`t an earthquake. It was Mike coming up my drive, wheeling a large box loaded on a sack truck. It was crammed with fossils, especially those of Carboniferous plants. In age they were anything between 354 million years and 290 million years old. I think at one time he had worked for the Coal Board. He was proud of his finds; one in particular. He couldn`t leave without showing it to me. He held out a piece of red sandstone.
"There is a small jawbone with teeth in this rock," he said. He believed the fossil to be from a small lizard. Suddenly he accidentally dropped it and it broke in two. He was very upset. After he left I stuck it together. Fossils are rarely perfect anyway, but fossil fragments are just as important as complete specimens.

After Mike and Jackie left the village, I spent hours examining the specimens. I soon realised there were several other pieces of sandstone from the same source. Most carried tiny bones. I noticed some bones were of great length compared to their cross-section. Then I discovered another jawbone. Eventually I came up with the idea that I was examining the bones of a small pterodactyl - a flying reptile from possibly as far back in time as the Triassic Age. England would have been just north of the Equator then. I took the specimens to Keele. They tended to agree with me. I was very pleased and felt my patience had been rewarded. There had been several different species of pterosaur. A very large one had the wing-span of a Spitfire, but there were also some with a wing-span of no more than five-and-a-half to six inches. The latter ate insects and probably caught them in flight.

It gives me great satisfaction to discuss geology with children and the elderly. I have given the occasional talk to Senior Citizens and other groups. Geology overlaps other sciences, such as archaeology, botany, biology, physics and chemistry, but it is considered to be more closely associated with physics.

I remember going on a field trip with Keele to Castleton in Derbyshire. In Castle Dale we were shown where magma had extruded from a fault and had flowed out over the country rock as molten lava. A mile away, bitumen was oozing from a fault in the limestone. This is limestone country and the limestone of Derbyshire is known to be over a mile thick. The calcium carbonate is the remains of ancient creatures of an invasive sea that covered the region millions of years ago. A quick way of seeing these fossils is to examine the local dry stone walls.

Another interesting feature in the area is Mam Tor, `the Shivering Mountain`. Resting on shale beds, it remains stable during dry spells. During wet spells it becomes unstable and starts a gravitational horizontal movement at the base. It has already engulfed a nearby public road, more than once.

Now that great advances have been made in the exploration of the planets of our Solar System, geologists are turning their attention more and more to the study of planetary rocks and rock formations. It is hoped by what they learn to throw more light on the understanding of our own planet, the workings and history of our Solar System and that of the Universe.

Page 206. The magnificent geode from Pottal Pool Quarry, Cannock Chase,
Staffordshire.

Owing to the great strides that have been made in winkling out the history of our planet, it is now estimated that the Earth and our Moon are approximately some 4.6 billion years old. This is considered to be almost half the life of the Sun (a star) and its solar system.

We are all children of the Universe and every one of us is unique. So be it, but we are only important to each other as a common species and to God, whatever we deem God to be.

*   *   *   *   *

CHAPTER THIRTY ONE

THE BELSEN MEMORIAL

My younger daughter Gillian and her husband Paul lived for six years in Army married-quarters at Fallingbostel in Germany. For some of that time Paul served as a sergeant (The Staffordshire Regiment) in the Middle East in the first Gulf War. He served as a medic out in the desert, with the tanks of the 7th Armoured Brigade .(Operation Granby). It was an anxious time for the family.

My wife and I paid them several visits during their time in Germany. During a stay in 1988 we visited Celle, a typical German town not far away. The return journey was uneventful until we came to a road sign for Belsen.

Paul decided to drive us there but when we arrived I declined to go through the gates of the Belsen Memorial, which had been erected on the site of one of the notorious Nazi concentration camps and ethnic cleansing factories. The shocking news pictures of that awful place, which appeared near the end of the war, are etched in the minds of my generation. I could sense, even outside the gates, what I can only describe as a strange presence. How surviving Jews or families of the murdered feel about such places is impossible to imagine. I feel sorry too for the decent Germans of today, for it is very easy to tar everybody with the same brush of shame. That cannot be right.

I still have difficulty in coming to terms with the fact that people did those terrible things to other people of the same species, just as though they were working on a conveyor belt in a factory. The Germans responsible for this evil had some essential traits missing from their human makeup. Those fiends left their nation an unhealthy legacy of shame and achieved nothing.

I know my younger grandson Damian, as he approached the entrance with his parents on a different occasion, said,
"Mum I don`t like this place." He also refused to go any further. He was then only five years old.

Paul told us about a British sergeant from the same base, who saw a notice at a nearby farm, advertising honey for sale. He was about to buy some and mentioned he had just visited Belsen. The German farmer said,
"Yes it is terrible what the British did to those people." The sergeant was so disgusted he refused to buy the honey and angrily left. Was it possible the farmer had been brainwashed by the German authorities of the time and he actually believed what he was saying ? I doubt it !

*　　*　　*　　*　　*

CHAPTER THIRTY TWO

A TELEVISION WEEKEND

In February 1990, at the age of sixty five, I retired from Rugeley Power
Station. They gave me a wonderful send-off. It took me a year to get used to my
new-found freedom. I hear of so many instances of people who retire, having no
specific interests. They sit in their comfortable armchairs in front of the `tele` and
within a year are no longer with us. I had no intention of going down that path if I
could possibly help it. And so I pursued my interest in geology, turned my hand to
artistic endeavours such as oil painting and carving, taught myself to play the
keyboard, joined a walking group and studied Prehistory. I hope this doesn`t sound
like boasting, but I am trying to make a point here. To stay comparatively young and
to keep one`s mind keen, I believe it is better to <u>live</u> life, than to watch others living
it on the television.

In 1992 a TV programme called `Help Squad` was a successful series for Michael
Parkinson. The TVS studio in Southampton invited people to write in for help with
`anything under the sun`. With tongue in cheek, I wrote in to say that I wanted to get
hold of a dinosaur toe bone to add to my geological collection. Not for one minute did
I expect to hear any more about it.

During the Spring I was planting tomato plants in the greenhouse. All of a sudden
my wife came out of the house and shouted up the garden,
"There is a call for you. He said he was some sort of manager." To cut a long story
short, I learned that I had been picked out of fifteen thousand applicants, to take part
in an episode of `Help Squad`. I would have to report to the TVS studio. The voice at
the other end said I could bring my wife, we would be put up at the Hilton Hotel and
all expenses would be paid. Was I interested ? How could I refuse ? We could not
believe our luck.

On the 1st May we set off and reached Southampton in two and a half hours, but
it took another half an hour to find the studio. My wife was ushered to a seat in the
studio, whilst I was led outside with a cameraman and several others.

A microphone with a furry jacket was thrust above my head and I was told to say
certain lines. I have never been much good at acting and I found it disconcerting that I
was not asked to say words of my own. I made a mess of two attempts, after which
everyone`s patience was beginning to wear thin. One of the group, in an exasperated
tone of voice, said,
"Oh, just say whatever comes into your head." I had no problem with that and
afterwards he said,
"Marvellous. That is just what we wanted." In effect I was required to explain what
help I wanted. I can`t remember my exact words now as it is so long ago, but
whatever I said must have made the right impression. That was a prerecording and
was sent out in the afternoon as an introduction to the live programme, which had a
studio audience.

A young man from the studio staff accompanied us at all times. This was to
ensure I put in an appearance at the studio at the appropriate times. He escorted us to
the dining room and sat with us for lunch. He explained TVS was being taken over by
Meridian and so this programme would be their very last. He also told us that he was
to be made redundant He still had three weeks of work and would be flying to
America the next day to interview Sylvester Stallone.

In the morning there was a rehearsal in the studio. We were each given a copy of the script. It was at this stage that I learned of two scientists from the Dinosaur Museum at Dorchester in Dorset, a man and a woman, who would be meeting me later in the afternoon. It was the woman Jackie Ridley with whom I would appear on the programme.

The programme consisted of a panel of three people who offered professional advice and were experts in their own field : Annabel Giles, Chris Donat and Jan Rowland. Michael Parkinson`s role was as interviewer and commentator.

I was introduced to the geologists when they arrived at the studio. They had turned up in a van which surprised me, but I was unaware of a twelve foot high dinosaur costume stowed in the back. The man proceeded to don the suit, helped by one of the staff. To get into it, he first laid the costume on the floor and then crawled into it. It was then zipped up from the outside. He had to be assisted, as it was impossible for him to get to his feet unaided. It was very amusing. He looked as though he was going to topple over at any minute. During the programme, I do remember thrusting out a steadying hand to him.

The live broadcast began. Michael Parkinson introduced the lady scientist. He quizzed her about dinosaurs and after giving her reply she was invited to present me with the dinosaur toe bone. I wisecracked during the broadcast,
"I didn`t ask for a dinosaur leg-bone because it would have been too big to get in my car !" That raised a few laughs.

After the programme finished, I was approached by the two geologists.
"We have something else for you," the lady said. She presented me with a wooden box with a hinged lid, which contained several fossils and fossil casts from museum specimens. I was especially pleased with a cast taken from dinosaur skin. There was also a small dinosaur footprint. Fossilised dinosaur skin would be a rare find, indeed . The other geologist said,
"I have something for you too," and he produced a large fossil which he had been hiding behind his back. It was a paddle bone from a plesiosaur - a large fearsome Jurassic marine reptile. I was thrilled . Some of those reptiles grew to a length of forty feet.

It was the last programme to go out from the TVS studio. A farewell party had been organised for the staff for that evening. Glad and I were kindly invited. They were a very nice bunch of people and I would imagine, great to work with. Knowing that Michael Parkinson spent a lot of his time in Australia, I told him about the incident just after WWII when I had climbed Sydney Bridge. He laughed and in his phlegmatic way said,
"You had better not show your face in Australia."

After the party we drove to the Hilton and stayed the night. It was nice to see how the `other half` lived, but I wouldn`t like to live at that pace every day. In the morning, the hotel did us a slap-up breakfast. My wife decided she could get used to this high life. I, after all my travels, just wanted a quiet life and an occasional celebration. My odd request for the dinosaur toe bone had certainly done some good for the Dinosaur Museum. It had received nation-wide publicity. I had been given some fine specimens for my collection and we had both had a very interesting, unusual and entertaining weekend. When we arrived home, I offered my family and friends my autograph but there were no takers.

*　　*　　*　　*　　*

CHAPTER THIRTY THREE

A MISAPPROPRIATION

In 1993 during a pleasant three-week holiday in Malta, an incident occurred which initially caused much concern to the hotel staff and subsequent amusement to our holiday group. It also caused some embarrassment to me. On this particular day, before setting out on our daily quest for historical mind-benders and lace-edged tablecloths, my wife armed herself with a hot-brush and proceeded along the corridor, to perform emergency hairdressing on one of her friends. To pass the time while I waited, I decided to return to our room to look up some map details.

When I reached the room the door was open and the head housekeeper (Mary Rose) was cleaning the room.

"Do you want me to go, only I have nearly finished?" she said.

"It is OK. You finish up first. I have only come back to look at a map. Pretend I`m not here," I said. I spread the map out on the bed. Shortly afterwards Mary had completed her task and she left. I locked the door after her.

A few minutes later there was a knock on the door. I thought it was my wife but it was the housekeeper. She was very agitated.

"Sir I cannot find the hotel master keys. May I look for them in your room?"

"Certainly," I said. "In fact I will help you search," and leaving the map spread out on the bed we both searched but drew a blank.

"Sorry to trouble you," she said and again left the room and again I locked the door behind her.

Shortly afterwards she returned, but this time with the janitor. I let them in and he immediately made a beeline for my bed. He lifted up the map. He did not find the keys. They both apologised profusely and left. My wife had not yet returned so I continued to peruse the map.

Suddenly there were loud anguished voices arguing in Maltese in the corridor . `Those blasted keys!` I thought. Without them of course, the housekeeper was unable to continue her cleaning duties and should they have fallen into the hands of some dishonest individual, that person would be able to gain access to every room in the hotel. Goodbye jewellery !

I unlocked the door and went out into the corridor. Mary Rose and the janitor were still babbling excitedly.

"Have you found those keys yet?" I asked.

"No sir, we have not."

"What about looking in that pile of sheets over there," I said, pointing and at the same time playing with my own large bunch of keys in my trouser pocket.

"We have already looked there," he said. The housekeeper had heard the rattle of my keys.

"You have some keys," she said pointing excitedly.

"Of course I have, everybody has keys," I said, pulling them from my pocket.

"These are my car keys," holding up the first bunch, then I placed my main bunch of keys on a small coffee table in the corridor. It was then that I realised that I had an extra bunch of keys with a tag attached, which bore the word `MASTER` boldly printed across it. They both laughed with relief but I was flabbergasted. Whenever I saw Mary Rose during the rest of our stay I would say,

"Have you seen any keys lately?" It always raised a laugh. Thinking over what had happened, we all agreed that when Mary Rose left the room on the first occasion, she must have left her keys on the inside of the door. I had then locked the door behind her and assuming them to be my keys had dropped them into my pocket. It was a wonder that I didn`t notice the tag or the fact that her bunch was bigger than mine. I know the mistake sent the hotel staff into a panic.

*　　*　　*　　*　　*

CHAPTER THIRTY FOUR

THE EXTRAORDINARY FRENCHMAN

In 1994 we were staying with my sister and her husband at their cottage in the village of Les-Eyzies-de-Tayac, in the Dordogne. We were introduced to some French friends of theirs, Pierre and Monique. They lived about three kilometres away in an area rich in prehistory. From their land you could look across the Verzere River, the main tributary of the Dordogne River and see on the far cliff bank the cave of La Madeleine, the type site of the Magdalenien and the last of the Upper Palaeolithic industries of Western Europe. The site dates back fifteen thousand years.

Pierre is an interesting man with a mischievous sense of humour. He is very unassuming but I would not care to get into a fight with him, as he holds a black belt in judo. He is a retired petrochemical engineer. He worked for many years in Russia on a contract for the installation of oil refinery equipment. His passion is Prehistory and he has an impressive collection of Palaeolithic flint tools, which he found over a span of forty years. I have learned a lot from him and now prehistory is one of my main interests. Pierre is also an astronomer. He has a massive telescope mounted on his land, which he originally acquired from a Paris university. It was dismantled when he bought it and it took six years to bring it back to its former glory.

Pierre and Monique invited us to dinner. In France a meal can last three hours. They do not consume for all that time, but intersperse the meal with conversation. Monique conjured up gastronomical miracles. We really enjoyed the meal. During the conversation in French, English and by gesticulation, Pierre suddenly produced two Russian medallions and a certificate signed by Leonid Brezhnev. One of the medallions was the size of a dinner plate, presumably intended to be hung on a wall.

The other side of Pierre`s character came to light during the meal, when he suddenly placed a model frog on the table. This was followed by another and another, until there was a whole row of them, in different shades of green and all put there by Pierre. His eccentric behaviour caused us much amusement. After the meal, he produced from his cellar a twenty-five year old bottle of calvados. That really complemented the meal.

After dining, we retired to the lounge and my eyes fell on a magnificent showcase. Pierre ushered me in that direction and proudly showed me his collection of Palaeolithic flint tools. I was full of admiration at the beauty of some of these and had a great respect for the skill involved in the fashioning of such tools. Axe heads, knives, points and scrapers abounded from the Middle and Upper Palaeolithic Period. It surprised me to learn that nearly all of these artefacts had been found personally by Pierre. He turned out to be an authority on Palaeolithic tools and I hung onto his every word, although he spoke very little English and my French was limited.

Pierre and I had some affinity, I as an amateur geologist and he as an archaeologist. Certain aspects of these two sciences overlap.

A few days after the dinner we were invited to go with Pierre on a field trip, to search for flint tools. He had to obtain permission from the Mayor of the district for us to accompany him to a unique site in the French countryside. When we arrived it was raining slightly and the field was muddy, so all three ladies sat in the car. The three men, Pierre, Dennis and I walked into this very large ploughed field. When I say `large`, I mean much larger than the average field in England.

We followed the furrows, looking for any piece of flint that might possibly be a

Stone Age tool. In a matter of three hours we found thirty tools. My initial efforts were unsuccessful but amusing. I was not entirely sure what I was supposed to be looking for, except that I knew whatever I picked up had to be of flint. After I had in my hand as much as I could carry, I walked over to Pierre.

"Pierre ici?" I quizzed, holding out my finds. He took the first piece.

"Non !" he said, throwing it over his shoulder. Then he took the second piece.

"Non !" he said again and that piece went the same way. He rejected all the pieces I had picked up. I smiled ruefully. It taught me a lesson and I realised there was more to this than meets the eye. I resumed my search, but was far more perceptive after that and found several small tools.

Later on the practical joker within Pierre surfaced. He noted which furrow I was following and without my noticing, placed on the ground a museum-quality flint tool which he had been carrying in his pocket. Shortly afterwards I spotted it and shouted excitedly to Pierre, waving the artefact above my head. He walked over grinning. "That is a very good biface. It is valuable," he said. I pocketed it in all innocence, thinking I had made a good find. Dennis started to laugh.

"What are you laughing at?" I asked. "I saw him put that on the ground. Pierre knew which furrow you were in. He knew you were bound to come across it," he said. I did not tell Pierre I had found him out. I didn`t want to spoil his fun and after all, I had ended up with a valuable artefact.(Page 215).

While searching for flints I came across some really fine Cretaceous fossils of corals and sponges. I realised this area must have lain beneath the sea, at least sixty five million years ago. These fossils could well have fallen under the gaze of Stone Age Man, although probably he would not have known what he was looking at, other than to regard them as special stones.

We returned to Pierre and Monique`s house and after some snacks and a glass of wine we got into the car. Dennis wound the windows down so that we could say our goodbyes. It was now dark. Suddenly Pierre placed a live frog in my sister`s hand. There were loud squeals and then he came up to the back seat of the car, where Glad and I were sitting and appeared to fling something into the car. My wife let out a yell because she thought it was another frog and she hated them, but then we thought he was only pretending and so we laughed.

The next day when my sister was to drive us to the airport, she found snail trails all over the seats. It was evident Pierre had unleashed `l`escargot` inside the car.

One of the tricks he played on Pat and Dennis was to send them a letter, written on Mayoral notepaper, informing them they were to be presented with a cow for their fields and that it gave good milk. Pierre was a good artist and in with the letter was a wonderful cow caricature. I think it had a swollen udder ! Pat and Dennis lived on the outskirts of the village of Les Eyzies, which has been described as `the cradle of prehistory`. A new French National Museum of Prehistory has recently been completed there, after seven years of work. During the building of this magnificent museum, mammoth bones were discovered on the site. It was in this village that the skeletal remains of Cro-Magnon man, the oldest evidence of modern man, were first discovered.

My sister and her husband had their field ploughed by a local farmer. I asked their permission to walk the furrows. I did not find any stone tools but I did find a medieval washer from an ancient plough and also a large fragment of Romano-Gaul pottery.

Back in England, I put together quite a collection of flint tools, mostly from Pierre, but including one or two that I found. The tool I am most proud of is a

Page 215.   Some Palaeolithic flint tools from the Dordogne region, SW France - a
hand axe , scraper and blade .

hammer stone, which I found when Pierre and I were walking across Pat`s fields. "These are becoming rare," he said and added, "You have the beginner`s luck." It had been slightly knapped and fitted perfectly into my hand. Holding this tool gave me a peculiar feeling. I thought about the hunter gatherer who must have used this flint as a percussion tool, thousands of years ago. In fact it was deeply pitted on the surface with the traces of ancient blows. It had obviously had much use.

*   *   *   *   *

CHAPTER THIRTY FIVE

A SMALL WORLD

In the late February of 1994, my wife and I flew to Cyprus for a holiday. We had hardly been in our hotel for more than half an hour when I switched on the radio. The news was being broadcast from the UK. We were not paying much attention until suddenly, we heard the name of our parish mentioned - Stowe by Chartley, of which Hixon at that time was a part. We could hardly believe our ears.

On the night of Friday 25th February there had been a plane crash in a blinding snow storm. When we had left England there had not been the slightest hint of snow. The aircraft (a Vickers Vicount cargo carrier G-OHOT) carrying four tons of mail as cargo, had only two people on board, an Australian pilot and a co pilot. The pilot was killed. The plane`s swathe of destruction in Anglesea Coppice halted on the edge of a site of special scientific interest -Chartley Moss. This is a prehistoric floating bog, unique in the UK and most of Europe - a legacy from the last Ice Age.

It is an extraordinary experience to walk on this bog. As you walk across it, the huge mass of rotting, floating vegetation moves before you in a wave-like motion. The raft of vegetation is between ten and fifteen feet thick in places and has accumulated over thousands of years. Trees which grow from the bog never reach maturity, because the roots are constantly in water. In effect the trees drown. The bog is thought to have first become established over an Ice Age kettle hole, brought about by melting ice.

On an escorted visit to Chartley Moss, I was shown where the aircraft had crash-landed, ploughing a giant swathe through many young trees and disintegrating as it progressed.(Page 218). Two local heroes, David Gregory and Vic Antcliff, rescued the injured co pilot, who survived his injuries. If the aircraft had crashed directly into Chartley Moss, the water of which is some fifty feet deep, it would have almost certainly been completely engulfed.

*　*　*　*　*

THE EARTH MOVED FOR US

My wife and I had liked Cyprus so much the previous year that we decided to go there on holiday again in 1995. We booked ourselves into a three-star hotel, The Mayfair, situated in Upper Pathos. On the second night, Thursday 23rd February, my wife had just put on her nightdress and was about to get into bed. I was still in my singlet and boxer shorts and was about to change into pyjamas.(Thank goodness I wasn`t in my Micky Mouse shorts !} Suddenly the earth moved for us ! There was a terrific double rumble, almost a bang and the building swayed. We were experiencing an earthquake ; the first severe one in Cyprus since 1953. Instinctively I knew what it was.
"Get out now," I shouted. Glad stood bemused, gazing at the ceiling.
"What was that?" she asked.
"It`s an earthquake," I shouted.
"I`ve just got to put on my slacks," she said.
"Get out <u>now</u>," I yelled, pulling her by the arm. I must confess to feeling quite claustrophobic at the time, as though the building was going to cave in on us at any

Page 218.   Aircraft crash swathe at Chartley Moss prehistoric bog.
            (*photo by kind permission of the Staffordshire Police and The
            Staffordshire Newsletter*)

second.

We ran for the lift ; a big mistake. We should have used the stairs. Luckily the electrics had not given out, but as we descended, the lift banged against the shaft, presumably from an aftershock. We reached the ground floor safely. Thankfully the lift doors opened and we rushed past the hotel reception towards the exit. I was suddenly aware of a crowd of guests behind us, who were all converging on the exit. "Don't panic!" I shouted, but we were the first guests outside.

After hanging about in the night air for a while we began to feel cold. During that time there was another strong aftershock. Finally I decided we should chance a return visit to our room. Apprehensively and very quickly I might add, we climbed the stairs. We frantically donned more clothes and descended to the lounge but soon went outside, as there was yet another strong aftershock. Eventually we returned to the lounge and dozed on the plush settees. We returned to our bed at about 3.30 am.

For those who may be interested, here are some facts :-

The earthquake was felt in Israel and Lebanon. The Cyprus seismology station reading was 5.8 on the Richter Scale.

Aftershocks that could be felt continued to the 6th March. It was strange that they all happened at night. There had been landslides and rock falls.

The epicentre was some 50 km out to sea, from Paphos and Limassol.

Over 900 dwellings in 70 villages were damaged. There were two fatalities and a number of people were injured. 60 of those villages were in the Paphos district ; the remainder being in the Nicosia area. 50 houses had to be demolished as unsafe whilst a further 30 were listed buildings and were to be renovated. The homeless were put into tents.

The effects of the `quake` on our hotel :-

The main lounge wall was cracked from top to bottom.

A balcony moved out about an inch from the wall.

Pictures tilted some two inches.

A large mirror flew off the wall and was smashed.

Ornaments were scattered.

At breakfast the next morning we were amused to see a man filling in the main lounge crack and painting it over. Subsequent guests would never have known the crack had ever been there.

I suppose on reflection one could say we were then nearer to God than at any time since World War Two.

Cyprus is a beautiful island, especially in the Spring, with pleasant temperatures, carpets of cyclamen and dwarf iris everywhere and the people are good natured. So don't let me put the reader off the island of Aphrodite. And if you are too warm you can always take to the Troodos Mountains, where the air is cool and the scenery breathtaking.

*   *   *   *   *

CHAPTER THIRTY SIX

SAXON GOLD

In 1997 we were staying with friends, the Lloyd family, at their house overlooking Bowleaze Cove, Weymouth. I decided I would go down and search the small beach for ammonites for my geological collection.

After a thorough search, I failed to find any ammonites. During my search I had come to an isolated rock. I nearly decided to move it. I`ve no idea why I did not. If I had done so, it would probably have changed my life dramatically for the better.

Some months later the Lloyd family wrote to me, enclosing a newspaper cutting from their local paper. It concerned a senior citizen, one Bernard Yarosz, aged 71, a former GI, of Wimborne, Dorset. He was searching the same small beach using a metal detector. When he came to the rock I have mentioned he got a strong signal, indicating there was something metallic beneath it.

Bernard rolled the rock over. You will never guess what he found. He had discovered a one thousand two hundred year old, gold manuscript pointer, believed to have belonged to King Alfred the Great.

A museum in America offered him three million pounds for it. He did not however, want the historic treasure to leave his `beloved` adopted country, as it was an important relic of English history. The grandfather offered the pointer to the British Museum. Needless to say it was gladly accepted. He was paid handsomely for it, but nothing like the amount he had been offered by the American museum .

What a man of quality - a true patriot. When at first I found out about it, I naturally felt a bit browned off. I must have been no more than a foot away from the relic. Never mind eh. What is to be will be, as they say.

*   *   *   *   *

CHAPTER THIRTY SEVEN

GRIEVING

On the 7th May 1998, after fifty one years of marriage, I lost my beloved wife and best friend Glad. Shortly before she died, my two lovely daughters presented her with a framed certificate which informed her that a star had been named after her. The star is very close to The Plough. Glad was very thrilled and moved and so was I.

We all have to suffer such losses. Those sad times are private and very personal, so I will not dwell on it, except to say my wife was very brave and that my family were like a rock, which is all anyone could ask for. I was broken hearted of course, but also grateful for what we had had. I decided the best way to try and deal with this awful emptiness was to get stuck in and do something - make myself busy. The last thing I wanted was to be a burden on my family.

In October 1998 I gave myself a challenge. I set out to produce a cave painting in my lounge, using the method thought to have been adopted by the cave artists of prehistoric times. I was amazed at how successful the mural turned out to be. (Page 222).

In that same month I was elected Chairman of the local Royal British Legion Branch and became involved in work for the Poppy Day appeal. Each year the Hixon and District Branch target was around £3,500, which we usually achieved and sometimes exceeded. This was a charity close to Glad`s heart.

In 2003 I decided it would be sensible to have a police escort to accompany Joyce, the poppy organiser and myself to the bank. £3,500 mostly in coinage is extremely heavy, so we stuffed the money into three suitcases. Each case was packed in a black bin bag. The policeman suggested we load the money into a supermarket trolley so that we could wheel it across the car park to the bank. I did point out to him that we could be done for stealing a supermarket trolley but he wasn`t amused.

I couldn`t help smiling to myself. Curious bystanders turned and stared. All they could see were two senior citizens wheeling large bags on a supermarket trolley, accompanied by a policeman. Perhaps they thought we were a couple of apprehended shoplifters. I know Glad would have laughed about this.

*   *   *   *   *

Page 222. The cave painting in my lounge - (Named by Pierre, my French friend, as
         LASCAUX III) .

CHAPTER THIRTY EIGHT

A VISITOR FROM THE WILD

On a day in the year 2000 I followed my usual daily routine of raking out the lounge fire, clearing out the ashes and taking the empty coal-scuttle outside, to refill it. When I reached the bunker I was surprised to find scattered on the path at least the equivalent of a sack of coal. At first I thought mischievous children had done it. I was wrong.

As I slid back the concrete bunker lid I received a shock. There, lying curled up asleep, was a fully grown male badger. It had hollowed out the coal until it had formed a comfortable den. I felt very privileged to see this wild animal bedded down at such close quarters. I carefully closed the lid, before summoning the RSPCA.

An inspector soon arrived in a van and a lady assistant appeared from the village to join him. They unloaded an oblong cage and carried it to the bunker. The inspector produced a short pole, which was fitted with a flexible steel noose.

He removed the bunker lid. The assistant opened one end of the cage and tilted it, ready to receive the animal. The inspector lowered the noose over the badger's head and tightened it. The badger was caught. It required considerable physical effort on the inspector's part to lift the badger out of the bunker. It struggled violently, snarling and showing its formidable teeth. There was a general sigh of relief when once it was safely secured in the cage.

The badger had a bloody abrasion on the head, thought to have been caused by falling coal when it was trying to make a cosy den.

I pushed my face close to the cage to get a good look at the animal. It was the first time I had seen a live badger. It snarled at me and face on, I thought how bear-like it looked. It also came across as an extremely tough creature. It just appeared to be a compact bundle of muscle, with teeth and claws. I am told badgers are quite capable of biting through the leather of a walking boot. I had no intention of putting my boots to the test.

The inspector said he would take the badger to the RSPCA depot in Uttoxeter, where the abrasion would be treated and the animal cared for, for about two weeks. It was interesting to learn that when once an animal is nursed back to health, the RSPCA is obliged to return it to the area where it was originally found.

Sure enough, two weeks later I received a phone call. The inspector said, "I am about to bring the badger back. Would you like to see it released?"
"Sure," I said. I rang two friends, Fred Mitchell and Allan Peake. They accompanied me. On the phone the inspector had told me he proposed to release the badger in an adjacent field and he would meet me in my lane. The only snag was the weather. Talk about a monsoon. There was no wind but the rain was unusually heavy - a deluge in fact.

It was now dark. Eventually the van appeared, followed by a second van. They both parked on the verge by a stile, leading to a path through thick bushes. We were now pretty well soaked. I wondered what the other van was there for. I soon found out. It turned out to be a television crew. The inspector had arranged it all, in connection with a Rolf Harris animal TV series.
"I hope you don't mind but I've brought a television crew along." Then addressing me he said, "Would you mind helping me to lift the cage over the stile?" I was surprised at the weight of it with the badger inside. We pushed through the bushes. I

can remember saying in the downpour,

"This reminds me of when I was in the jungle."

We set the cage down in the field and with the TV crew hovering about with camera and lights, the cage door was opened. Nothing happened. The badger did not seem keen to come out. The TV director, a woman, asked me to stand behind the cage. The inspector prodded the animal from behind with his pole and suddenly it came out. It slowly waddled off, making a bee line for a hedge.

"Isn`t that amazing!" I said, feeling very grateful to have witnessed this event.

Then a strange thing happened. The TV director asked me to stand behind the cage again.

"Will you repeat what you said before ? Pretend the animal is just coming out of the cage, as we didn`t get all of the shot the first time." I scratched my head to think of what I had previously said. Then, standing immediately behind the cage and looking down at it I said,

"Isn`t that marvellous." I felt really foolish standing there in the pouring rain, soaked to the skin, cold and in the dark, talking to an empty box as though the badger was still inside and watched by several bemused and thoroughly soaked onlookers.

*   *   *   *   *

CHAPTER THIRTY NINE

NINE - ELEVEN

After spending an enjoyable month in France with my sister Pat and brother-in-law Dennis, it was time for me to return to England. My flight was due to take off at 11am, on 11th September 2001. It was an internal flight from Perigueux Airport to Orly Airport in Paris. Unbeknown to the passengers and crew, at the exact time of our take-off, two passenger aircraft were deliberately being crashed by fanatical terrorists into the Twin Towers in Manhattan, New York. My flight to Orly took little over an hour, during which time no special announcements were made to the passengers.

On arrival at Orly, I was obliged to recover my baggage from the carousel, as there was no onward baggage routing to Charles de Gaulle airport, where I was destined to catch a flight back to England. I trundled my baggage to a waiting bus for the forty minute journey to Charles de Gaulle airport. Everything seemed to be perfectly normal at Orly - certainly no signs of concern or extra security checks.

Things were very different when I reached Charles de Gaulle airport. I was still not aware of the outrage in New York. My baggage was taken on board in the usual way, but when the time came to enter the departure lounge, the place was swarming with security personnel of one sort or another.

I managed to find a seat very near the boarding gate. I was sitting next to a Catholic priest. The departure lounge was bursting at the seams with frustrated passengers of many delayed flights. The departure time for my flight came and went. I turned to the priest and asked him the reason for the hold up.
"Haven`t you heard ?" he exclaimed, with considerable surprise. "Terrorists have deliberately crashed two planes into the Twin Towers in New York." I was very shocked.

My flight was now two hours late. An English couple was sitting near me. The woman was very flustered. Their flight was due to take off immediately prior to mine. The woman approached the boarding gate and asked the attendant if she could change some money into francs, so that she could ring her daughter who was waiting at Heathrow, to explain the delay. The attendant told her she was unable to help her. I had already changed my francs into sterling so I was unable to help out either. Thinking he might be able to help, I turned to the priest and said,
"That poor woman is in a state."
"It is her own fault," he said. "She should not have changed all her money."
`What an attitude,` I thought. It turned out that although he was English, he worked permanently in Paris for the Church.

Just then passengers for the Heathrow flight were allowed through the gate. At last things were moving. Passengers for my flight to Birmingham were the next to be called. We streamed down the gangway holding our boarding passes and passports, which were checked for the umpteenth time, but instead of being allowed to board the plane we were mustered on the tarmac by the side of our aircraft.

All baggage had been unloaded from every aircraft throughout the entire airport, and was laid out on the tarmac by each plane. We were all instructed to stand by our personal luggage. Two officials slowly passed along the row of passengers, who were asked individually to point out their own luggage. As soon as a passenger confirmed their baggage it was manhandled on board.

I assumed the disaster in New York had sent out shock waves to every civil airport in the western world, so passengers needed to show tolerance and patience towards the airport staff. They were doing their best, but I couldn`t help wondering how a terrorist with a suitcase on the tarmac would appear to act any differently from any of the other passengers, even though there might be a bomb in their case. The two officials were not asking passengers to open their luggage, so all a terrorist had to do was to keep their cool and respond to the question, "Is that your luggage ?" in exactly the same way as the rest of us. The officials would be none the wiser.

My plane eventually took off three hours late. We lost a further thirty minutes detouring a massive thunderstorm, which could be clearly seen to the west, beyond the Isle of Wight.

*   *   *   *   *

CHAPTER FORTY

PASTURES NEW

In 2002, my sister and her husband in France, now in their old age, decided that the work in their fields was becoming too much for them to cope with. Very courageously at their age, they decided to try for pastures new. They chose to move to Vancouver in Canada, where Pat's daughter lived and eventually they settled on Vancouver Island. This meant that I was able to stay with them there for my annual holiday.

In 2004 I stayed for the whole of September. On one of the days I had an appointment with Graham Beard, director of the Vancouver Island Palaeontology Museum Society, based at the Qualicum Museum. My sister and brother-in-law accompanied me, as subsequently they were going to call at their bank. Graham had just returned from the small town, where he discovered someone had just robbed <u>his</u> bank.

When we left the museum we drove into Qualicum, parking outside a bank. They left me sitting in the car while they headed round the corner to their own bank. While in the stationary car watching the world go by, I noticed there was a police tape strung around the building. I thought, `this must be the bank that was robbed`. Just then a police car with a policewoman at the wheel slowly cruised by. She was looking away from me.

I assumed the police were still looking for the bank robber, because shortly afterwards the same police car slowly cruised by again. The policewoman was again not looking in my direction. She must have driven round the block of shops several times.

The next day in the local paper were all the details of the robbery. There was a good CCTV picture of the robber. I had a shock. Facially, he was my double ! Not only that. He had a beard like mine, the same build and was wearing a Tilley hat like mine. The likeness was uncanny. It was lucky for me that the policewoman had been looking elsewhere.

A month later back in England, I was talking to my sister on the phone. "We didn`t know you also did a job in Ladysmith," she said jokingly. Apparently a bank had since been robbed in that town. CCTV showed it to be the same guy.

Soon afterwards the same man robbed a bank in Victoria, but someone managed to get the registration number of his getaway vehicle. The number was passed on to all city patrol cars. When one of the police cars received the message, they realised that the car travelling immediately in front of them was the one they were looking for. The days of easy money were over for that bank robber.

I said to my sister, "Before I come to Canada again, I think I had better change my appearance."

*   *   *   *   *

EPILOGUE

They say that a sign of getting old is when your back goes out more than you do. I haven`t quite yet got to that stage. Now I am eighty two years old I have nearly run my race, but all things considered I have to be extremely grateful for a life full of love, variety and interest. My family have been, and still are, my inspiration. My door is still slightly ajar, so I am looking forward with optimism to what life may yet bring.

One of my walking group, Allan Peake, who you will remember was with me when the badger was released, once said to me,
"Some blokes attract beautiful women but you attract unusual incidents." He was only half right, because my beloved wife was really beautiful, both in her looks and in her nature.

On the date of our anniversary ten days after my wife died, I was given an anniversary card on which Glad had written, `I shall always be near you`. I know that she is. To share our memories together, I have only to look up at the night sky, to her star.

APPENDIX A

Armament of warships served by the Author :-

King George the Fifth (BS) 10 x 14" guns, 16 x 5.25" guns, 48 pompoms, numerous 20 mm and 40 mm AA weapons

Duke of York (BS) Same as KGV

FFS Richelieu (BS) 8 x 15" guns, 9 x 6" guns, 56 x 40 mm and 50 x 20 mm AA weapons

Iron Duke (BS) 10 x 13.5" guns

Furious (AC) 12 x 4.5" dual purpose guns, 48 pompoms, 22 x 20 mm AA weapons

Rodney (BS) 9 x 16" guns, 12 x 6" guns, 8 x 4" guns, 48 pompoms, 16 x 40 mm and 61 x 20 mm AA weapons

Wager (DS) 4 x 4.7" guns, 8 x 21" torpedo tubes, several 20 mm AA weapons

Bermuda (CR) 12 x 6" guns, 6 x 21" torpedo tubes, 8 x 4" guns, numerous 20 mm AA weapons

Bigbury Bay (FR) 4 x 4" guns, 6 x 40 mm and 4 x 20 mm AA weapons

Mauritius (CR) 12 x 6" guns, 6 x 21" torpedo tubes, 8 x 4" guns, numerous 20 mm AA weapons

Liverpool (CR) Same as Mauritius

NOTE : - Due to the vulnerability of ships to air attack AA armament was increased wherever possible as the war progressed.

KEY:- BS = BATTLESHIP   AC = AIRCRAFT CARRIER   CR = CRUISER
     DS = DESTROYER   FR = FRIGATE
.   FFS. = FREE FRENCH SHIP

APPENDIX B

Summary of British Commonwealth Navies losses during World War Two :-

WARSHIPS

BATTLESHIPS	4
AIRCRAFT CARRIERS	5
CRUISERS	33
DESTROYERS	154
SUBMARINES	90
CORVETTES	38
AUXILIARY and MINOR	1,035
LANDING SHIPS and CRAFT	1,326

*   *   *   *   *

Casualties of The Royal Navy, The Royal Naval Reserve and The Royal Naval Volunteer Reserve

KILLED	50,758
MISSING	820
WOUNDED	14,663
PRISONERS of WAR	7,401

Womens Royal Naval Service.

KILLED	102
WOUNDED	22

*   *   *   *   *

Casualties of The British Merchant Navy.
KILLED or MISSING   30,248 (*Note :* This is only a fraction of the total Merchant Navy losses, as many of the seamen were of foreign nationality).

APPENDIX C continued..............

BIBLIOGRAPHY

Bhatt, J.R, *Animal Life,* Associated Newspapers, (Ceylon 1946).

Hawkes, Ellison, Captain RA, *Britain's Wonderful Fighting Forces,* Odhams
Press, (London 1940).
Jane's Fighting Ships 1943 - 44, Sampson Low, Marston & Co Ltd.

Jane's Fighting Ships 1944 - 45, Sampson Low, Marston & Co Ltd.

Kemp, P, *Convoy,* Brockhampton Press, (1999).

McWhan, Forrest, *The Falkland Islands Today,* Stirling Tract Enterprise
(Scotland 1952).
RAF Welfare Publication, *The Jungle Hiker,* 222 Group Indian Ocean, (1945).

Ruegg, R and Hague, A, *Convoys to Russia 1941 - 1945,* The World Ship Society,
(1992).
Spittel, R. L, *Far - Off Things,* The Colombo Apothecaries Co Ltd, (1933).

Spittel, R. L, *Wild Ceylon,* General Publishers Ltd, Colombo, (1945).

Winton, John, *An Illustrated History of the Royal Navy,* Salamander Books (2000)

*and finally, from jotted data from a book of the 70s, Send Her Victorious (source
unknown), concerning Operation 'Iceberg'.*